✴ *The Confederate General* ✴

Volume 4

⋆ *The Confederate General* ⋆

Volume 4

Kelly, John to Payne, William H.

William C. Davis, Editor

Julie Hoffman, Assistant Editor

A Publication of the
National Historical Society

Library of Congress Cataloging-in-Publication Data
The Confederate General / William C. Davis,
    editor; Julie Hoffman, assistant editor.
        p. cm.
        ISBN 0-918678-67-6 (v. 4) : $29.95
        Contents: v. 4. Kelly, John to Payne, William Henry.
        1. United States—History—Civil War, 1861-1865—
Biography. 2. Confederate States of America. Army.—Biography. 3.
Generals—Confederate States of America—Biography. 4.
Generals—Southern States—Biography. 5. Generals—United States
—Biography.
I. Davis, William C., 1946-   II. Hoffman, Julie.
    E467.C76   1991
    973.7'42'0922 [B]   91-8508

Editorial Assistant, Eleanor Mauck
Designed by Art Unlimited
Printed in the United States of America

✳ *Contents* ✳

✷ *John Herbert Kelly* ✷

The almost painful youthfulness of John Kelly is all too evident in this, his only known photograph in a uniform, taken as a West Point cadet sometime between 1857 and 1860. Kelly is seated second from the right. (Alabama Department of Archives and History, Montgomery, Ala.)

John Herbert Kelly was born on March 31, 1840, in Carrollton, Alabama. Orphaned at the age of six, he was reared by his maternal grandmother in Pineapple, Alabama. Through the political connections of relatives Kelly received an appointment to West Point in 1857 but resigned from the academy on December 29, 1860, at the beginning of Southern secession. He immediately traveled to Montgomery and was commissioned a 2d lieutenant of artillery in the Regular Confederate Army. After a brief stay at Fort Morgan, Alabama, Kelly joined the staff of Brigadier General William Hardee in Missouri as a captain and served for a brief time as his assistant adjutant general. On September 23, 1861, Kelly was commissioned a major in the 14th Alabama.

The next year at Shiloh Major Kelly was in temporary command of the 9th Arkansas Battalion in the brigade of Sterling A. M. Wood. His battalion formed Wood's skirmish line on April 6 during the initial Confederate assault. As the Confederates fell back on April 7, Wood ordered the brigade to counterattack near Shiloh Church. Kelly was again in command of the skirmish line that day but now led his men in attacking across a waist-deep pond into an open field. Wood wrote, "Major Kelly here displayed the greatest gallantry. He was on the right, and, dashing through the pond, sat on horseback in the open ground and rallied his men in line as they advanced." The Arkansans managed to push the Yankees back, then resumed the retreat. Kelly lost half of his battalion in the two-day fight.

For his gallantry at Shiloh Kelly was promoted to colonel and was given command of the 8th Arkansas Infantry in May 1862. Assigned to St. John R. Liddell's brigade, he participated in the autumn invasion of Kentucky and was said to have personally captured the colonel of the 22d Indiana at Perryville October 8. At Murfreesboro Kelly attacked the Yankees on December 31, 1862, and fought until his regiment ran out of ammunition. After refilling his men's cartridge boxes Kelly resumed the advance until about 1:30 P.M., when he was shot in the arm. One source described the wound as being serious, but Liddell classified it as slight. In any case, Kelly was out of the fight.

At Chickamauga Kelly commanded a brigade of inexperienced North Carolina, Georgia, Kentucky, and Virginia infantry in Brigadier General William Preston's division. On September 20, 1863, his brigade joined in the last series of attacks against Snodgrass Hill. In savage fighting his horse was killed under him as his brigade closed to within fifteen yards of the enemy. The Confederates took the Union position, and Kelly held it against three Union counterattacks. Finally the Yankees cried out that they surrendered. Kelly walked out to talk with their commander, who hesitated when ordered to surrender his men. The Yankees suddenly opened fire on Kelly, and a confused fight erupted again. At that point Kelly was ordered back to consult with Preston, and in his absence the enemy surrendered. His brigade lost 303 men out of 852 engaged at Chickamauga. Because of his good conduct during the battle Kelly was recommended for promotion by Preston, Liddell, and Major General Patrick Cleburne. The latter wrote, "I know of no better officer of his grade in the service."

On November 17, 1863, Kelly received his appointment as brigadier general, becoming at the age of twenty-three the youngest Confederate general at that time. While outside Chattanooga during the winter of 1863–64, he was embroiled in some controversy when he signed Cleburne's famous memorandum calling for the enlistment of blacks into the army. The incident apparently did not hurt his reputation, however, for on May 8, 1864, Kelly was given command of a division of cavalry under Major General Joseph Wheeler and took on the duties and responsibilities of a major general.

During the Atlanta Campaign May 1–September 2, 1864, Kelly earned the reputation of being a good divisional commander. He served Wheeler well throughout the campaign and participated in the raid against Union Major General William T. Sherman's supply line in late summer. During that raid he was mortally wounded in a skirmish at Franklin, Tennessee, on September 2, 1864. He probably died on September 4 at the house of William H. Harrison. Wheeler wrote, "To my brave division commander, General Kelly, who gave up his life at Franklin, while gallantly fighting at the head of his division, I ask the country to award its gratitude. No honors bestowed on his memory could more than repay his devotion." Kelly was buried in the Harrison yard, but his body was exhumed in 1866 and reinterred at Mobile, Alabama.

Terry L. Jones

Wheeler, Joseph, *Alabama*, Vol. VII in Evans, *Confederate Military History*.

Colonel James Kemper of the 7th Virginia Infantry, taken probably before June 1862. (Cook Collection, Valentine Museum, Richmond, Va.)

⋆ *James Lawson Kemper* ⋆

Kemper was born at Mountain Prospect in Madison County, Virginia, on June 11, 1823, the son of William and Mary Elizabeth (Allison) Kemper. Kemper's primary education was received at Locust Dale Academy, then he graduated in 1842 from Washington College (now Washington and Lee University) with a B.A. degree. While at the college he participated in the "school of the soldier" classes and drills sponsored by nearby Virginia Military Institute. After leaving Lexington, Kemper read law and opened an office at Madison Court House.

After war began with Mexico, he was commissioned captain of volunteers on January 30, 1847, and assigned to duty as quartermaster of the 1st Virginia Infantry. He and his unit reported to Brigadier General Zachary Taylor in March at Camargo, too late to participate in the bitter battles waged in northeastern Mexico.

Upon being mustered out, Kemper returned to his Madison County law practice. In 1853 he married Cremora Conway Cave and was elected to the first of five successive terms in the Virginia House of Delegates. There he chaired the committee on military affairs and was president of the Virginia Military Institute board of visitors. He was house speaker from December 1860 to March 1861.

Kemper initially opposed secession but changed his stance following the bombardment of Fort Sumter and President Abraham Lincoln's call for seventy-five thousand volunteers. After brief service as a brigadier general of the 1st Brigade, 2d Division of the state militia, Kemper was mustered into the Confederate Army on May 2, 1861, as colonel of the 7th Virginia Infantry. Kemper first saw combat July 21 at First Manassas as the Army of the Potomac's quartermaster, and oversaw the "preparation for and execution" of the evacuation of Fairfax Court House by Brigadier General Milledge L. Bonham's brigade and its withdrawal behind Bull Run, for which he was commended. On the afternoon of July 21 Kemper and his Virginians battled the Federals on Chinn Ridge.

In the aftermath of First Manassas Kemper's regiment was brigaded with the 1st, 11th, and 17th Virginia under Brigadier General James Longstreet. Kemper spent the first winter of the war in and around Centreville. On March 8, 1862, General Joseph E. Johnston evacuated the Centreville area, and the army retired behind the Rappahannock. By this time the brigades had been organized into divisions, and Brigadier General A. P. Hill led the brigade and Longstreet the division. Mid-April found Kemper and his Virginians on the Yorktown-Warwick line. He saw desperate fighting at Williamsburg on May 5, near Fort Magruder, and was cited by General Hill for his "conspicuous...daring and energy."

On May 27 A. P. Hill was placed in command of a newly constituted division, and Kemper, as senior colonel, assumed command of the Virginia brigade. Four days later, May 31, at Seven Pines, he and his Virginians hammered the IV Corps on the Williamsburg road, earning the approbation of General Longstreet, who wrote: "The severest part of the work was done by Major Gen. D. H. Hill's division, but the attack of the two brigades...one commanded by Colonel Kemper...the other by Col. M. Jenkins—was made with such spirit and regularity as to have driven back the most determined foe. This decided the day in our favor."

Upon the recommendation of General Robert E. Lee, who had succeeded Johnston as army commander, Kemper was appointed brigadier general on June 2, 1862, effective the following day. Kemper's was one of six brigades that constituted Longstreet's division during the Seven Days', but it only saw action on June 30 at Glendale, where more than one-fourth of his troops were casualties, and their general was cited by Longstreet for gallantry. By mid-July General Lee had organized the Army of Northern Virginia into two corps—Longstreet's and Major General "Stonewall" Jackson's. On August 13 Longstreet's Corps was ordered to Gordonsville, and upon arriving there General Kemper, as senior officer present, assumed

A slight variant, taken at the same sitting. No photo from Kemper's service as a brigadier has come to light. (U.S. Army Military History Institute, Carlisle, Pa.)

command of a three-brigade division that he led during the Second Manassas Campaign. Before crossing the Potomac on September 5, Kemper's division was consolidated with Major General D. R. Jones' division. Kemper and his understrength brigade—the 1st, 7th, 11th, 17th, and 24th Virginia—fought at Turner's Gap on September 14 and on the Confederate right against Burnside's IX Corps at Antietam on the afternoon of the 17th.

On October 27 a reorganization of the army found Kemper and his brigade assigned to the five-brigade division to be led by Major General George E. Pickett, whose return to duty was momentarily expected following the severe wound he had received at Gaines' Mill. At Fredericksburg, late in the afternoon of December 13, Kemper reinforced the troops defending Marye's Heights against Burnside's human wave attacks.

Kemper and his Virginians accompanied General Longstreet to the Southside in the early spring of 1863 and participated in the ill-starred—for the Confederates—March 30 to April 20 siege of Washington, North Carolina. Kemper rejoined the Army of Northern Virginia in mid-May. Kemper's was one of the three brigades that Pickett took across the Blue Ridge on the march north to Gettysburg, camping on Marsh Creek on July 2. The next afternoon Kemper formed his brigade on the left of Brigadier General Richard B. Garnett's and at 3 P.M. participated in Pickett's Charge. After crossing the Emmitsburg road and obliquing toward the angle, Kemper, who had gone into action mounted, was shot in the groin and unhorsed.

Following the Confederate repulse, General Lee learned that Kemper was being carried to the rear. Riding over to his litter, Lee inquired, "General, I hope you are not badly hurt?" Kemper replied, "Yes, I'm afraid they have got me this time." Lee, clasping Kemper's hand, exclaimed, "I trust not, I trust not."

Kemper's wounds, which caused a temporary paralysis of his legs, were so severe that he was hospitalized and left behind when the Confederates retreated. Captured by the Federals, he was held for three months as a prisoner at Fort Delaware and when it seemed unlikely that he would serve again, was exchanged for Brigadier General Charles K. Graham on September 22. No longer fit for field duty, Kemper was assigned administrative positions, first as commander of Virginia's Reserve Forces and then as officer-in-charge of the Confederate Conscription Bureau. He

was promoted major general, to rank from September 14, 1864. He was surrendered and paroled at Danville May 2, 1865.

Kemper returned to Madison Court House and despite his civil war injuries, reestablished his law firm and reentered politics. In the latter, he was a moderate, championing the conservative party in 1869 and in 1872 stumped the state as an elector on the Horace Greeley ticket. In 1873 Kemper, appealing to the white voters of the Piedmont and former soldiers, wrested the party's nomination for governor from Colonel R. E. Withers, a Bourbon, and defeated the Republican candidate in the general election. His four-year administration (1874–77) was characterized by his independence. He supported African-Americans in their civil rights campaign, and vetoed a bill placing the Petersburg city government under a commission as contrary to the principle of local government, though professing sympathy with the city's desire to escape black majority rule. He unsuccessfully urged Congress to share the task of state education for blacks and to assume the state's debts as they were war-related. Much to the dismay of the bankers, he promoted a workshop with the state's creditors aimed at securing equality of creditors and reduction of the debt. The conference collapsed, and Kemper allied himself with the "Debt-payers," to the dismay of the "Readjusters." Plagued by pains from his Gettysburg wound, he declined to be a candidate for election to the U.S. Senate in 1877 and upon the end of his term retired from politics and returned to Madison.

In the early 1880s he commenced building a country home in Orange County, which he named "Walnut Hills." He relocated his family there in 1886 after selling his Madison home. Kemper never fully recovered from his Civil War injuries, and his last years were spent as an invalid. He died on April 7, 1895, and was buried at Walnut Hills.

Edwin C. Bearss

Hotchkiss, Jedediah, *Virginia*, Vol. III in Evans, *Confederate Military History*.

Woodward, Harold, *For Home and Honor* (Madison, Va., 1990).

✷ *John Doby Kennedy* ✷

Born in Camden, South Carolina, on January 5, 1840, John Doby Kennedy attended local schools until he entered South Carolina College in 1855. He left college in the fall of 1857 to study law in the office of W. Z. Leitner and to marry Elizabeth Cunningham. Not admitted to the bar until January of 1861, a month after South Carolina's secession, Kennedy practiced law until April when he joined the army.

Commissioned captain of Company E in Colonel Joseph B. Kershaw's 2d South Carolina Infantry, Kennedy was present during the bombardment of Fort Sumter in April of 1861. Transferred to Virginia, the regiment arrived in time to participate at the First Battle of Manassas. On the morning of July 21 while engaged in the Union attack against the Confederate left flank, Kennedy was struck by a Minié bullet. He recovered from the wound and was able to return to duty in the field. When Kershaw assumed command of the brigade in January of 1862, Kennedy succeeded him as colonel of the regiment.

On June 1 Kennedy led the 2d South Carolina in a skirmish on the Nine-mile road near Richmond during the fighting at Fair Oaks and in the fighting at Savage's Station on June 29 during the Seven Days' battles. Immediately after the fight at Savage's Station Kennedy was incapacitated by fever, but he recovered in time to participate in the capture of Harpers Ferry. On September 17 his brigade was the first to arrive from Harpers Ferry and come to the assistance of Major General Thomas J. "Stonewall" Jackson on the Confederate left. Kershaw's South Carolinians repeatedly counterattacked the advancing enemy and eventually drove the Federals from their front, but Kennedy had fallen with a painful wound during their first charge.

At Fredericksburg, on December 13 Kennedy led his own regiment and the 8th South Carolina Infantry to reinforce Brigadier General Thomas R. R. Cobb's Georgians at the stone wall fronting Marye's Heights, where the South Carolinians substantially contributed to the repeated repulses of the Union attacks. During the Chancellorsville Campaign April–May 1863, Kennedy participated in General Robert E. Lee's holding action on May 2 while Lieutenant General Jackson made his famous flanking march. After pressing the advantage gained by Jackson the previous evening, Kennedy's regiment withdrew on May 3 and marched eastward toward Fredericksburg to stop Federals who had broken through. The Confederates thwarted this threat at Salem Church on May 4, but before Kennedy and his comrades could return to Chancellorsville, the enemy had retreated across the Rappahannock River. On July 2 during the Battle of Gettysburg Kennedy was severely wounded while leading a charge against a Union battery near the Peach Orchard.

Recovering in time to accompany Lieutenant General James Longstreet to Georgia, Kennedy, apparently unable to lead his regiment when it penetrated the Union line at Chickamauga on September 20, did participate in the sieges of Chattanooga and Knoxville before returning to Virginia in 1864. While in the Western theater Kennedy, when fit for duty, commanded the

No uniformed portrait of General Kennedy has been found; this dates from the 1880s. (Miller, *Photographic History*)

brigade whenever Kershaw was called upon to command the division.

In May 1864 Kennedy fought in the Wilderness and was among the first to arrive at Spotsylvania Court House and to secure that important road junction for the Confederates. After fighting in the ensuing engagement there and at Cold Harbor, Kershaw was permanently assigned to command Major General Lafayette McLaws' division on June 4, and Brigadier General James Conner was assigned to command the brigade. After a few weeks in the trenches protecting Petersburg, Kennedy accompanied the division when it was ordered north to support Lieutenant General Jubal A. Early's operations in the Shenandoah Valley. Kennedy was absent during much of this campaign, presumably because of wounds. When Conner lost a leg as a result of a wound during a skirmish near Cedar Creek on October 13, Kennedy was not present to assume command of the brigade during the Battle of Cedar Creek six days later, when Colonel George M. Love of the 116th New York Infantry won the Congressional Medal of Honor by personally capturing the regimental colors of Kennedy's 2d South Carolina. Kennedy resumed command of the brigade shortly thereafter and was appointed brigadier general on February 8, 1865, to rank from December 22, 1864, by which time the brigade occupied a section of the trenches surrounding Petersburg.

After the fall of Atlanta, South Carolina Governor Andrew G. Magrath requested that Kershaw's brigade be transferred to defend his state against the anticipated invasion of Union Major General William T. Sherman. On January 3, 1865, Kennedy was ordered to take his brigade to South Carolina. The brigade was assigned to the division of their previous commander, Major General McLaws, which formed part of Lieutenant General William J. Hardee's corps. Kennedy fought at Averasborough and Bentonville before being included in the surrender of General Joseph E. Johnston. Kennedy was paroled with Major General Edward C. Walthall's division of Lieutenant General Alexander P. Stewart's corps at Greensboro, North Carolina, on or about May 1, 1865. In all Kennedy had been wounded in six different engagements and had been struck by fifteen spent bullets.

After the war Kennedy resumed his law practice in Camden, South Carolina. Elected to Congress in December of 1865, he was denied his seat because he refused to take the Ironclad Oath. Kennedy then worked to redeem his state from the Republican carpetbaggers and to restore white Democratic supremacy. He voted for Samuel Tilden at the National Democratic Convention in St. Louis in 1876. A member of the state executive committee of the Democratic party that year, he was its chairman in 1878. He served two terms as state representative (1878, 1879), was elected lieutenant governor in 1880, and was defeated for the Democratic nomination for governor in 1882. His first wife died in 1876; six years later he married Harriet A. Boykin. A presidential elector-at-large on the Democratic ticket in 1884, Kennedy was appointed by President Grover Cleveland to serve as consul general in Shanghai, China, a position he held from 1885 to 1889. Active in fraternal and Confederate veterans' organizations, Kennedy assisted in the establishment of Camp Kirkland. On April 14, 1896, he died suddenly from a stroke of apoplexy in his home in Camden, where he was buried.

Lawrence L. Hewitt

Capers, Ellison, *South Carolina*, Vol. V in Evans, *Confederate Military History*.

An outstanding previously unpublished portrait of Brigadier General Kershaw, dating at the earliest from February 1862. (Museum of the Confederacy, Richmond, Va.)

Kershaw's blouse buttons suggest a brigadier, but more likely he is shown here as colonel of the 2d South Carolina, indicated by the three stars on his collar, in what would be an 1861 image. (Southern Historical Collection, University of North Carolina, Chapel Hill)

⋆ *Joseph Brevard Kershaw* ⋆

Joseph Brevard Kershaw was born on January 5, 1822, in Camden, South Carolina. His parents were John and Harriette DuBose Kershaw. His mother's father was Isaac DuBose, a member of Francis Marion's staff during the American Revolution. Joseph, on his paternal side, was a third-generation South Carolinian; his grandfather—a 1748 emigrant from England—was an active participant in public affairs both during and after the American Revolution. His father had also been a public servant—mayor of Camden, county judge, member of the state legislature, and a representative in the United States Congress (1812–14).

Kershaw received his primary and secondary education in the Camden District schools and at the Cokesbury Conference School in the Abbeville District; read law in John M. DeSaussure's Camden office; and was admitted to the South Carolina bar in 1843. He enlisted February 6, 1847, in the Palmetto Regiment for service in the Mexican War and was elected 1st lieutenant in the DeKalb Rifle Guards. Kershaw was stricken by fever while in Mexico and returned, a physical wreck, to Camden in June. He was nursed back to health by his wife, Lucretia Douglass, whom he had married in 1844.

He resigned his commission and resumed his law practice, and in 1852 he was elected to represent the Camden District in the state legislature. He was reelected in 1854. In the weeks following John Brown's October 1859 Harpers Ferry raid Kershaw became active in the militia and was elected colonel of the local regiment. In December 1860 he was a member of the Charleston Convention that enacted the state's secession ordinance.

In response to a call by Governor Andrew Pickens, Kershaw turned out his militia regiment and proceeded to Charleston and was assigned duty on Morris Island. During the first months of 1861 he organized the 2d South Carolina and on April 9 was named its colonel. He and his regiment were ordered to northern Virginia and assigned to Milledge L. Bonham's brigade, then posted in and around Fairfax Court House.

Kershaw saw his first action at Mitchell's Ford on July 18. At First Manassas on July 21 he, with the 2d and 8th South Carolina and the Alexandria Virginia Artillery, was rushed from Mitchell's Ford and played a key role in the Confederate victory in the Henry Hill struggle and the pursuit of the enemy to Cub Run. In mid-January, while the South Carolina brigade was in winter quarters near Bull Run, General Bonham resigned. Kershaw, as senior colonel, assumed command of the brigade and on February 15, 1862, was promoted brigadier general, to rank from February 13.

Kershaw's brigade, along with other units of General Joseph E. Johnston's army, abandoned its winter camp on March 9 and withdrew behind the Rappahannock. Kershaw and his South Carolinians were among the first of Johnston's troops to be sent to the Peninsula to reinforce Major General John B. Magruder's army, then menaced by George B. McClellan's Army of the Potomac. Kershaw reached the Yorktown-Warwick line in mid-April. During the Confederate retreat up the Peninsula to the Richmond

Kershaw's best-known pose, probably from 1862 or 1863. (U.S. Army Military History Institute, Carlisle, Pa.)

11

approaches following the May 3 evacuation of the Yorktown fortifications, Kershaw fought the Yankees on the 5th at Williamsburg.

Kershaw was with Magruder's wing south of the Chickahominy on June 26 when Robert E. Lee, on the second day of the Seven Days' battles, assailed McClellan's troops posted behind Beaverdam Creek. On the 19th Kershaw's brigade was in the forefront at Savage's Station, and on July 1 at Malvern Hill he entered the fight at 6 P.M., passing over three waves of Confederates who had preceded him. His "gallantry, cool yet daring courage and skill in the management of his troops" at Savage's Station earned for Kershaw the commendation of division commander Lafayette McLaws.

Kershaw and his South Carolinians, along with other units of McLaws' division, missed the campaign that ended with the Confederate victorious at Second Manassas. They rejoined Lee's army for the Maryland campaign, September 4–22, 1862, crossing the Potomac at White's Ferry on September 6. Kershaw and his people seized Maryland Heights on the 13th, thus playing a key role in the surrender of Harpers Ferry and the capture of eleven thousand Union soldiers, and spearheaded the Confederate onslaught that routed John Sedgwick's II Corps division in Antietam's West Woods. In late November the brigade was bolstered by a reorganization that saw the 15th South Carolina Regiment and the 6th South Carolina Battalion reporting to General Kershaw.

At Fredericksburg, December 13, Kershaw's brigade reinforced the Georgians and North Carolinians posted behind the stone wall fronting Willis and Marye's Heights, and from midafternoon until dark beat back the waves of attacking Federals while suffering frightful losses. As senior officer present, Kershaw commanded the defenders.

Detached from Lieutenant General James Longstreet, Kershaw and his South Carolinians, along with McLaws' division, remained on the Rappahannock and participated in the 1863 Battle of Chancellorsville. May 1–3 Kershaw fought under General Lee's eyes as he hammered his way westward toward the Chancellor house. He was engaged on the 4th as Lee's attack on Major General John Sedgwick at Salem Church misfired.

In mid-May upon the return of Longstreet from the Southside, General Lee reorganized his army into three infantry corps, each of three divisions, and in late June crossed the Potomac and for the second time

carried the war into the North. At Gettysburg on July 2 Kershaw led the advance of McLaws' four-brigade division and in savage fighting played a key role in driving troops of Daniel E. Sickles, Winfield S. Hancock, and George Sykes from the Rose Farm, Stony Hill, the Peach Orchard, and Rose's Wheatfield. But in doing so, more than one-half of his men became casualties.

Kershaw and his South Carolinians went west with Longstreet in mid-September. At Chickamauga on September 20, as senior officer present, Kershaw led McLaws' division in Longstreet's charge at the Brotherton Cabin that broke the Union line, shattered three enemy divisions, and precipitated a panic on the Union right. With Major General John B. Hood wounded, he then met his match when George H. Thomas held Snodgrass Hill and gained his *nom de guerre*, the "Rock of Chickamauga." Upon McLaws' late-September arrival, Kershaw resumed command of the brigade as General General Braxton Bragg's army invested Chattanooga.

In early November Kershaw accompanied Longstreet to East Tennessee. On the 17th Longstreet's columns, having failed to trap Ambrose E. Burnside's army at Campbell's Station on the previous day, laid siege to Knoxville. Kershaw and his men were spared the Fort Sanders disaster on November 29, and they, along with Longstreet's army, retreated to Rogersville upon the December 4 approach of William T. Sherman's army. In mid-December Kershaw saw action at Bean's Station before going into winter quarters at Russellville. Disenchanted with McLaws' leadership during the autumn campaigns, particularly for the botched Fort Sanders assault, Longstreet sacked the long-time division commander and named Kershaw to act in McLaws' stead.

Longstreet returned to Virginia with Kershaw's and Major General Charles W. Field's divisions in mid-April 1864, reported to General Lee, and went into camp in and around Gordonsville. On May 6 Kershaw and his division, along with Field's, were committed in the Battle of the Wilderness. They first checked and then hurled back Hancock's legions that had overwhelmed the Army of Northern Virginia's III Corps.

Kershaw had earlier that day been riding up the Orange Plank Road with Longstreet and Micah Jenkins when the latter two officers were accidentally shot by Brigadier General William Mahone's Virginians. Kershaw, who apparently led a charmed life, escaped injury, while Longstreet fell wounded and Jenkins took a fatal bullet through the brain.

Kershaw's division helped General Lee win the race to Spotsylvania, where on the morning of May 8 they stood tall at Laurel Hill and beat back repeated V Corps attacks. Kershaw held this position for the next two weeks before moving on to the North Anna, where Lee's army confronted the Army of the Potomac from May 23 to 27. Meanwhile Kershaw was promoted major general on February 15, to rank from February 13, 1862.

Kershaw and his division saw desperate fighting at the First Battle of Cold Harbor on June 27, 1862. On the former day Kershaw failed to coordinate his attack, and one of his brigades was mauled by Union cavalry fighting dismounted. Two days later Kershaw's division, fighting from behind breastworks, decimated the XVIII Corps' assaulting columns. On June 18 the timely arrival of Kershaw's division on the Petersburg lines helped break the back of Ulysses S. Grant's four-day attempt to seize that city, which for the next nine and one-half months was the unbreakable lock to Richmond. On July 13 Kershaw's troops were pulled out of the works, took position north of the James River, and battled a Union column led by General Hancock at Deep Bottom on July 27–29.

Reaching Front Royal on August 12 Kershaw next reinforced Jubal A. Early in the Valley. During the next month he marched many miles, advanced as far as Halltown, and engaged the foe at Cedarville August 16, Halltown August 26, and Abrams Creek September 13. On September 16 Kershaw and his division headed back to join General Lee. Word of Confederate defeats in the Valley reached Kershaw at Gordonsville, and he rejoined Early's army near Brown's Gap. At Hupp's Hill on October 13 Kershaw thrashed the Yankees, and at Cedar Creek on October 19 Kershaw and his division crossed at Bowman's Mill Ford and routed Thoburn's division. At 4 P.M. the tide turned, and Early's army suffered a crushing defeat. In November Kershaw returned to the Richmond area and took position in the earthworks north of the James, where he again came under the command of General Longstreet, who had returned to duty.

The Union victory at Five Forks, followed by Grant's all-out April 2 assault on the Petersburg lines, compelled the Confederates to evacuate that city as well as Richmond. Kershaw fought his last battle at Sayler's Creek on April 6, as part of Richard S. Ewell's force. His division was overwhelmed, and Kershaw and large numbers of his officers and men were captured.

Kershaw was sent as a prisoner of war to Fort Warren, Massachusetts. Following his August 13, 1865, release, he returned to Camden and resumed his law practice and political career. Elected to the state senate that autumn, he served as its president *pro tem* until the imposition of a reconstruction government in 1866. Four years later, as a member of the Union Reform party convention, he authored the resolutions recognizing the Reconstruction acts. In 1874 he was an unsuccessful Democratic candidate for Congress, but three years later, with South Carolina "redeemed," he was elected judge of the state's fifth circuit, a position he held until 1893, when failing health compelled his resignation. In February 1894 President Grover Cleveland named him postmaster of Camden, but he held this position less than two months, dying on April 13. He is buried in his hometown's Quaker Cemetery.

Kershaw—successively a regimental, brigade, and division commander—repeatedly demonstrated that he was without peer as a combat leader. He and his commands were always in the forefront of battle, and during their four years of service compiled a record for valor and self-sacrifice that few units, either in blue or gray, could equal, and none surpass.

Edwin C. Bearss

Capers, Ellison, *South Carolina*, Vol. VI in Evans, *Confederate Military History*.

Dickert, D. Augustus, *History of Kershaw's Brigade* (Dayton, 1973).

✯ *William Whedbee Kirkland* ✯

The only known wartime pose of General Kirkland dates from after August 1863. (Virginia Historical Society)

A native of North Carolina, William W. Kirkland was born on the family farm, "Ayrmont," near Hillsboro on February 13, 1833. Following education at the local schools he was given an appointment to the U.S. Military Academy at West Point in 1852. He attended only three years before leaving the academy, probably because an immediate commission as 2d lieutenant in the United States Marines became available. He wore the Marine uniform until August 1860 and then gave his allegiance to the new Confederacy even before his native state decided to secede. On March 16, 1861, he was appointed a captain in the Regular Army, but when North Carolina followed her sister states into the new Confederacy, Kirkland quickly went home to help recruit the 11th North Carolina Infantry. The men elected him their colonel.

Kirkland got his regiment to the front in Virginia just prior to the opening engagements along Bull Run and was there to participate at Blackburn's Ford July 18 and First Manassas July 21 in Milledge L. Bonham's brigade, being posted in defense of the Stone Bridge through much of the day of the latter battle. Following the breakup of Bonham's brigade Kirkland and his regiment, soon to be designated the 21st North Carolina, were reassigned to two Virginia brigades before going to the Shenandoah in early 1862. At Winchester on May 25 Kirkland was among those commanders who opened the Confederate attack, Kirkland himself taking a serious wound in the sharp fighting.

His wound took him out of active field service for nearly a year, though while recuperating he went west to the Army of Tennessee and attached himself as a volunteer staff officer with Major General Patrick

Cleburne's headquarters during the Battle of Stone's River (December 31, 1862–January 2, 1863). Following his recovery Kirkland rejoined the Army of Northern Virginia and resumed command of his regiment, now brigaded with two other North Carolina regiments under the command of Brigadier General Robert Hoke, who was absent at the time. He was heavily engaged during the Battle of Gettysburg on July 1 and 2 and especially on the first day in the fighting around the Alms House on the Heidlersburg Road and in the July 2 attacks on Cemetery Hill led by Major General Jubal A. Early.

Following Gettysburg Kirkland was appointed a brigadier on August 31, to date from August 29, 1863, but he had little time to enjoy his new status before another wound at Bristoe Station on October 14 put him out of action while leading Brigadier General James J. Pettigrew's old brigade, the 11th, 26th, 44th, 47th, and 52d North Carolina. This new wound put him out of active service for nearly eight months, and when he did return to duty in May 1864, assuming command of Hoke's old brigade, he did so only to be wounded yet again at Gaines' Mill on June 2.

This time Kirkland recuperated rapidly, returned to his command, and served on the north side of the James River during the Petersburg operations until December, when he and his men were sent to Wilmington, North Carolina. They arrived just in time to go into the Christmas Day fighting that repulsed the landing and attack aimed at Fort Fisher. General Kirkland was thereafter engaged in all of the operations around Fort Fisher and Wilmington, covering the final retreat to the latter place. Afterwards he took his brigade to join with the remnant army under General Joseph E. Johnston, seeing his last major fight at Bentonville March 19–21, 1865, and reportedly earning the praise of Johnston for his conduct on that field, as he had won plaudits from several commanders previously.

Kirkland surrendered with the rest of Johnston's army in April and soon thereafter removed to Savannah, Georgia, working as a commission merchant for several years. Late in the century he moved to New York City, perhaps in part because his daughter was achieving success on the Broadway stage, and there he worked in the post office until being completely invalided. He lived in the Washington, D.C., soldiers' home until May 12, 1915, when he died and was taken to Shepherdstown, West Virginia, for burial.

Kirkland gave universal satisfaction as a brigade commander, and had he only been able to stay out of the way of Yankee bullets, he might well have risen to higher responsibility. At Bentonville, the story goes, Johnston himself was well pleased when he learned that heavy firing came from the direction of Kirkland's brigade. "I am glad of it," said the army commander. "I would rather they would attack Kirkland than any one else."

William C. Davis

Gragg, Rod, *Confederate Goliath* (New York, 1991).

Hill, D. H., Jr., *North Carolina*, Vol. IV in Evans, *Confederate Military History*.

James H. Lane post-November 1862, showing wonderful detail in his full uniform, from regulation kepi to striped trousers. (Cook Collection, Valentine Museum, Richmond, Va.)

⁂ James Henry Lane ⁂

From first to last James H. Lane's Confederate fortunes were united with the army in Virginia. He was himself a native of the Old Dominion, born at Mathews Court House on July 28, 1833. He attended the Virginia Military Institute at Lexington, where he compiled an exemplary record, graduating in 1854. After that he attended the University of Virginia in Charlottesville, where he studied science. Following graduation in 1857 he worked for a brief spell on the hydrographic survey of the York River before taking an appointment as assistant professor of mathematics at his alma mater V.M.I. He also taught tactics but seems not to have been interested in staying put anywhere for long. He soon left to teach the same subjects at the Florida State Seminary and then moved on to Charlotte's North Carolina Military Institute, where he taught natural philosophy and military studies.

At the outbreak of the war Lane and his fellow professors went to work raising troops and training volunteers, Lane himself becoming drill master and adjutant at the Raleigh camp of instruction, where the 1st North Carolina was raised under Colonel D. H. Hill. The men then elected Lane their major, and he went to Virginia with the regiment in time for the first "battle" of the war at Big Bethel in June. Dubbed the "little major" because of his diminutive stature, Lane moved up to lieutenant colonel when Hill was given a generalcy, and at a subsequent reorganization of North Carolina volunteers for new terms of service Lane was chosen colonel of the 28th Infantry, the first twelve-months regiment to reorganize for the full indefinite term of the war.

Lane took his regiment back to Virginia after its reorganization and was assigned to the brigade of Lawrence O. Branch. Lane was subsequently engaged in the Peninsula and Seven Days' campaigns (March–August and June 25–July 1, 1862, respectively) and won praise for his performance at Hanover Court House, where his inexperienced men were bested in spite of considerable courage. Later at Cold Harbor Lane felt the enemy lead for the first of three times in

his career and hardly had time to recuperate from the superficial wound when he was hit again at Frayser's Farm, taking a hit in the face, despite which he continued to command.

Lane went on into Maryland with the Army of Northern Virginia, performing admirably September 17 at Antietam, where he assumed command of the brigade after the death of Branch in the closing hours of the fight. Now commanding the 7th, 18th, 28th, 33d, and 37th North Carolina, Lane covered the retreat of the army back into Virginia.

Recognizing the "little major's" capacity, President Jefferson Davis appointed him a brigadier on November 1, to date from the same day, and thereafter his men affectionately called him the "little general." His command presented him with a new sword and sash, as well as saddle and bridle, to honor the occasion. At Fredericksburg the next month Lane held the center of Major General A. P. Hill's line on the right flank of General Robert E. Lee's army and was badly broken up by Union Major General George G. Meade's attacks, though the line managed to hold out. Just over four months later on the evening of May 2, 1863, he was in the forefront of Lieutenant General Thomas J. "Stonewall" Jackson's attacking flank column at Chancellorsville. He renewed his attacks at dawn the next day on the Orange Plank Road until beaten back by Yankee artillery.

On the subsequent march into Pennsylvania, General Lane and his brigade were among the first engaged in the July 1 fighting at Gettysburg. On the second day when Major General William D. Pender fell with a mortal wound, Lane temporarily assumed command of the four-brigade division of South Carolina, Georgia, and North Carolina troops. The next day Major General Isaac Trimble replaced him and Lane returned to his brigade and was at its head, mounted on his horse, on July 3 when it went forward in the Pickett-Pettigrew assault. His command suffered nearly fifty percent casualties, and his own horse went down under him. When Trimble himself went down

Lane as colonel of the 28th North Carolina, probably in 1862. (Cook Collection, Valentine Museum, Richmond, Va.)

and was captured, Lane again took command of the remnant of the division, though only for a week until the battered command was consolidated with Major General Henry Heth's division.

Lane continued with the Army of Northern Virginia throughout the coming months of relative inactivity. In May 1864 he helped hold a vital position at the Bloody Angle at Spotsylvania and fought on in the Overland Campaign until the fierce fighting in June at Cold Harbor, where he took a wound in the groin that put him out of action for the rest of the year. He rejoined his brigade in the trenches around Petersburg and accompanied it on the retreat to Appomattox, where he was surrendered in April 1865 along with the rest.

After the war Lane returned to teaching, struggling to rebuild the fortunes of his desolated family. He taught at the Virginia Agricultural and Mechanical College (later the Virginia Polytechnic Institute); did a stint as professor of mathematics at Missouri State University; then moved to the Alabama Agricultural and Mechanical College, later Alabama Polytechnic Institute, at Auburn. Frequently he doubled as commandant of cadets at these combined civilian and military academies and was still active at his last position when he died on September 21, 1907. He was buried at Auburn, where his four children survived him. The Army of Northern Virginia never had a more devoted or able brigade commander, his many wounds testifying that Virginia was as much of his blood as he was of hers. Testimony to the regard in which he was held after the war was his selection to join in the guard of honor for President Jefferson Davis' funeral in New Orleans.

William C. Davis

A very slight variant of the previous image of Colonel Lane. (William A. Turner Collection)

Coddington, Edwin B., *The Gettysburg Campaign* (New York, 1968).

Hill, D. H., Jr., *North Carolina*, Vol. IV in Evans, *Confederate Military History*.

✴ *Walter Paye Lane* ✴

General Walter P. Lane in the 1870s. No uniformed portrait has come to light. (University of Texas at Austin)

Walter Paye (or Page) Lane was born on February 18, 1817, in County Cork, Ireland. His parents brought him to the United States when he was four years old, and the family settled in Guernsey County, Ohio. As a teenager Lane moved to Louisville, Kentucky, where he made the acquaintance of Stephen F. Austin, who persuaded him to emigrate to the Republic of Texas. Lane arrived in Texas in March 1836; he fought in the Texas War for Independence at San Jacinto on April 21 in Henry W. Karnes' cavalry. He was promoted to 2d lieutenant for his valor during the fight. After Texas gained independence, Lane participated in several Indian battles. He was wounded in 1838 during the Surveyors' Fight in Navarro County.

In the years before the Civil War his occupations varied from service on a privateer in the Gulf of Mexico to teaching school. He served in the Mexican War as a 1st lieutenant in Kit Archland's Ranger Company. This group captured the mayor of Salado while out on a scouting expedition and forced him to return the bones of some Texans executed there years earlier. Lane was "ruthless and careless of [Mexican] property...[but] so brave and efficient as a scout that he made himself indispensable." He also fought in the battles of Monterrey and Buena Vista and won a promotion to major for gallantry.

At the end of the Mexican War he settled in Marshall, Texas, but also headed for California when gold was discovered and from 1849 until 1853 mined there and in Nevada, Arizona, and Peru. He made and lost money several times before he finally settled in Marshall, where he became a businessman. When the

Civil War began, Lane joined a unit from East Texas and was elected lieutenant colonel when the regiment reorganized in Dallas on June 13, 1861.

The 3d Texas Cavalry (also known as the South Kansas–Texas Regiment) arrived in Arkansas under Colonel Elkanah Greer in July 1861 and joined Ben McCulloch. Lane fought on August 10, 1861, at Wilson's Creek, where his "gallant bearing" received much notice. "He had his horse shot [from] under him in the charge," reported Greer, "and fought on foot until he mounted another horse [whose rider had been killed], and continued the fight." Under James McIntosh the regiment went to the Indian Territory where Lane took part in the battle of Chustenallah on December 26, 1861. At Pea Ridge (Elkhorn Tavern) in March the following year Greer said Lane "joined in the charge, and afterwards performed good service in aiding and assisting in dismounting and forming the cavalry."

Lane's regiment crossed the Mississippi River with Major General Earl Van Dorn and joined General P. G. T. Beauregard in May at Corinth. Beauregard wrote in June 1862: "The general commanding takes great pleasure in calling the attention to the army of the brave, skillful, and gallant conduct of Lieutenant-Colonel Lane, of the Third Regiment Texas Dismounted Cavalry, who with 246 men, on the 29th ultimo, charged a largely superior force of the enemy, drove him from his position, and forced him to leave a number of his dead and wounded upon the field. The conduct of this brave regiment is worthy of all honor and imitation."

Lane fought at Iuka in September and again at Corinth in October but returned in 1863 to the Trans-Mississippi, where he continued to be an adventurous sort who tended to make his own rules. In May 1863 William Steele, commander of the Indian Territory, complained that Lane was not following orders. "I have heard that Colonel Lane is trying to get ordered in another direction," wrote Steele. "This regiment is out of the Indian Territory without authority, having been ordered only to Red River to refit and get back the absentees."

Lane's 1st Texas Partisan Rangers served in James Major's cavalry brigade and fought in southern Louisiana in the summer and fall of 1863. Major reported that the regiments under the command of Lane had "behaved with gallantry" during the Louisiana operations. Lane returned to Texas with Major in December but returned to Louisiana to take part in the Red River Campaign, March–May 1864. He was wounded at Mansfield April 8, and his replacement noted that "before he was disabled [he] was ever in the front rank encouraging his men by his voice and example. I know I express the feelings of the entire brigade when I say we wish for no braver or more experienced officer to command us."

On October 28, 1864, E. Kirby Smith recommended him for promotion, saying he was a "superior cavalry officer." Jefferson Davis recommended him for promotion on December 23, 1864. He was not, however, promoted for three more months, to rank from March 17, 1865, and the promotion was confirmed by President Davis and the Senate on the last day it met, March 18.

After the war Lane returned to tend his business interests in Marshall. One historian described Lane as a "colorful fellow, full of blarney and bombast, but his courage and resourcefulness under fire would vindicate his own high opinion of himself." Lane promulgated this image when he wrote his war memoirs in 1887. He also was prominent in several veterans' organizations after the war. Lane died at Marshall on January 28, 1892, and was buried there.

Anne Bailey

Lane, Walter P., *The Adventures and Recollections of Walter P. Lane* (Marshall, Tex., 1928).

General Evander Law posed sometime during or after October 1862 for this, his only known portrait as a brigadier. (Albert G. Shaw Collection, Virginia Historical Society, Richomond, Va.)

✴ Evander McIvor Law ✴

Born August 7, 1836, at Darlington, South Carolina, Evander McIvor Law attended public schools and Old St. John's Academy before entering the South Carolina Military Academy. Graduating in 1856, Law served as an instructor during his senior year and as assistant professor of history and belles lettres in 1857. After serving as professor of history and belles lettres at Kings Mountain Military Academy at Yorkville from 1858 to 1860, Law moved to Tuskegee, Alabama, where he cofounded and taught at the Military High School. He also studied law.

When the Civil War erupted, Law recruited and became captain of a company largely composed of his students. When the company became part of the 4th Alabama Infantry at Pensacola, Law became the lieutenant colonel of the regiment. Ordered to Virginia on May 12, 1861, the 4th arrived at Harpers Ferry within nine days. The regiment fought with distinction July 21 at First Manassas, where its colonel was killed and Law was severely wounded. Law recovered sufficiently to return to field duty and was commissioned a colonel in October.

Transferred to the Peninsula, the regiment served in Brigadier General William H. C. Whiting's brigade. Law commanded the brigade at Seven Pines and again during the Seven Days' battles. Major General Thomas "Stonewall" Jackson praised his penetration of the Union lines at Gaines' Mill on June 27, 1862. After fighting July 1 at Malvern Hill, Brigadier General John Bell Hood assumed command of a demi-division of his own and Law's brigades. Law led the 4th Alabama, the 2d and 11th Mississippi, and the 6th North Carolina in the campaigns of Second Manassas, Sharpsburg, and Fredericksburg; although they saw little action at the latter.

At Second Manassas August 29–30 the two brigades played a prominent role in the counterattack that drove the Union army from the field. September 17 at Sharpsburg the two brigades were the first to come to Jackson's support. Their ferocious charge through the Cornfield caused Hood to remark later that day that his division lay "dead on the field." Law's corps commander, Major General James Longstreet, commended him for his performance at Manassas, Boonsboro, and Sharpsburg.

Law was promoted to brigadier general on October 15, 1862, to rank from October 2. His brigade was reorganized in January 1863 and afterward consisted of five Alabama regiments; it was in southeastern Virginia throughout early 1863. Law's brigade held the Confederate extreme right at Gettysburg on July 2, 1863, when he initiated the attack on the Round Tops. After nearly securing his objective Law had to assume command of the division following the wounding of Major General Hood. Law claimed afterward that the repulse of the division was General Robert E. Lee's fault, because Lee had not concentrated his troops against the Round Tops. On July 3 Law skillfully repulsed a Federal cavalry attack against Lee's right rear.

Believing Hood unfit for further field duty, Longstreet urged the promotion of Brigadier General Micah Jenkins, whose commission predated that of Law's by two months. Despite Law's seniority with the division and President Jefferson Davis' support Longstreet remained adamant. The controversy ended when Hood resumed command.

At Chickamauga in September Hood acted as corps commander and Law, because Jenkins failed to reach the battlefield, led the division. Although Longstreet reportedly expressed "his admiration and satisfaction" at his handling of the division, Jenkins commanded the division during the sieges of Knoxville and Chattanooga. Twice during that period Jenkins accused Law of failing to support him. The animosities between the two rivals finally influenced Law to submit his resignation on December 19, along with a request for a transfer to the cavalry. Longstreet brought charges against Law and threatened to resign if Law was not court-martialed. The War Department ignored the wishes of both men, and both remained in their former positions.

Returning to Virginia in 1864, Law fought at the Wilderness, at Spotsylvania Court House, and along the North Anna River. At Cold Harbor on June 2 Law reinforced Lee's right with his own and another brigade. He deployed his men where the Confederates had been driven back the previous day. Fortifying their position during the night, Law's men inflicted over three thousand casualties in their repulse of the Union XVII Corps the following day, at which time Law was severely wounded.

After recovering from his wounds Law renewed his request for a cavalry command. Sent to South Carolina, he commanded the former brigade of Major General Matthew C. Butler. While in charge of the evacuation of Columbia (which had been captured on February 17, 1865) Law was commissioned a major general on March 20 upon the recommendations of General Joseph E. Johnston and Lieutenant General Wade Hampton. As a member of Johnston's staff during the fighting at Bentonville on April 19 Law assumed command of Butler's division the following morning. Despite his rank Law apparently commanded only Butler's old brigade when he received his parole in North Carolina in May.

On March 9, 1863, Law married Jane Elizabeth Latta. Immediately after the war Law became administrator of his father-in-law's estate, which included extensive agricultural holdings and railroad interests. Returning to Tuskegee in the late 1860s, Law organized the Alabama Grange in 1872 and was associated with the Kings Mountain Military Academy until it closed in 1881.

Anxious to establish a military academy modeled after the Citadel, Law moved to Florida in 1881. In 1894 he opened the Southern Florida Military Institute at Bartow. Going public in 1895, the South Florida Military and Educational Institute received state support through county scholarships. Law operated the school until he resigned in 1903. He edited the *Bartow Courier-Informant* (1905–15), served as a trustee of the Sumerlin Institute (1905–12), and was a member of the Polk County Board of Education from 1912 until his death. Law's efforts in the field of public education constituted a major contribution to the foundation of public education in Florida.

Active in Confederate veterans' activities, Law served as division commander of Florida from 1899 to 1903, helped organize a chapter of the United Daughters of the Confederacy in Bartow, and wrote several articles about the war. Law was the last Confederate major general to die, doing so on October 31, 1920, in Bartow, where he was buried.

Lawrence L. Hewitt

Wheeler, Joseph, *Alabama*, Vol. VIII in Evans, *Confederate Military History*.

Law, seated at center, as colonel of the 4th Alabama Infantry, probably in 1862. (Cook Collection, Valentine Museum, Richmond, Va.)

A little-known portrait of General Lawton, apparently taken early in the war. (Museum of the Confederacy, Richmond, Va.)

✶ *Alexander Robert Lawton* ✶

A capable Confederate officer whose rise to prominence would be tainted by controversy, Alexander Lawton was born in the parish of St. Peter, near Beaufort, South Carolina, on November 4, 1818, to a prestigious local family. His connections thus gained him an appointment to the U.S. Military Academy, where he matriculated in 1835, graduating four years later to be appointed 2d lieutenant in the 1st United States Artillery. Lawton's tenure in uniform was brief, however, for he resigned in 1841 to enter Harvard Law School, and upon graduation in 1842 he moved to Savannah, Georgia, forming an association with that city that would last the rest of his life.

Lawton spent seven years in private practice before turning his West Point engineering training to the presidency of the new Augusta & Savannah Railroad, which he ran until 1854. When he left the railroad, he changed careers once more by seeking and winning a seat in the Georgia legislature, serving 1855–56 and then moving into the state senate, 1859–60, where he increasingly allied himself with the ardent Southern-rights faction.

When the secession crisis erupted, Lawton won the colonelcy of the 1st Georgia Volunteers and led his regiment in the seizure of Fort Pulaski on January 3, 1861, more than two weeks before Georgia actually seceded. It was not much of an achievement, the fort being guarded only by a sergeant and a caretaker, but it brought Lawton to sudden prominence among the state's military leaders. As a result, when President Jefferson Davis passed out appointments following the formation of the Confederate government, Lawton was one of the early brigadiers, receiving his commission on February 17, to rank from the same day.

At first Lawton took command of the Georgia military district, which at the time was a backwater promising little action. Early in 1862 he took command instead of a brigade composed of the 13th, 26th, 31st, 60th, and 61st Georgia infantries and in late spring was attached to the division that Major General Thomas J. "Stonewall" Jackson commanded in the

Shenandoah Valley. Briefly brought to aid in the defense of Richmond, Lawton was sent back to the Valley in June but hardly arrived before returning with Stonewall for the Seven Days' Campaign, participating with distinction at Gaines' Mill on June 27. In the absence of specific orders Lawton rushed his men to the aid of Ewell's command, his thirty-five hundred men stabilizing the Gray line long enough for reinforcements to reverse a near-crisis.

Lawton's performance brought him conspicuously to Jackson's attention. After Second Manassas, in which Lawton was attached to Major General Richard Ewell's division and in which Ewell himself lost a leg, Lawton was given command of the division. At Antietam September 17 he figured importantly in the fighting around the Dunkard Church and took a severe wound in the vicious fighting on the Mumma farm and in the Cornfield. Lawton remained in the field long enough to see reinforcements arrive.

It took many months for the general to recover his health, and his active field service was permanently at an end. Meanwhile Quartermaster General Abraham C. Myers fell out with Davis, many said because Myers' wife had criticized Varina Davis. In response the president relieved Myers and appointed Lawton to the post on August 10, 1863. Administration foes in Congress immediately made Lawton's appointment a focal point for their general campaign of opposition to Davis, declining to confirm the appointment and even maintaining that Myers was still the legitimate quartermaster. The battle continued off and on for months before Lawton was finally confirmed. Meanwhile, his own varying health frequently prevented him from exercising his duties.

Nevertheless Lawton performed his role as capably as possible under the circumstances. Certainly no groundswell outcry against him ever emerged as it did against Commissary General Lucius Northrop, and Lawton served to the end of the war under two secretaries of war, even when changes in administration led to house cleanings in other bureaus. He reportedly made occasional requests to be returned to field duty, but Davis declined and Lawton did not again take to the saddle until the last days during the evacuation of Richmond. After the government had fled and the bridges and warehouses were destroyed, Lawton was one of the last officials to leave Richmond, in company with the secretary of war. He briefly joined Lee's retreating army, then located the fleeing government and traveled with it until May 4 when Secretary of War John C. Breckinridge officially disbanded the War Department at Washington, Georgia.

It was but a short trip back to his home in Savannah after that. Lawton returned to the law and politics, taking a seat in the legislature in 1870, acting as vice president of the state constitutional convention in 1877, and leading state delegations to Democratic conventions in 1880 and 1884. He lost a U.S. Senate bid in 1880, but in 1885 his name was proposed as minister to Russia. This fell through, but two years later he was confirmed as minister to Austria. On July 2, 1896, while on a visit to Clifton Springs, New York, General Lawton died and was returned to Savannah for burial. Wounding had taken an able division commander from the field and buried him in the backwater and political in-fighting of an administrative post, but he gave satisfaction wherever he served.

William C. Davis

Davis, William C., *Jefferson Davis: The Man and His Hour* (New York, 1991).

Evans, Clement A., *The Civil History of the Confederate States*, Vol. I in Evans, *Confederate Military History*.

Lawton's receding hairline and generally older appearance suggest that this is a late-war portrait. (Museum of the Confederacy, Richmond, Va.)

✶ *Danville Leadbetter* ✶

No uniformed portrait of General Leadbetter has come to light. This is an early 1850s image. (U.S. Army Military History Institute, Carlisle, Pa.)

Danville Leadbetter was born at Leeds, Maine, on August 26, 1811. He graduated third in his class at West Point in 1836. Though commissioned originally in the artillery service, he was transferred shortly to the engineer corps. Leadbetter served on garrison duty from 1839 to 1845 and then took charge of the engineer agency in New York City. In 1853, by which time he had been promoted to captain, he was assigned to Mobile, Alabama. There he superintended repair work at Fort Morgan, began construction of Fort Gaines, and had charge of construction of the custom house. Leadbetter resigned from the army on December 31, 1857, and became chief engineer for the state of Alabama.

When that state seceded in January 1861, Governor Andrew B. Moore made Leadbetter one of his aides. The Confederate War Department appointed him a major of engineers on March 16. One month later he received orders to inspect the defenses at Mobile and make a full report to the government. Colonel William J. Hardee, commander at Mobile, ordered Leadbetter to work on the defenses at Fort Gaines after Leadbetter had filed his report. At this early stage of the war, he recognized the strategic importance of Mobile and concluded that the preparation of the city's defenses was worth all that could be spent on it. He wrote: "...we must, if necessary, spend our all in this business, certainly hundreds of millions, and I know of no point more worthy the application of a half of one million than Mobile Bay." Leadbetter also anticipated the Union's use of ironclad steamers against the forts at the mouth of Mobile Bay and advised making the masonry walls as strong as possible.

On August 3 Leadbetter received orders to go to Richmond, Virginia, to assume command of the Confederates' Engineer Bureau. He served as acting chief of the bureau until November 11, 1861. With the rank of colonel, he was ordered to eastern Tennessee to restore and maintain the railroad line between Bristol and Chattanooga, which had been damaged in several places by Union sympathizers. Leadbetter established his headquarters first at Greeneville in Greene County, which he called "the headquarters of insurrection." Within several weeks his troops had captured and hanged several of the men involved in burning the railroad bridges. Eventually he moved his headquarters to Knoxville. It was Leadbetter who ordered leading Unionist William G. "Parson" Brownlow taken into custody.

Leadbetter was promoted to brigadier general on March 6, 1862, to rank from February 27. When Major General Edmund Kirby Smith assumed command of the District (soon Department) of East Tennessee on March 8, he reorganized his command, and Leadbetter became commander of the district's 1st brigade. He continued operating against the Unionists until after the Battle of Shiloh, April 6–7, when he received orders to go to Chattanooga and protect it against advancing Federal forces. On April 29 the enemy drove his forces back from Bridgeport and forced them to destroy the bridge there. Leadbetter called for reinforcements in June when elements of Major General Don Carlos Buell's army advanced against him. The Federals had surprised Leadbetter and captured intact the railroad bridge over the Tennessee River. He fell back into his entrenchments at Chattanooga, where his troops had to endure a bombardment by Union forces.

The action at Bridgeport and Leadbetter's subsequent conduct convinced Kirby Smith that he needed another commander at Chattanooga. Brigadier General Henry Heth relieved Leadbetter on July 1 and assumed command of the 2d Division of Kirby Smith's army. Leadbetter retained command of a brigade under Heth. In this capacity he participated in Kirby Smith's invasion of Kentucky in August and September. He exercised temporary command of his own and Colonel William G. M. Davis' brigades at Frankfort for a brief time in September.

On October 19 the War Department ordered Leadbetter to Mobile as chief engineer, and he arrived there on November 4. For the next year he worked hard to improve the defensive posture of Mobile despite having to face frequent shortages of labor, construction supplies, and artillery pieces. Leadbetter designed and supervised construction of a line of redoubts and entrenchments around the city, and his men had completed most of the work by May 1863. Largely through the efforts of Leadbetter and his engineers, Mobile became one of the most strongly fortified places in the Confederacy.

In October 1863 Leadbetter left Mobile to become General Braxton Bragg's chief engineer and superintend the construction of fortifications on Missionary Ridge southeast of Chattanooga. He assumed that position on October 23. It is unclear to what extent Leadbetter was responsible for the extremely poor placement of Confederate defensive positions on Missionary Ridge, a factor that led to the startling Union victory there on November 25. Shortly before the latter battle, Bragg ordered Leadbetter to go to Knoxville and consult with Lieutenant General James Longstreet concerning the latter's operations against that city. Since he had supervised so many of the entrenchments there, it was felt that Leadbetter could provide valuable advice. Brigadier General Edward P. Alexander strongly criticized Leadbetter after the war for the influence he had exerted over Longstreet's plans. According to Alexander, Leadbetter advised against an attack planned for November 26. Then several days were wasted in searching for the most favorable point to attack. Finally, Leadbetter apparently persuaded Longstreet to conduct a predawn surprise assault on Fort Sanders rather than one during daylight hours when artillery support might have given it a chance to succeed. The resulting attack was repulsed with heavy losses.

Leadbetter left Knoxville on the morning of November 29 and reached the Army of Tennessee at Dalton on December 3. He remained chief engineer of the army until he resigned his commission on April 7, 1864, due to ill health. Leadbetter went to Mobile and was there in early August when Admiral David G. Farragut's Union fleet fought its way into Mobile Bay. The chief of the Engineer Bureau in Richmond telegraphed him to offer whatever assistance he could to Major General Dabney H. Maury, commander of the District of the Gulf. Leadbetter apparently remained in Mobile until the end of the war, though he was not captured or paroled. He went to Mexico after the fall of the Confederacy and soon made his way to Canada. He died on September 26, 1866, at Clifton. Later his body was reinterred in Magnolia Cemetery at Mobile.

Arthur W. Bergeron, Jr.

Bergeron, Arthur W., Jr., *Confederate Mobile, 1861–1865* (Jackson, 1991).

Owen, Thomas M., *History of Alabama and Dictionary of Alabama Biography,* 4 vols. (Spartanburg, S.C., 1978).

Wheeler, Joseph, *Alabama,* Vol. VIII in Evans, *Confederate Military History.*

Colonel Edwin G. Lee, probably taken while in Richmond in 1863. (William A. Turner Collection)

⋆ Edwin Gray Lee ⋆

Of the seeming host of generals named Lee in the Confederate service, surely the least known of all was one of the youngest, Edwin Gray Lee, born May 27, 1836, at the family home, "Leeland," near Alexandria, Virginia. Though distantly related to the more illustrious Lees, young Edwin did not seem to enjoy the kind of first-families connection that so benefited the others socially and politically. He attended Hallowell's elementary school in Alexandria, then entered Williamsburg's College of William and Mary when he was fifteen. Three years later, however, he withdrew prior to graduation and finished his education at the Alexandria Boarding School for boys, graduating in June 1855.

The family had removed to the western part of the state, and at Shepherdstown (now West Virginia) he first came to public notice as a speaker of prominence in 1856, helped no doubt by being the great-grandson of Richard Henry Lee. Thereafter he attended the law school presided over at Lexington by Judge John W. Brockenbrough and completed his studies in 1858 to join his father's Shepherdstown practice. Young Lee also joined the town's militia unit, the Hamtranck Guards, and marched with them to Harpers Ferry in December 1859 when John Brown attempted to take the United States Arsenal. Young Lee performed well during the brief crisis, enough so to attract the attention of his distant kinsman Robert E. Lee, commanding the U.S. forces sent to subdue Brown. "Though a youth he displayed great bravery and firmness," recalled the elder Lee. The young lawyer married the next year, becoming the son-in-law of future general William Nelson Pendleton.

When Virginia seceded in 1861 and the call went out for her sons to rally to the colors, Lee marched with his militia company to join the 2d Virginia Infantry, of which he was immediately made adjutant. The appointment to a staff position may have reflected Lee's fragile health, for he had been diagnosed the previous year with tuberculosis, and his health seems to have been almost continuously fragile. Lee continued in staff work when Brigadier General Thomas J.

"Stonewall" Jackson soon made him an aide-de-camp with the rank of 1st lieutenant.

Lee was present with Jackson July 21, 1861, at First Manassas and performed well enough there despite his health that he was soon given a field assignment as major in the 33d Virginia of the Stonewall Brigade. Thereafter he rose to lieutenant colonel and served with the regiment through Jackson's Valley Campaign (May–June 1862) and the Battle of Antietam (September 17). Just after the latter battle he was captured by Federals while visiting his family in Shepherdstown but was exchanged in time to assume the colonelcy of his regiment December 13 at the First Battle of Fredericksburg. Active service had ravaged his system, however, and almost immediately afterward he resigned his position and took a lengthy leave of absence to recuperate.

During the next year, while supposedly resting, Colonel Lee occasionally led clandestine assaults on Federal boats on the Potomac River and by May 17, 1864, felt well enough again to accept a command at Drewry's Bluff just prior to the Federal attack. On June 3 he received orders sending him to the Shenandoah to command the post at Staunton and organize Valley defense forces. On September 23 the president appointed him a brigadier to date from September 20, but within two months his health was so weakened by his labors that he once again received a leave of absence.

Nevertheless, behind the scenes there had been much discussion of Lee in Richmond, and Jefferson Davis and Secretary of State Judah Benjamin decided to send him to Canada to assist with the Confederate commission sent there to help foment unrest in the North. Traveling as "W. Gray," General Lee arrived after a lengthy sea journey via Bermuda and Nova Scotia. However, when he reached Montreal on April 3, 1865, the war was all but over. Lee worked with agent John Surratt to investigate the possibilities of effecting a massive breakout of the fifteen thousand or more prisoners held at Elmira, New York, prison camp, but nothing came of it and Lee soon had to help spirit Surratt out of Canada when he was charged with complicity in the murder of Lincoln.

Lee remained in Canada until 1866 when it was safe to return to Virginia, but the old infirmity gave him little peace, and almost immediately he moved to the warmer, drier climate of Seguin, Texas. Thereafter Lee wintered in the Deep South for his health and earned his living by writing and publishing, chiefly poetry. But his health was shattered, and at Yellow Sulphur Springs, Virginia, during the night of August 24–25, 1870, he died in his sleep after months of being a complete invalid. The thirty-four-year-old general was buried in Lexington Cemetery among so many other Confederate luminaries who lived and died for their cause.

William C. Davis

Hotchkiss, Jedediah, *Virginia*, Vol. III in Evans, *Confederate Military History*.

Levin, Alexander Lee, "The Canada Contract," *Civil War Times Illustrated*, XVIII (June 1979).

General Lee, photographed during the last seven months of the war. (National Archives)

✹ *Fitzhugh Lee* ✹

Fitzhugh Lee, the grandson of "Light Horse Harry" Lee, great-grandson of George Mason of Gunston Hall, and nephew of Robert E. Lee, was born on November 19, 1835, at "Clermont" in Alexandria, Virginia. He attended private schools until his 1852 admission to West Point, where his gregarious personality and carefree nature clashed with the rigid discipline of the academy. The recipient of numerous demerits, he earned the wrath of the superintendent—his uncle, R. E. Lee—when he and other cadets wandered from their quarters without permission. Colonel Lee demanded that they face dismissal or a court-martial, but classmates swore they would abide by the rules that Fitz had violated, and convinced the colonel to drop the charges. A year before he graduated Lee confessed: "I entered this Academy a wild, careless, and inexperienced youth,…but I begin to see the 'folly of my ways,' and shall try to amend." Despite conduct he managed to complete his studies at West Point and ranked forty-fifth of forty-nine in the class of 1856.

Commissioned a brevet 2d lieutenant in the 2d Cavalry on July 1, 1856, Lee spent a year as a cavalry instructor at Carlisle Barracks, Pennsylvania, before joining his outfit. He advanced to 2d lieutenant on January 1, 1858, and reported to his regiment on the Texas frontier. Comanches and oppressive heat greeted Lee, who received an arrow through both lungs during one scuffle with the Indians in 1859 and "thought certainly I was going to die." At the end of 1860 he returned to West Point as an instructor of cavalry tactics. He was promoted to 1st lieutenant on March 31, 1861, but this did little to relieve his anxiety over the election of Abraham Lincoln. He complained to his father that he "was tired of serving a Black

Republican administration." After Virginia had left the Union on April 17, 1861, Lee offered his resignation from the U.S. army on May 16 (accepted May 21).

He entered the Southern army as an aide to Brigadier General Richard S. Ewell but saw no fighting at First Manassas. In September 1861 he was appointed to lieutenant colonel of the celebrated 1st Virginia Cavalry. He took command of the regiment on April 23, 1862, receiving promotion to colonel the same day. June 12–15, 1862, Lee and his regiment accompanied Major General "Jeb" Stuart on his famous ride around the Army of the Potomac. Impressed by his subordinate, Stuart claimed that no other Southern officer possessed "more of the elements of what a brigadier of cavalry ought to be than he." Lee was appointed to brigadier general, effective July 24, 1862, but not everyone believed that merit had been the basis of his rapid rise in the army. Colonel Thomas R. R. Cobb of Georgia wrote on July 28: "I confess that I was a little annoyed this morning by the announcement of the promotion of Fitzhugh Lee…. I suppose in a few days we will see the balance of the Lee's promoted also."

Lee's actions during the Second Manassas Campaign in August and September did little to quiet the critics. His failure to arrive with his brigade at Verdiersville by August 17 almost resulted in the capture of Stuart, who scolded Lee for his dilatory behavior. Lee redeemed himself, however, in a raid against John

On the way to becoming one of the most photographed Confederate generals, Fitz Lee sat for this portrait probably in late 1862 or early 1863. (Museum of the Confederacy, Richmond, Va.)

Lee as he appeared at the outbreak of the war, while still a 1st lieutenant in the U.S. army. (William A. Turner Collection)

Lee as a general in the middle of the war. (U.S. Army Military History Institute, Carlisle, Pa.)

Pope's headquarters on August 22 and at the gaps of South Mountain on September 15. He also successfully protected the rear of Lee's retreating column when it trudged back to Virginia following the Battle of Antietam on September 17.

During the fall and winter of 1862 Lee's horsemen frequently dashed behind enemy lines to disrupt communications and raid supply depots, though he missed Stuart's ride around McClellan in October. On March 17, 1863, Federal cavalry splashed across Kelly's Ford on the Rappahannock River, stormed past Confederate outposts, and charged into Lee's command. The Union troopers fought exceptionally well and inflicted significant casualties on Lee's troopers before retiring. At Chancellorsville on May 2, 1863, Lee discovered the Federal right flank along the Orange Turnpike, information that prevented Lieutenant General "Stonewall" Jackson's launching a frontal assault down the Orange Plank Road, where the end of the Northern army supposedly was positioned.

Rheumatism forced Lee to relinquish command of his brigade at the Battle of Brandy Station on June 9; however, he returned to the saddle for Stuart's fruitless ride around the Army of the Potomac during the Gettysburg Campaign. On July 1 Lee burned Carlisle Barracks, where he had served as cavalry instructor, and two days later led his brigade in the inconclusive cavalry fight east of Gettysburg. After the Army of Northern Virginia limped back across the Potomac, Lee informed his mother that he had "survived some narrow escapes but with exception of my four horses being shot again, escaped without harm."

With the reorganization of Stuart's cavalry into two divisions after Gettysburg, Lee received his commission as major general on September 3, 1863, effective August 3. Robert E. Lee's endorsement of his promotion read: "I do not know any other officer in the cavalry who has done better service." Standing five feet, eight inches tall, possessing broad shoulders, a full beard, and sparkling blue eyes, Fitz competently carried out his new duties. On May 8, 1864, his cavalry slowed the Federal march down the Brock Road toward Spotsylvania Court House, gaining time for Confederate infantry to block U. S. Grant's advance to the south. At Yellow Tavern on May 11, Stuart fell with a mortal wound. As Lee assumed command on the battlefield, the dying officer cried, "Fitz will do as well for you as I have done."

Wade Hampton praised Lee's performance at Trevilian Station, June 11–12, 1864, after which Fitz and his division reinforced Jubal Early's army in the Shenandoah Valley during the middle of August 1864. On September 19 Lee "was shot through the thigh and carried from the field" at the Third Battle of Winchester. Returning to his division in January 1865, he received command of all the horsemen north of the James River in February. At the Battle of Five Forks on April 1 Lee's behavior recalled his conduct at the academy. Instead of devoting attention to their heavily out-numbered troops, he and George E. Pickett dined on shad while Philip J. Sheridan delivered an assault that sent the Confederates flying from the field in disorder. Robert E. Lee subsequently stripped Pickett of any responsibility in the army but allowed his nephew, whose behavior was equally inexcusable, to remain on duty until Appomattox. Fitz took part in Lee's last council of war; refusing to sur-render, he slipped through Grant's lines but turned himself over to Federal authorities on April 22, 1865.

For twenty years after the war Lee tilled the Virginia soil at "Richland," in Stafford County. In 1879 he entered the political arena; after failing to capture a seat in the state senate, he won the governor's race in 1885. When Lee lost a bid for election to the U.S. Senate in 1893, President Grover Cleveland named him consul general to Cuba, a position he resigned when hostilities erupted with Spain. Given a commis-sion of major general of volunteers on May 4, 1898, Lee did not see any fighting. He was honorably discharged on March 2, 1901, having received a brigadier-general-ship in the regular army on February 11 of that year. In addition to his military and political endeavors, Lee became one of the leading spokesmen of the myth of the Lost Cause. In 1894 he published *General Lee*, which offered a Christ-like portrayal of the Southern chieftain and stinging criticism of James Longstreet.

Lee died in Washington, D.C., on April 28, 1905, and his remains were interred in Hollywood Cemetery in Richmond.

Peter S. Carmichael

Hunter, Robert W., "Fitzhugh Lee. An Address Delivered on Fitzhugh Lee Day at the Jamestown Exposition," in *Southern Historical Society Papers*, Vol. 35.

Nichols, James L., *General Fitzhugh Lee: A Biography* (Lynchburg, 1989).

One of a later war series of poses, probably while Lee was a major general, though nothing on his uniform indicated exact rank. (Museum of the Confederacy, Richmond, Va.)

Another pose from the same sitting. (William A. Turner Collection)

Possibly still from the same sitting or a variant of an earlier pose. (Southern Historical Collection, University of North Carolina, Chapel Hill)

A maturing General Lee. (William A. Turner Collection)

✫ *George Washington Custis Lee* ✫

George Washington Custis Lee as a colonel during his years as aide to President Davis. (Medford Historical Society, Medford, Mass.)

Custis Lee in April 1865, with his father and Colonel Walter Taylor, posing for Mathew Brady. His buttons show that he is a general, though, like his father, he persists in wearing a colonel's collar insignia. (University of Texas at Austin)

Georgia Washington Custis Lee was born on September 16, 1832, at Fort Monroe, Virginia. The eldest child of Robert E. and Mary Custis Lee, he was named for his maternal grandfather and called "Custis" by his family. Like his father, he chose a military career, graduating first in his class at West Point in 1854. Assigned to the engineers, Custis Lee stayed in the army until the Civil War broke out, resigning his commission on May 2, 1861.

Commissioned a captain in the Confederate army, Lee performed engineering duties on the Richmond fortifications. Although he preferred field service, Lee was selected by President Jefferson Davis for his staff. By the spring of 1862 Lee held the rank of colonel and frequently carried out important missions for Davis. Ill health plagued Lee throughout the war and hampered his efforts to attain field command. He wanted to be assigned as chief of staff to his father, but the elder Lee opposed it.

Promoted to brigadier general on June 25, 1863, Lee continued to serve as a trusted member of the president's staff. In the spring of 1864 he declined command of the District of Southwest Virginia. Lee was promoted to major general effective October 20, 1864, with permanent confirmation on February 3, 1865. During the war's final months Lee organized the clerks and mechanics of Richmond for the capital's defenses.

When Confederate forces retreated from Petersburg and Richmond in April 1865, Lee's command was attached to Richard Ewell's corps. At Sayler's Creek on the 6th the Federals attacked Ewell's troops and routed the Confederates. Lee and other generals were captured in the debacle. The Federals, however, paroled Lee because of his mother's illness, and he joined her in Richmond.

After the war Lee accepted a professorship of mathematics at Washington College in Lexington, Virginia, where his father had assumed the presidency. When Robert E. Lee died in October 1870, his eldest son succeeded to the presidency. Custis Lee served in the position for over a quarter of a century, resigning in 1897. He lived his remaining years at "Ravensworth," the family's ancestral home near Alexandria, where he died on February 18, 1913. He was eventually buried in the Lee family crypt on the campus of Washington and Lee University.

Jeffry D. Wert

Freeman, Douglas Southall, *Lee's Lieutenants: A Study in Command* (New York, 1942–44).

Nagel, Paul C., *The Lees of Virginia: Seven Generations of an American Family* (New York, 1990).

A variant pose made at the same sitting. (University of Texas at Austin)

Richmond photographers Minnis and Cowell made this little-known 1862 portrait of General Robert E. Lee. (Courtesy of Mark Katz)

✳ *Robert Edward Lee* ✳

Robert Edward Lee, perhaps the best loved and most famous of American soldiers, was born in Westmoreland County, Virginia, on January 19, 1807, the son of General "Light Horse Harry" Lee of revolutionary war distinction. Young Lee entered the U.S. Military Academy in 1825 and quickly compiled an outstanding record. He ranked third academically after his first year, trailing only William H. Harford of Georgia and Charles Mason of New York. At graduation in 1829 Lee stood second among forty-five graduates and finished his full term at West Point without receiving a single demerit. Future Confederates who graduated with Lee included Joseph E. Johnston (thirteenth) and Theophilus H. Holmes (forty-fourth).

For more than three decades after graduation Lee served in the U.S. Army, starting as a 2d lieutenant of engineers and progressing through the ranks to colonel in this fashion: 1st lieutenant, September 21, 1836; captain, July 7, 1838; lieutenant colonel, 2d Cavalry, March 3, 1855; and colonel, 1st Cavalry, March 16, 1861. During his antebellum career Lee performed such disparate duties as flood control on the Mississippi at St. Louis, building Fort Carroll in Baltimore harbor, serving as superintendent at his alma mater, and commanding cavalry in Texas just before the Civil War.

The military experience that best prepared Lee for his future role came during the Mexican War. While serving on the staff of General Winfield Scott at Cerro Gordo and Churubusco, Captain Lee executed reconnaissances that opened the way to American victories. His energy and skill won for the captain three brevets during the war, to major, lieutenant colonel, and

colonel. He also impressed Scott so thoroughly that the general-in-chief of the army later called Lee "the very best soldier that I ever saw in the field."

Upon the secession of Virginia Lee became briefly the commander of all military forces of his native state. On May 14, 1861, he was commissioned as brigadier general in the Regular Army of the Confederate States; precisely one month later he became a full general. For nearly one year General Lee labored in relative obscurity and without notable success. His attempt to impose order on fractious Southern generals in mountainous western Virginia around Cheat Mountain resulted in disappointment and failure. In a mission to the South Carolina coast during the war's first winter, Lee contributed to planning defensive positions that later proved their worth, but he had no opportunity for substantive command. The next spring Lee filled the thankless post of military advisor to Jefferson Davis. He quietly engineered some significant results while in that job despite the president's obsession with managing even the smallest details of matters that caught his fancy.

The opportunity to exercise an important command came to Lee on June 1, 1862, when General Joseph E. Johnston fell wounded at Seven Pines. The association between Robert E. Lee and the Army of Northern Virginia that began that day lasted for nearly three years and turned both the man and the organization into legend. Three weeks later the general put his army into action for the first time. With the audacity

Another Minnis & Cowell portrait, probably also made in 1862. (Southern Historical Collection, University of North Carolina, Chapel Hill)

Lee's first full-length portrait in uniform, with field glasses around his neck.
(Courtesy of Dementi Studio, Richmond, Va.)

Perhaps Lee's best-known bust portrait, taken probably in 1863 by Julian Vannerson. (William A. Turner Collection)

Probably at the same sitting, Vannerson made this famous full-length portrait, with Lee holding his famed "Maryland" sword. (Courtesy of Mark Katz)

A variant Vannerson portrait from the same sitting. (Cook Collection, Valentine Museum, Richmond, Va.)

Late in the war Lee sat for his only portrait without a vest. (William A. Turner Collection)

that marked his command style throughout the war, Lee assailed the Federal army besieging Richmond. In the Seven Days' Campaign, June 25–July 1, despite dreadful problems with controlling his far-flung units, poor staff arrangements, and breakdowns by subordinate officers, Lee hurled the enemy from the gates of his country's capital. By late August he had moved north to the plains of Manassas, where he collaborated with "Stonewall" Jackson on a fabulous flanking initiative that bemused and routed Union General John Pope. During the Second Battle of Manassas, August 29–30, Lee engaged in the same sort of personal reconnaissance to the front of friendly lines that had made him famous in Mexico—and came back with the mark of a Northern sharpshooter's bullet on his face as vivid evidence of a close call.

When Lee led his army across the Potomac into Maryland early in September 1862, he climaxed an astonishing metamorphosis in the military situation that stood the war on its ear. Near the end of June Federals had swarmed around the outskirts of Richmond; barely more than two months later Lee was threatening the Northern capital city. While Lee's decision to raid into Maryland cannot rationally be gainsaid, his operational determination to stand at Sharpsburg, when the campaign faced its difficult climax there, is hard to defend. The army's valor on the field on September 17 won a tenuous draw, which was all that could have been expected. Lee ended the 1862 campaigns with an easy defensive victory at Fredericksburg in December that ranks as the most lopsided major campaign in the Virginia theater.

General Lee's leadership style became apparent early during his tenure in command. He divided his army into corps groups months before such arrangements had any basis in Confederate law, and before the ranks of lieutenant general existed. When the Congress caught up with his system in November 1862, Lee gave formal commands and ranks to Jackson and James Longstreet. After Jackson's death the army operated with three infantry corps. This structure allowed Lee to employ a *laissez faire* system that produced his greatest successes, particularly when Jackson operated at his freewheeling best, but that later led to some disappointments. Lee's personal style also became a recognizable part of the army's environment. Only weeks after he assumed command Lee wrote of a querulous Georgia colonel eager to press some grievance against another officer, "Why give our enemies the advantage & pleasure of our differences?…He can do his duty, though others may do wrong." The commanding general had ample opportunity to apply his calm and poised code of duty in an army full of contentious officers, including several of exalted rank.

Junior officers and enlisted men soon began to recognize in Lee a symbol of what seemed to them to be the virtues of their country. A physician called in to treat the general during the winter after Fredericksburg wrote home to his children, "I know you would all love him if you saw him, but with a deep quiet admiration which would find expression in a desire to imitate his actions and arrive at his excellencies…." The effect of this admiration on the fortunes of the army extended through most of its history and became especially important late in the war.

The first campaign in 1863 resulted in what must be considered Lee's greatest battle; it was also "Stonewall" Jackson's last. In the thickets around Chancellorsville in early May the two Virginians, using fewer than half as many men as Union Major General Joseph Hooker had available, routed a Northern host. After Jackson's remarkable flank march and surprise attack on the far Union right on May 2 and his subsequent mortal wounding, Lee sealed the great victory by pressing his enemy against the river. When news of rear-guard trouble near Fredericksburg reached him, Lee went to that quarter himself to rectify the situation. "The word soon went down the line 'All is right, Uncle Robert is here, we will whip them,'" wrote a North Carolina major. "There was no cheering, the men leaned on their muskets and looked at him…as tho' a God were passing by."

Lee's second venture north of the Potomac River resulted in disaster at Gettysburg in July 1863. The causes of the reverse will be argued forever to the complete satisfaction of no one, but the Southern defeat certainly counted among its salient contributors the crippling absence of Major General "Jeb" Stuart and his cavalry, Lieutenant General Richard S. Ewell's equivocation (Lee later said that he would have won had Jackson been present), Longstreet's stubbornly bad attitude, and Lee's own determination to strike hard against the enemy even after his good options had expired. After the army returned to Virginia, Lee sent Longstreet away with a sizable body of troops to help in the Western theater. Lee maneuvered the remaining portion of his army skillfully in campaigns

A slight variant of the previous portrait, showing only a rearrangement of the bow tie. (Library of Congress)

Lee's only known wartime photo mounted on Traveler, taken in Petersburg in the fall of 1864. (Courtesy of Dementi Studio, Richmond, Va.)

In April 1865 Mathew Brady came to Lee's home and persuaded the general to pose for his last series of images, just days after surrendering. (University of Texas at Austin)

Lee sits between his son General Custis Lee on the left, and military secretary Lieutenant Colonel Walter Taylor. (University of Texas at Austin)

A variant of the portrait with his son and Taylor. (University of Texas at Austin)

Lee's only full seated portrait in uniform, by Brady in April 1865. (University of Texas at Austin)

Lee on Traveler once more in an early postwar portrait, included because he has donned his uniform once more. (Miller, *Photographic History*)

around Bristoe Station and Mine Run during the fall of 1863, with low-key defensive success for results.

When Longstreet's troops returned from a miserable campaign in Tennessee, Lee held a welcoming review for them in late April 1864. Brigadier General E. P. Alexander, a sharp-eyed observer not at all given to romantic rushes, wrote that on seeing Lee, "we shout & cry & wave our battleflags.... The effect was that of a military sacrament, in which we pledge anew our lives." Some of the troops in the admiring throng were called upon for precisely that sacrifice a few days later when they joined Lee in the Wilderness as his army's life hung in the balance. The Army of Northern Virginia tangled with the Army of the Potomac, newly under the direction of Lieutenant General Ulysses S. Grant, in the Wilderness of Spotsylvania May 5 and 6, 1864. Longstreet's troops arrived early on the second day just in time to thwart a tremendous Federal onslaught. The Texas brigade that had become famous under Hood sent Lee to the rear when he tried to lead them into the breach. Again at Spotsylvania Court House a few days later the general three times attempted personally to lead troops in desperate assaults. He was losing the means to wage aggressive war, and in consequence felt a great frustration. The fighting at Spotsylvania from May 8 to May 21 inaugurated a new kind of warfare that featured continuous contact. Grant, unable to handle Lee in the open field, settled into a war of attrition after absorbing brutal losses at the Wilderness and Spotsylvania. On June 3 at Cold Harbor Lee's men butchered Grant's in a brief and ghastly repulse that came to typify military futility. In resisting Grant's drive from the Rapidan to the James, Lee inflicted during a period of one month as many casualties on his enemy as his own army had men in its ranks.

Grant cleverly stole a march on Lee in mid-June, crossing the James toward Petersburg in such secrecy that the Confederates lagged far behind. Lee did not believe the reports coming in from south of the river, where at one moment a wildly visionary General P. G. T. Beauregard pleaded in vain for the help that he genuinely needed, but then caromed to wildly optimistic hopes based on impossible schemes. By the time Lee reacted to the serious threat at Petersburg, he nearly was too late. The savage bloodletting that had enervated the Federal army during May left it unresponsive to the opportunity, and Lee's men squirmed through a rapidly closing door to save Petersburg.

The siege of Petersburg and Richmond that followed for the next nine months presaged the static warfare of the early twentieth century. The Battle of the Crater at the end of July and a series of struggles for control of the railroads highlighted operations during the rest of 1864 and early 1865, but most of the long siege was given over to dreary and intermittently deadly little battles over trenchlines. Grant stretched his left and Lee stretched his right. The war of stretching and attrition eventually, inevitably, produced results for the side with the big battalions. Near the end Lee held his army together in part by virtue of his personality and character. "You are the country to these men," one of his officers told Lee late in the war. "They have fought for you.... Their devotion to you and faith in you have been the only things which have held this army together."

The stretched lines snapped at the beginning of April after Lee's last offensive gesture on March 25 at Fort Stedman. At Five Forks and Sayler's Creek the Army of Northern Virginia lost most of its pathetic remaining strength, and Lee surrendered it on April 9 at Appomattox Court House. By then he was almost as much a legend to his foemen as to his soldiers. At the end of the month a Federal officer still could hardly believe that Lee no longer stood in his path. "He was like a ghost to children," the officer wrote home, "something that haunted us so long...."

Robert E. Lee devoted the next five years remaining to him to education of young men in an effort to rebuild his beloved Virginia and the South, serving as president of Washington College. There he imparted to both students and interested onlookers what a modern professor at the institution has aptly called "the Lee legacy of spirituality, courtesy, self-denial, self-control, [and] self-sacrifice...." He died on the college campus on October 12, 1870, and was buried there.

Robert K. Krick

Freeman, Douglas Southall, ed., *Lee's Dispatches* (New York, 1915).

Freeman, Douglas Southall, *R. E. Lee* (New York, 1934–35).

Lee, Robert E., Jr., *Recollections and Letters of General Robert E. Lee* (New York, 1924).

Stephen D. Lee was a captain on Beauregard's staff at the time of Fort Sumter, when this portrait was taken. (Courtesy of Mark Katz)

⋆ *Stephen Dill Lee* ⋆

Stephen Dill Lee was born September 22, 1833, at Charleston, South Carolina. He was distantly related to the Lees of Virginia, but by the era of the Civil War no one in either of the lines knew of the linkage. Stephen's mother died when he was quite young, leaving him and a sister to be raised by their widowed—and financially unsuccessful—physician father. Stephen was named for one of his uncles, with whom he became close. This uncle briefly had attended the U.S. Military Academy and subsequently ran a military boarding school for young boys. There Stephen received all of his formal education.

Possessing a strong affinity for the military life and needing a free college education, Stephen sought and attained appointment to West Point. There he was an average student, excelling only in artillery and cavalry studies, which he took under Professor George H. Thomas, who impressed him greatly. Two men served as superintendent of the academy during Lee's tenure, both of them potent influences on his life: Henry Brewerton and Robert E. Lee. Stephen Lee graduated in 1854, seventeenth out of forty-six, near the top of the middle third of his class. William Dorsey Pender was Lee's closest friend at West Point. His other intimate chums included Oliver Otis Howard, Custis Lee, John Pegram, and James E. B. Stuart.

Lee spent nearly seven years on active duty in the United States Army with the 4th Artillery Regiment. He saw combat in Florida during the 3d Seminole War and subsequently along the Kansas-Missouri borderland. Just prior to the Civil War he was stationed at Fort Randall, Dakota Territory. Lee impressed his superiors with his organizational and administrative capabilities, and this led—both before and during the early part of the Civil War—to his being assigned to a number of paper-shuffling jobs. Being tagged a "staff officer" inhibited his chances for early promotions to higher command.

The young Lee displayed no deep concern for politics, but his sentiments were unquestionably proslavery and thoroughly Southern. Yet, when South

Carolina seceded from the Union, he delayed for nearly two months before resigning his commission and returning to offer his military services to his home state. One of his friends later asserted that Lee had taken the step with regret and that "he was never sanguine of the success of the Southern movement for independence."

Lee was appointed a captain in the state of South Carolina's regular artillery service. These forces soon were melded into the Confederate army, and Lee served during the Fort Sumter episode as an aide-de-camp to Brigadier General P. G. T. Beauregard. Lee was with the party that delivered the ultimatum demanding Sumter's surrender; with the group that delivered the orders to the field battery to open fire; and with the delegation that formally accepted the capitulation terms. Lee kept a diary, possibly during the whole conflict, but only the pages for the early months have been found. It contains a remarkably sensitive observation concerning the firing of the war's first shot: it "woke the echoes from every nook and corner of the harbor, and in this dead hour of night, before dawn, that shot was a sound of alarm that brought every soldier in the harbor to his feet, and every man, woman, and child in the city of Charleston from their beds. A thrill went through the whole city. It was felt that the Rubicon was passed."

During the next year Lee grew enormously as a commander. This period was the high point of his practical military education. He emerged distinguished from the mass of other junior officers, himself reflecting and always infusing professionalism. Quite simply, he was *good* at training soldiers! He was inspirational and talented. Above all else he had a certain air of competence. Some observers perceived him to be dashing and inspiring, and many were impressed with his ingenuity and his courage. But he was in no way eccentric, and although he was bold in combat and committed his men to great dangers—some critics later would say he was audacious to a fault—he never attracted notice for any oddity of behavior nor for any foolish or less than competent management. He was

Lee's insignia are indistinct in this portrait, but he appears to have the three collar stars of a full colonel, dating the image to mid-or late 1862. (George H. and Katherine M. Davis Collection, Tulane University Library, New Orleans)

A hint of a wreath on the collar suggests that this image dates from November 1862 or later, showing Lee as probably a brigadier. (William A. Turner Collection)

Lee is definitely a general in this later war image, which shows his aging. (U.S. Army Military History Institute, Carlisle, Pa.)

A badly damaged image that appears to show him after his August 1863 promotion to major general. (Library of Congress)

supremely self-confident and yet modest. One newspaper reporter noted that Lee was "a man of commanding presence, exquisite courtesy, and superior intelligence...the center of every circle." Jefferson Davis later asserted that Lee was "one of the best all-round soldiers which the war produced."

Lee rose eventually to become a lieutenant general, appointed March 16, 1865, effective June 23, 1864, and at thirty the youngest man in the war to attain that rank. But he had to earn every single promotion from captain. He did not attain independent command until 1863 and oversaw only small bodies of troops until August 1864. It is reasonable to assert that he should have been elevated much more rapidly, but on the other hand a great deal must be said for his having had beneficial experience at each level. Ironically, the one job for which he was perhaps singularly best suited—division command in a major army—was one that he never had.

Lee commanded an artillery battery during late 1861, an artillery battalion in the Peninsula Campaign; briefly headed the 4th Virginia Cavalry in mid-1862; won great notice and was distinguished as an artillery commander at Second Manassas in August and at Sharpsburg in September; defeated Major General William T. Sherman at Chickasaw Bluffs in December 1862; helped with the defense of Vicksburg; commanded all the cavalry in Mississippi in late 1863 and early 1864; rose to military department command; was the only one of Major General Nathan Bedford Forrest's superiors to work well with that eccentric genius; and finally Lee attained a corps command with the Army of Tennessee.

Late in the war Lee married a Mississippi girl and thereafter lived in his wife's home, which is now a museum and Historical Pilgrimage headquarters. The Lees had one child, a son. After the war Lee was an insurance salesman; served in the Mississippi Senate; headed the A & M College of Mississippi; was deeply committed to and involved with the establishment and early management of the Vicksburg National Military Park; and helped found the United Confederate Veterans, rising to be that organization's commander in chief during the last four years of his life. He died May 28, 1908, and was buried in Friendship Cemetery, Columbus, Mississippi.

Herman Hattaway

Capers, Ellison, *South Carolina* Vol. V in Evans *Confederate Military History.*

Unlike others of his name, William Henry Fitzhugh Lee spent very little time in front of the camera. This shows him as colonel of the 9th Virginia Cavalry prior to September 1862. (U.S. Army Military History Institute, Carlisle, Pa.)

⋆ *William Henry Fitzhugh Lee* ⋆

William Henry Fitzhugh Lee was born on May 31, 1837, at Arlington, Virginia. The third child and second son of Robert E. and Mary Custis Lee, "Rooney," as the family called him, was educated at Harvard but withdrew from school before completing his degree. Like his father and older brother, Custis, Rooney wanted a military career, and when he failed admission to West Point—a horse had chopped off the tips of his fingers when he was eight years old—he was commissioned directly as a 2d lieutenant in the 6th Infantry in 1857. He served in the army during the Utah campaign and in California before resigning in 1859. He farmed at the "White House," a plantation on the Virginia Peninsula that he had inherited from his maternal grandfather, until the outbreak of the Civil War.

Rooney Lee was commissioned a captain of cavalry in May 1861 and soon thereafter a major in the Confederate army. During the summer and fall of 1861 he served as chief of cavalry in Brigadier General William Loring's campaign in western Virginia. Months later Lee was appointed lieutenant colonel and assigned to the 9th Virginia Cavalry. In March 1862 he assumed command of the regiment with the rank of colonel.

Lee initially distinguished himself during Major General "Jeb" Stuart's famous ride around the Union army June 12–16, 1862, and during the Seven Days' Campaign at the end of the month. Following the operations Stuart recommended Lee for promotion to brigadier general, asserting that the twenty-five-year-old colonel rivaled his cousin Fitzhugh Lee in "the daring exploits of the expedition" and had "established a like claim to promotion of the same grade." Fitzhugh, however, was the senior officer and received the promotion.

An acquaintance of Rooney Lee described him during this period, writing that the cavalry officer was "an immense man, probably six feet three or four inches tall...I remember that I wondered, when I first saw him, how he could find a horse powerful enough to bear him.... His hands and feet were immense, and in company he appeared ill at ease. His bearing was, however, excellent, and his voice, manner, and everything about him bespoke the gentleman."

A steady, reliable, and modest officer, Lee earned increasing regard during the campaigns of the summer and fall of 1862. He rendered valuable service in the defense of Turner's Gap during the Sharpsburg campaign in September. He was severely bruised when unhorsed and trampled at a bridge near Boonsboro, Maryland, prior to the September 17th battle at Sharpsburg. In October he temporarily commanded Fitzhugh Lee's brigade in Stuart's raid into Chambersburg, Pennsylvania.

Stuart again recommended Rooney for promotion, as did his father, who commanded the army. Robert E. Lee wrote to his other son, Custis, that he considered Rooney "one of the best cavalry officers" in Stuart's command. On November 10 Rooney received his brigadier-generalcy and command of a newly organized brigade comprised of the 2d North Carolina and the 9th, 10th, 13th, and 15th Virginia Cavalry.

During the Chancellorsville Campaign in May 1863 Lee led his brigade and two additional regiments against George Stoneman's Union cavalry as the Federals raided through Virginia. At the June 9 Battle of Brandy Station Lee's regiments fought valiantly in the fierce combat. He suffered a serious thigh wound as he led his men in a charge against John Buford's Federals. After the battle Stuart again praised Lee for "the handsome and highly satisfactory manner" in which he handled his brigade.

Lee recuperated at "Hickory Hill," the plantation of his in-laws. There, however, near the end of the month a Federal raiding party captured him. He initially was imprisoned at Fort Monroe and later at Fort Lafayette. While incarcerated he learned that his wife was dying of tuberculosis, and Union officials refused his request for a parole so he could join her before she died. Finally exchanged in March 1864, Lee rejoined the army and was promoted to major general on April 23,

A minutely differing variant from the same sitting. (Cook Collection, Valentine Museum, Richmond, Va.)

1864, to rank from the same day. He was the youngest officer of that rank in the Confederate cavalry.

During the campaigns of 1864 he commanded two brigades and in August commanded the entire cavalry force at Globe Tavern in the Petersburg Campaign. When Lieutenant General Wade Hampton, who had succeeded Jeb Stuart, was transferred to South Carolina in January 1865, Lee commanded the cavalry on the south side of the James River and reported directly to his father. At Five Forks on April 1 his cavalry held the Confederate right and fought well in the disastrous defeat. Five days later at Sayler's Creek his troopers covered the army's rear. He surrendered with his father's army at Appomattox.

Although Union troops had burned the White House during the Peninsula Campaign, Lee resumed the life of a planter. He remarried in November 1867, served as president of the Virginia Agricultural Society and as a member of the state senate for four years. In 1887 he was elected to the House of Representatives and died during his third term on October 15, 1891, at "Ravensworth," the family's ancestral home near Alexandria. He was buried in the family plot until 1922, when his remains were placed in the Lee family crypt at Washington and Lee University in Lexington.

Rooney Lee had carved out his own distinguished Civil War career. A diligent officer, he had fought with bravery and skill. By war's end he had been one of the finest generals in the cavalry corps of the Army of Northern Virginia.

Jeffry D. Wert

Freeman, Douglas Southall, *Lee's Lieutenants: A Study in Command* (New York, 1942–44).

Longacre, Edward G., *The Cavalry at Gettysburg* (South Brunswick, 1986).

Nagel, Paul C., *The Lees of Virginia: Seven Generations of an American Family* (New York, 1990).

Thomas, Emory M., *Bold Dragoon: The Life of J. E. B. Stuart* (New York, 1986).

✶ *Collett Leventhorpe* ✶

Collett Leventhorpe was born May 15, 1815, at Exmouth, Devonshire, England, of distinguished lineage. A paternal forebear was an executor of Henry V and another married Dorothy, a sister of Jane Seymour, third wife of Henry VIII. His mother was Mary Collett, a descendant of a brother of the First Lord of Suffield. Leventhorpe was educated at Winchester College and at seventeen was commissioned ensign in the 14th Regiment of Foot by William IV. He was promoted captain of grenadiers, served three years in Ireland, several years in the West Indies, and a year in Canada. He sold his commission in 1842, returned to Great Britain, and emigrated to the United States, settling in North Carolina, where his business acumen and professional character redounded to his advantage. In 1849 he married Louisa Bryan of Rutherfordton, a daughter of General Edmund Bryan.

Upon the secession of North Carolina, the six-foot-six-inch Leventhorpe tendered his sword to his adopted state, and when the 34th North Carolina Infantry was organized, he was elected colonel. His commission was dated October 25, 1861. Versed in the military arts by background and training, he instituted an effective training program, highlighting the "school of the soldier" that made the 34th a well-disciplined unit both in the field and in camp. His skills in this regard elicited favorable comments from his superiors, and he was placed in charge of a brigade that included the 33d, 34th, 36th, and 37th North Carolina regiments.

Ordered into the field in the first winter of the war, Leventhorpe and his regiment—the 34th North Carolina—were assigned to the District of Cape Fear, which included those sections of North Carolina threatened by Union amphibious forces that had penetrated into Albemarle and Pamlico sounds, captured Roanoke Island, and threatened Goldsboro. Mid-February 1862 found him overseeing efforts to prevent Union gunboats from ascending the Roanoke River. Upon a reorganization of the Confederate armies mandated by the Conscription Act of April 16, 1862, he was elected colonel of the 11th North Carolina Infantry, which traced its lineage to the 1st North Carolina Infantry of Big Bethel fame. Ordered to Wilmington, Leventhorpe was placed in charge of a brigade that included the 11th, 43d, and 51st North Carolina, and Company E, 1st North Carolina Artillery. He commanded at Wilmington until August 18, when General Thomas L. Clingman was named as his replacement. An outbreak of yellow fever prevented the transfer of command until mid-September. He and his unit were then ordered to Virginia's Blackwater. There he reported to General Samuel G. French, was given responsibility for the security of a twenty-six-mile front, and twice repulsed enemy columns that in early December advanced from Suffolk and sought to cross that river, earning for Leventhorpe a commendation from French as "a most able officer."

Leventhorpe and the North Carolinians assigned to the defenses of the Blackwater were recalled in the second week of December and concentrated at Goldsboro to oppose the powerful eleven-thousand–man column led by John G. Foster that had sortied from New Berne and on the 14th occupied Kinston after a sharp engagement in which they captured more than four hundred Confederates and seventeen cannon. At White Hall on

---

No genuine uniformed portrait of Leventhorpe has been found; this one is early postwar. (Virginia Historical Society)

the 16th Leventhorpe assailed Thomas J. G. Amory's brigade and, before being withdrawn from the field, three times drove Yankee cannoneers from their guns and as often prevented the infantry regiments from forming line in their front. At this time Leventhorpe's regiment was reported to be one of the best-drilled regiments in the Department of Virginia and North Carolina, and he received several commendations. The regiment was frequently barred from "drilling contests," a tribute to the soldiers' training.

Leventhorpe and his 11th North Carolina participated in the Siege of Washington (March 30–April 15, 1863) and battled F. B. Spinola's column that had marched from New Berne to the relief of the beleaguered Blount's Creek garrison on the 9th.

In late April he and his regiment were assigned to General J. Johnson Pettigrew's brigade. Ordered to Virginia, Pettigrew's brigade reported to the Army of Northern Virginia at Hanover Junction on May 11, and when Robert E. Lee reorganized his army, Pettigrew's brigade was assigned to Henry Heth's II Corps division. On the afternoon of July 1 at Gettysburg Leventhorpe led his regiment across Willoughby's Run and slugged it out with the Iron Brigade in McPherson's Woods. The North Carolinians drove the Yankees from the woods, but at a terrible cost. Among the casualties was Colonel Leventhorpe, who fell seriously wounded. When the Confederates abandoned the field on July 4 and began the retreat back to Virginia, Leventhorpe was left behind in a hospital and captured. The doctor found it necessary to cauterize his wound with nitric acid.

Leventhorpe was held prisoner at Fort McHenry and on October 5 was informed that he would only be paroled or exchanged on receipt of "positive intelligence that the authorities at Richmond have released a number of officers of colored regiments constituting an equivalent to a colonel." He was released from the Point Lookout prison pen and exchanged at Aiken's Landing, Virginia, on March 10, 1864.

He was promoted brigadier general of state troops by North Carolina Governor Zebulon Vance and ordered to Kinston, where he assumed command of troops charged with guarding the Wilmington & Weldon Railroad against Union raiding parties operating out of the New Berne and Plymouth enclaves. General Lee recommended to the War Department in late January 1865 that Leventhorpe be commissioned a brigadier general in Confederate service, as he was

the "best officer" in the Department of North Carolina. On February 18, by order of President Davis, Leventhorpe was nominated and confirmed by the Senate as a brigadier general. He, however, declined the appointment on March 6. Early April found Leventhorpe's brigade deployed to guard the North Carolina Railroad—with troops posted at Salisbury, Lexington, High Point, and the Yadkin bridge—then under threat of attack by George F. Stoneman's four-thousand–man mounted column that had departed its East Tennessee base and was wreaking havoc on the railroads in western North Carolina and southwest Virginia. He was surrendered by Joseph E. Johnston and paroled at Greensboro May 1, 1865.

After the war he entered into various business adventures, traveled to Great Britain on several occasions, and resided in New York. In the 1880s he returned to Yadkin Valley and made his home with his wife's sister and her husband at "The Fountain" in Wilkes County. Leventhorpe died there December 1, 1889, and was buried in the Episcopal Cemetery in Happy Valley, near Lenoir, North Carolina.

Edwin C. Bearss

Henderson, Archibald, *North Carolina, The Old North State and the New* (Chicago, 1941).

Hill, D. H., Jr., *North Carolina*, Vol. V in Evans, *Confederate Military History*.

⭐ *Joseph Horace Lewis* ⭐

The only known uniformed image of General Lewis dates from after September 1863. (Library of Congress)

Joseph H. Lewis, the last commander of the famed Orphan Brigade and the one of longest duration, was born October 29, 1824, in Barren County, Kentucky, in or near the town of Glasgow. He attended Centre College in Danville, graduating in 1843, and then read law before being admitted to the commonwealth's bar two years later. He also became an early adherent to the old Whig party, staying allied to its tenets even after its decline and death in the early 1850s. As a Whig he was elected to three terms in the legislature at Frankfort and twice unsuccessfully sought a congressional seat.

In the years immediately prior to the war Lewis was engaged with a local militia unit, and when the war erupted and Kentuckians had to start choosing sides, he turned his loyalties to the new Confederacy and led many of his fellow militiamen with him to the recruiting camps across the state line at Camp Boone, Tennessee. Several other companies of volunteers preceded him, and Kentucky Confederate regiments started forming as early as July 1861. On November 19 the 6th Kentucky Infantry was formally organized with Lewis appointed its colonel despite his lack of any military training or experience. The new regiment joined with several others to form the 1st Kentucky Brigade, later to be known to posterity as the Orphan Brigade.

Lewis commanded his regiment in all of the subsequent campaigns of the brigade, from Shiloh (April 6–7, 1862), where his bravery was commended in the attacks on the Hornets' Nest to Vicksburg and Baton Rouge that summer; the disastrous January 2, 1863, attack at Stone's River; and on to Chickamauga

September 19–20, when he won commendation in the reports of his division and corps commanders. With the death of Brigadier General Ben Hardin Helm he also assumed command of the Orphan Brigade, which he retained till the end of the war. With the command came promotion to brigadier general on October 1, 1863, to rank from September 30.

Lewis' brigade now consisted of the 2d, 4th, 5th, 6th, and 9th Kentucky infantry regiments and two batteries, and he led it during the operations culminating in the Battle of Missionary Ridge (November 25), where most of the brigade artillery was lost. Lewis wintered with his command at Dalton, Georgia, then participated in the retreat toward Atlanta and in the battles for the city itself. The Battle of Jonesboro on September 1, 1864, so ravaged the brigade that it could no longer operate effectively as infantry, and soon thereafter the War Department issued orders converting it to mounted service. Unfortunately, this late in the war horses were hard to find, as was requisite equipment, and the brigade never would completely succeed in getting mounted. It split into mounted and dismounted commands, the latter being left idle behind the lines in the Georgia interior while Lewis commanded the mounted portion—only a few hundred strong—in harassing Major General William T. Sherman's advance toward Savannah.

The Kentucky general was attached to Major General Joseph Wheeler's cavalry in the division of Major General P. M. B. Young during the 1865 Carolinas Campaign, taking part in the hopeless resistance to Sherman's advance. In April Lewis attempted to hold Camden, South Carolina, unsuccessfully and on April 21 was forming for a charge against the Federals confronting him when word came that General Joseph E. Johnston had agreed upon an armistice. Lewis was seen with tears in his eyes at the news as he announced it to his men. Ordered to bring his command to Washington, Georgia, for parole, Lewis arrived on May 6, only days after President Davis passed through on his flight south. The next day he gave his parole.

Lewis returned to Kentucky, where he lived for nearly forty years after the war, honored and respected. He returned to the law but in 1868 won his old legislature seat again and in 1870 was finally successful in winning a seat in Congress, where he remained for three terms. He was then appointed an associate judge of the commonwealth court of appeals and in 1894 became chief justice. He returned to Scott County four years later and lived out his days as a farmer, dying July 6, 1904, and being laid to rest in Glasgow.

Lewis had been an unfailingly competent though rarely colorful commander. He never held independent command and so never had the chance to display any talents or initiative of a higher sort, but he never disappointed a superior and earned and held for decades the regard and love of his men. That was good enough for any general.

William C. Davis

Davis, William C., *The Orphan Brigade* (New York, 1980).

Johnston, J. Stoddard, *Kentucky*, Vol. IX in Evans, *Confederate Military History*.

⋆ *William Gaston Lewis* ⋆

The only known uniformed portrait of General Lewis dates from the last year of the war. (North Carolina Division of Archives and History, Raleigh, N.C.)

William Gaston Lewis was born in Rocky Mount, North Carolina, on September 3, 1835. A descendant of revolutionary war veterans, Lewis attended Lovejoy's Military School in Raleigh before enrolling at the University of North Carolina, from which he was graduated in 1854. He taught school in his native state and in Florida, worked as a government surveyor in Minnesota, and returning to North Carolina, served as an assistant engineer during the construction of the Wilmington & Weldon Railroad from 1858 to 1861.

When North Carolina seceded, Lewis enlisted as a 3d lieutenant in Company A, 1st North Carolina. The regiment fought at Big Bethel, Virginia, in June 1861. Seven months later on January 17, 1862, Lewis was elected major of the 33d North Carolina. The regiment participated in the defense of New Berne during March. Several weeks later on April 24, Lewis accepted the lieutenant-colonelcy of the 43d North Carolina.

The 43d North Carolina, a unit in Junius Daniel's brigade, spent another year in its native state before being transferred to Virginia in May 1863. On July 3 at Gettysburg the regiment's commander, Colonel Thomas S. Kenan, fell wounded during the fighting on Culp's Hill, and Lewis assumed command of the regiment. Daniel subsequently in his report praised Lewis for his "bravery and coolness." Lewis and the 43d remained in Virginia throughout the summer and fall, participating in the Bristoe Station and Mine Run campaigns.

By the spring of 1864 Lewis had returned to North Carolina under the command of Major General Robert Hoke. On the night of April 18–19 Hoke's forces attacked the Union garrison at Plymouth. When his brigade commander was killed in the assault, Lewis took direction of the unit, performing so capably that he earned his colonelcy.

Within a month Hoke's troops were rushed to southern Virginia where they participated in the operations on Bermuda Hundred. Lewis commanded Hoke's former brigade, comprised of the 6th, 21st, 54th, and 57th North Carolina and the 1st North Carolina Battalion. Assigned to Major General Robert Ransom's division, Lewis' brigade fought valiantly in the Battle of Drewry's Bluff on May 16. On June 2 Lewis was promoted to brigadier general, to date from May 31, 1864, and his brigade assigned to the division of Major General Stephen Dodson Ramseur in the II Corps, Army of Northern Virginia.

Two weeks later the II Corps under Major General Jubal A. Early raced westward to the Shenandoah Valley. The command thwarted a Federal advance on Lynchburg and then turned northward, crossing into Maryland and threatening Washington, D.C. Lewis' brigade acted in a reserve role at the Battle of Monocacy on July 9. During Early's withdrawal into Virginia, Ramseur's division advanced against a Union force on July 20. At Rutherford's Farm, or Stephenson's Depot, a few miles north of Winchester, Ramseur's three brigades collided with William W. Averell's Federals. Lewis' brigade held the left front, and when the enemy overlapped his flank and charged, two of Lewis' regiments panicked and unhinged the entire Confederate line, resulting in a Union victory.

Although the records are unclear, Lewis evidently took an extended leave of absence within a month after the defeat. Newly exchanged and appointed brigadier Archibald C. Godwin assumed command of the brigade, leading it until his death at Third Winchester on September 19. Ranking colonels directed the brigade at the defeats of Fisher's Hill and Cedar Creek before Lewis returned to duty in November. By the end of the year the II Corps had returned to the army at Petersburg.

On April 7, 1865, at Farmville, during the Confederate retreat before Appomattox, Lewis fell wounded while rallying a portion of the 54th North Carolina and was captured. After his parole Lewis returned to North Carolina, where he worked as a civil engineer for over three decades. At one time he was the chief engineer of the Albany & Raleigh Railroad and served for thirteen years as state engineer of

North Carolina. The capable if undistinguished brigadier died in Goldsboro on January 7, 1901, and was buried there.

Jeffry D. Wert

Clark, Walter, ed., *Histories of the Several Regiments and Battalions from North Carolina in the Great War 1861–65* (Raleigh, 1901).

Hill, D. H., *North Carolina*, Vol. IV in Evans, *Confederate Military History*.

Robertson, William Glenn, *Back Door to Richmond: The Bermuda Hundred Campaign, April–June 1864* (Newark, 1987).

✲ *St. John Richardson Liddell* ✲

St. John R. Liddell was born on September 6, 1815, at Elmsley Plantation near Woodville, Mississippi. He received an appointment to West Point in 1833 but resigned under murky circumstances a year later. Some sources blame poor grades for the resignation, others claim Liddell was forced to leave after wounding a fellow cadet in a duel. Liddell's wealthy father then bought him a plantation in Catahoula Parish, Louisiana. There he became involved in a blood feud with Charles Jones that would eventually cost Liddell his life. The cause of the feud is unclear but may have involved a female friend of Liddell's who shot and wounded Jones. Whatever the cause, the feud was eventually deadly. Liddell was later arrested for the murder of two of Jones' friends, but a court acquitted him in 1854.

When the Civil War began, Liddell had numerous connections with ranking Confederate officers. He was an old acquaintance of Generals Braxton Bragg, William Hardee, and P. G. T. Beauregard and was also known to the family of Jefferson Davis. In the summer of 1861 Liddell traveled to Richmond to try for a command. On the way he met Hardee, who promised him a position on his staff as a volunteer aide. Liddell was at Manassas during that battle July 21 but finally returned to Hardee's command in Missouri and was given the rank of colonel. He accompanied Hardee to Kentucky shortly afterward and sometimes was entrusted to carry Albert Sidney Johnston's confidential reports to Richmond. He continued to serve as a staff officer without pay until May 1862 when he was given command of a small two-regiment brigade at Corinth, Mississippi.

On June 17, 1862, Liddell was promoted to brigadier general, effective June 12, 1862, and was given a brigade of Arkansas infantry. His first engagement was at Perryville, Kentucky, on October 8. There his brigade was posted a mile in advance of the main line to observe the enemy. The Federals advanced and forced Liddell to withdraw. His brigade then served as a reserve until sunset, when it was brought up to the firing line. At first confused as to the identity of the force fronting them, the Arkansans held their fire until Major General Leonidas Polk rode up and ordered them to open up on the Yankees. Polk described it as "one of the most deadly volleys I have ever witnessed." The brigade "well-nigh annihilated" the Yankee force and earned Liddell the praise of Polk and Hardee.

Liddell stayed with the Army of Tennessee after the Kentucky invasion and fought again at Murfreesboro. On December 31, 1862, his brigade was on the left of Brigadier General Patrick Cleburne's division and attacked the same Federals it had faced at Perryville. The fighting was vicious, but Liddell cracked two Union lines. When numerous Yankee prisoners asked him what they were to do, he astonishingly replied that while they would not be molested as long as they were unarmed, he would not object to their trying to escape if they promised not to fight again! The brigade continued to battle its way toward the Nashville Pike, and Liddell's artillery shelled a Federal supply train before he fell back. Liddell's men had fought well, sometimes hand to hand, but had suffered 589 casualties, the most of any of Hardee's brigades. Cleburne praised Liddell when he wrote, "Brigadier

---

No genuine uniformed portrait has been found of General Liddell. This image had insignia added on by an artist, but is almost certainly a civilian view. (Miller, *Photographic History*)

General Liddell led his brigade with a skill, courage and devotion which, I believe, saved my left flank from being turned by the enemy."

When William Rosecrans maneuvered General Braxton Bragg out to Tennessee in the summer of 1863, Liddell again performed well. His brigade, with the subsequent help of another, held Liberty Gap against two Union divisions from June 24 to 27 at a cost of 120 men. Liddell fell back with the rest of the army until a stand was made at Chickamauga Creek, Georgia. There he was given a small division comprised of his own and Edward Walthall's brigades in W. H. T. Walker's corps. On September 18 he was ordered to take control of Alexander's Bridge but ran into a Yankee force armed with Spencer breech-loading rifles. He captured the bridge but only after losing 105 men. Liddell wrote, "I can only account for this disproportion from the efficiency of this new weapon." On September 19 his force advanced and collided with Union Major General George Thomas' men who were also advancing through the thick woods. Liddell captured almost one thousand prisoners and numerous cannons but was sent reeling back when his division was struck on the flank. On September 20 he was moved to the far right to hit the Union flank. He attacked twice but failed to break the strong Union line. The three days at Chickamauga cost Liddell's small division 3,123 casualties, almost half of its strength.

Liddell's last service with the Army of Tennessee was at Chattanooga. When the Federals routed Bragg from Missionary Ridge in November, Liddell gave Cleburne valuable aid in holding the rear guard. Cleburne wrote, "General Liddell was absent on leave, but hearing of the fight returned and rendered me all the assistance in his power. He selected and reformed the new line after we withdrew from our first position."

Liddell became disillusioned with the personal bickering among the army's generals and upon his request in December 1863 was transferred to Louisiana. There in January 1864 he assumed command of the Sub-district of North Louisiana. With only a few hundred ill-disciplined cavalry, Liddell spent the next few months chasing jayhawkers and gathering up draft evaders. On April 1 he moved to the Red River to cooperate with Major General Richard Taylor in stopping Union Major General Nathaniel Banks' move against Shreveport. Liddell skirmished constantly with the Union gunboats on the river and almost as much with Taylor, whom Liddell detested. After much disagreement over tactics Liddell finally requested to be transferred out of Taylor's jurisdiction.

From Louisiana Liddell was sent to command the Confederate forces in southern Mississippi for a few days and then was given control of the defenses of eastern Mobile Bay. There he stayed from September 1864 until the end of the war. In November he took a cavalry force and stopped a column of black troops who were raiding the Montgomery & Mobile Railroad. Liddell defended Spanish Fort throughout its bombardment and evacuated it in early April 1865. On April 9 he was captured when Federal troops overran Fort Blakely.

After the war Liddell returned to Louisiana, where his feud with Charles Jones came to a tragic conclusion. While on a Black River steamer, Liddell was confronted by Jones and his two sons on February 14, 1870. The meeting ended in gunfire, with Liddell being shot seven times and killed. He was buried on the family plantation in Catahoula Parish. Jones and one of his sons were later killed by a mob.

Terry L. Jones

Conrad, Glenn, *A Dictionary of Louisiana Biography* (New Orleans, 1988).

Liddell, St. John R., *Liddell's Record: St. John R. Liddell, Brigadier General , C.S.A., Staff Officer and Brigade Commander, Army of Tennessee* (Dayton, 1985).

The only known wartime uniformed photo of Robert Lilley shows him sometime after July 1864, when he lost his arm. Though his collar insignia indicates a colonel, he had been a brigadier for at least two months. (U.S. Army Military History Institute, Carlisle, Pa.)

✶ *Robert Doak Lilley* ✶

Robert D. Lilley was born near Greenville, Augusta County, Virginia, on January 28, 1836. A graduate of Washington College in Lexington (today Washington and Lee University), Lilley sold surveying instruments invented by his father. While in Charleston, South Carolina, in April 1861, the young businessman witnessed the attack on and surrender of Fort Sumter. Returning home, Lilley recruited and organized the Augusta Lee Guards and was chosen its captain during May. On July 1 the guards were enrolled as Company C, 25th Virginia.

Assigned to western Virginia, the 25th Virginia participated in the operations in the region beyond the Allegheny Mountains during the summer and fall. On July 11 at Rich Mountain Union forces broke the Confederate line. During the retreat numbers of the regiment were captured, but Lilley led part of his company across the mountain and escaped. Three months later on October 3 at Greenbriar River the Confederates redeemed themselves, repulsing two Federal assaults and holding the field.

In the spring of 1862 the 25th Virginia was assigned to the brigade of Jubal Early and fought in the series of engagements of the 1862 Shenandoah Valley Campaign. At Cedar Mountain on August 9, under the watchful presence of Early, Captain Lilley seized the regimental flag and with a small group of men rallied the regiment after it had broken under a Federal assault. Weeks later at Second Manassas Lilley commanded the brigade's skirmish line and was commended for his role in repulsing the enemy attacks. Lilley and the regiment also fought at Sharpsburg in September and at Fredericksburg in December.

Lilley was promoted to major in January 1863. During April and May 1863 the 25th Virginia served in western Virginia in Brigadier General John Imboden's command. Subsequently returned to the Army of Northern Virginia, the regiment fought at Gettysburg in the brigade of John M. Jones. A short time after the campaign Lilley received his lieutenant-colonelcy.

Jones' brigade participated in the Mine Run, Wilderness, and Spotsylvania campaigns, during which time Lilley was promoted to colonel and to command of the regiment. On May 31, 1864, he received his brigadier-generalcy and was assigned to Early's former brigade, comprised of the 13th, 31st, 49th, 52d, and 58th Virginia. Lilley and the five veteran regiments then marched westward with Early's II Corps, participating in the latter's raid into Maryland and against the defenses of Washington, D.C.

On July 20 at Rutherford's Farm, or Stephenson's Depot, Lilley's brigade was routed in the defeat of Major General Stephen Dodson Ramseur's division by Union forces under William W. Averell. While endeavoring to rally his shattered ranks, Lilley suffered three wounds and became a prisoner. Later that day Federal surgeons amputated one of his arms. Four days later when the Union troops abandoned Winchester, they left Lilley behind.

Lilley had recovered from his wounds by fall and on November 28 was assigned to command of the Reserve Forces of the Valley District. He held this post until the surrender of Confederate forces in Virginia in April 1865. For Lilley, his service as a Confederate general was limited and undistinguished. The defeat at Rutherford's Farm, however, was not as a result of his conduct.

After the war Lilley devoted his life to the welfare of his alma mater and his church. He served as financial agent of Washington and Lee and a member of the Presbyterian Synod of Virginia. Lilley died in Richmond on November 12, 1886, while attending a meeting of the synod. He was buried in Staunton.

Jeffry D. Wert

Hotchkiss, Jedediah, *Virginia*, Vol. III in Evans, *Confederate Military History*.

Krick, Robert K., *Stonewall Jackson at Cedar Mountain* (Chapel Hill, 1990).

⭐ *Lewis Henry Little* ⭐

No wartime uniformed pose of General Little has appeared. This one in his old United States uniform dates from the 1850s and shows him as a captain. (National Archives)

Born in Baltimore, Maryland, on March 19, 1817, Lewis Little would one day drop the use of his first name and be known to friends and associates as Henry. His father, Peter Little, was a War of 1812 veteran and a congressman from Maryland, and the latter influence probably accounts for his son being given a direct commission into the army as a 2d lieutenant without benefit of West Point training. Little had attended St. Mary's College in Baltimore, but once embarked in the military, he never again put off his uniform.

Assigned to the 7th United States Infantry, Little went to Mexico in 1846 and soon stood out for his bravery and conduct at the Battle of Monterrey, winning a captain's brevet. On August 20, 1847, he received full promotion to a captaincy and thereafter remained in Mexico and out on the frontier following the end of the war. He served under Sidney Johnston in the 1858 Mormon Campaign in Utah and was serving at Fort Smith, Arkansas, when the secession crisis erupted.

In February 1861 he was ordered with his company to Jefferson Barracks, Missouri, and was almost immediately caught up in the fervor surrounding St. Louis. Little found himself deeply torn in his sentiments between loyalty to his uniform and adherence to the South. On April 20 he received orders to go to Wisconsin to muster in volunteers responding to Lincoln's call for seven hundred and fifty thousand men. Five days later he started on the journey, then found he could not go through with it. He returned to St. Louis and sent in his resignation, which was accepted on May 7.

Little thought at first to sit out the conflict, moving to Boonville, Missouri, with his wife and daughter. Almost immediately he began to feel sympathetic pulls to offer his services to the new Confederacy, but as he confessed, "it is hard to give up the *old flag*." By May 9, however, he was talking with Governor Claiborne Jackson and three days later had agreed to be what he called "a kind of Nondescript Ad Genl" for Major General Sterling Price. On May 18 he was appointed a colonel in the secessionist Missouri state forces.

Little served with Price during the chaotic weeks that followed until Unionist forces compelled the secessionists to abandon St. Louis and flee to the southwestern part of the state. Little left Price then and went to Richmond, where he received both a commission as a major in the infant Confederate Regular Army and a colonelcy in the provisional forces. In November, when a Missouri infantry brigade was raised by Price for the Confederacy, Little was given command of the 1st Missouri Brigade. His men found him "quick and active in his speech and movements, with a look and manner somewhat French." He was already a great favorite with Price, who entrusted him with covering the retreat of his small army into Arkansas in February 1862.

At Elkhorn Tavern on March 7 Little opened Price's attack and pressed the enemy hotly during the day, sometimes overseeing the artillery placement and firing personally. Price and Brigadier General Earl Van Dorn both praised him highly in their reports, and Little's reward was an appointment as brigadier on April 16, to date from the same day. Following Shiloh April 6–7, Little was ordered to join the army concentrating under General Pierre G. T. Beauregard at Corinth, Mississippi. In June he assumed command of Price's division in that commander's absence, and when Price returned to take command of the Army of the West, Little permanently retained the division's four predominantly Missouri brigades. By August Price was starting a letter campaign to get Little promoted to major general, but circumstances would intervene to render such efforts wasted.

Early in September Price began his march toward Rosecrans' Federals at Iuka, Mississippi. Little advised him against the movement, but in vain, and himself accompanied the advance in an ambulance at times, suffering from a variety of fevers probably related to malaria. At times he was unable to sit on his horse, right up until the opening of the Battle of Iuka on September 19, but he pulled himself into the saddle to join Price, General Louis Hébert, Colonel John

Whitfield, and others at the front when Rosecrans' attack hit them. Little was wearing his old U.S. army uniform tunic—"once more in Uncle Sam's blue," he quipped—and seated on his horse conferring with Price when a Yankee bullet passed beneath Price's arm and struck Little in the forehead at the scalp line just above his left eye, stopping just beneath the scalp on the opposite side. Little was killed instantly and fell from the saddle into the arms of an aide. Price was almost unhinged by the loss of his close friend. "My Little, my Little," he cried over and over, "I've lost my Little." Buried first in Iuka, Little's remains were reinterred after the war in Baltimore's Greenmount Cemetery.

Unfailingly able and unassuming, Little left behind associates who paid unexcepted tribute to him as a man and officer.

William C. Davis

Anderson, Ephraim, *Memoirs: Historical and Personal...of the First Missouri Confederate Brigade* (Dayton, Ohio, 1972).

Castel, Albert, ed., "The Diary of General Henry Little, C.S.A," *Civil War Times Illustrated*, XI (October 1972).

Thomas Logan as a captain in the Hampton Legion in 1861—62. (Museum of the Confederacy, Richmond, Va.)

✯ *Thomas Muldrup Logan* ✯

Thomas Muldrup Logan was born in Charleston, South Carolina, on November 3, 1840. The son of a prominent judge, he graduated first in the South Carolina College class of 1860. During the bombardment of Fort Sumter Logan served as a volunteer private in the Washington Light Artillery. He then helped organize Company A of the Hampton Legion and was elected the company's 1st lieutenant.

At First Manassas July 21, 1861, Logan saw action when the Hampton Legion helped defend Henry House Hill during a crucial part of the battle. Promoted to captain after the fight, he led his company in the Seven Days' Campaign (June 25—July 1, 1862) and was severely wounded at Gaines' Mill on June 27. Although not fully recovered from his wound, Logan rejoined his men and fought at Second Manassas in August. There the Hampton Legion charged and captured a Union battery near the Chinn House. Logan's superior wrote that "Capt. T.M. Logan, by his brilliant fighting, won the admiration of every one." After again being cited for "great bravery" at Antietam September 17, Logan won a major's commission.

Logan soon afterward joined Micah Jenkins' brigade and was promoted to lieutenant colonel. In the spring of 1863 he won a commendation for leading a reconnaissance patrol fifteen miles beyond the Confederate lines near Suffolk, Virginia. After accompanying Lieutenant General James Longstreet's corps to Georgia in September 1863, Logan took command of the sharpshooters in Major General John Bell Hood's division during the sieges of Chattanooga and Knoxville (October to December). Upon arriving at Knoxville, Logan was ordered to push the Yankees back toward town to prevent them from entrenching. He did so with his sharpshooters and captured a number of enemy soldiers. Then on the night of November 28 his men preceded Longstreet's main attack by advancing to capture a line of Union trenches and sixty prisoners. Longstreet wrote of Logan that he "had at various times through the campaign control of the line of skirmishers of Hood's division, and always managed it with courage and skill."

Returning east in early 1864, Logan served on unattached duty with General P.G.T. Beauregard's staff during the fighting at Drewry's Bluff in May 1864. He played a significant role in the battle by serving as a courier between Beauregard and his generals. On May 19 he was promoted to colonel and given command of the Hampton Legion. Soon afterward Logan was severely wounded during a skirmish at Riddell's Shop on June 13.

Upon recovering from this second serious wound, Logan proceeded to the Carolinas to take command of Matthew G. Butler's cavalry brigade under Major General Wade Hampton. When he was recommended for promotion, Fitzhugh Lee, his divisional commander, endorsed it as "the best appointment that can be made for this brigade." His promotion to brigadier general on February 23 became effective on February 15, 1865. At twenty-four years old, Logan was the youngest general then in the Confederate army. He served throughout the Carolinas Campaign and led the last Confederate assault of the war at Bentonville, March 19—21. Logan then accompanied General Joseph E. Johnston to the surrender ceremony at Durham Station. There Major General William T. Sherman found it hard to believe that this "slight, fair-haired boy" was a brigade commander.

A month later Logan borrowed five dollars from a friend and married a Virginia girl. Settling in Virginia, he studied law in Richmond and began buying stock in the Richmond & Danville Railroad. Logan became a major railroad tycoon after the Civil War, buying and consolidating a number of lines. Sometimes associated with John D. Rockefeller, he won and lost several fortunes. In 1894 his railroad holdings were renamed the Southern Railway. In additioin to his railroads, Logan took an interest in politics and in Wall Street, marketing such inventions as the telautograph. He was chairman of the Virginia Democratic Executive Committee in 1879 and of Virginia's Gold Democrat party in 1896.

While identification cannot be positive, this may be Logan in late 1860 or early 1861 when he served as a volunteer prior to and during the bombardment of Fort Sumter. (Courtesy of Dale S. Snair)

Logan died in New York City on August 11, 1914, and was buried in Richmond's Hollywood Cemetery.

Terry L. Jones

Capers, Ellison, *South Carolina*, Vol. V in Evans, *Confederate Military History*.

Roman, Alfred, *The Military Operations of General Beauregard in the War Between the States, 1861 to 1865* (New York, 1883).

Logan's collar is indistinct and may be an artist's addition. Since he was only promoted to brigadier in February 1865, he likely did not have time to alter his uniform and sit for a portrait. The uniform is nevertheless genuine, though only that of a colonel, lieutenant colonel, or major. (Museum of the Confederacy, Richmond, Va.)

✶ *Lunsford Lindsay Lomax* ✶

An excellent late-war portrait of Major General Lomax taken after August 1864.
(William A. Turner Collection)

Lunsford Lomax was born on November 4, 1835, in Newport, Rhode Island, the son of an army captain and a member of an old Virginia family. Lomax was educated in the schools of Richmond and Norfolk before entering the United States Military Academy, from which he was graduated in 1856. Brevetted a 2d lieutenant, he served with the 2d United States Cavalry on the frontier. He resigned his commission on April 25, 1861, one month after receiving promotion to 1st lieutenant.

Lomax accepted a position of captain in the Virginia state forces and the position of assistant adjutant general on the staff of General Joseph E. Johnston. He served under Johnston during the operations of 1861. Transferring to the west, he served as inspector general on the staff of Brigadier General Benjamin McCulloch until the latter's death at the Battle of Pea Ridge March 7—8, 1862. Lomax subsequently accepted the post of acting adjutant and inspector general of the Army of West Tennessee under the command of Major General Earl Van Dorn.

On February 8, 1863, Lomax was promoted to colonel and assigned to the command of the 11th Virginia Cavalry in the Army of Northern Virginia. Returning to his native state, Lomax joined his regiment in the brigade of William E. "Grumble" Jones. The 11th Virginia fought at Brandy Station on June 9 and participated in the cavalry actions of the Gettysburg Campaign. Lomax's performance in these operations elicited praise and the recommendation of General Robert E. Lee for promotion to brigadier general. Within weeks after the Gettysburg Campaign he received a brigadiership on July 30, to rank from June 23, 1863, and command of a brigade comprised of the 5th, 6th, and 15th Virginia and the 1st Maryland Cavalry.

During the Overland Campaign of May 1864 Lomax's brigade served in the division of Fitzhugh Lee. At Yellow Tavern on May 11 his command held the Confederate left and fought valiantly. By September Confederate authorities had transferred Lomax to the Shenandoah Valley where he commanded a cavalry division in Lieutenant General Jubal Early's Army of the Valley in operations against Philip Sheridan's Union Army of the Shenandoah.

In the Shenandoah Valley Campaign of 1864 Confederate cavalry was overwhelmed by their superior Union counterpart. Lomax's reputation and those of other cavalry officers suffered accordingly. At Third Winchester on September 19 the Southern horsemen fought stubbornly until Federal numbers and armament prevailed. Three days later at Fisher's Hill Lomax's brigades held the vulnerable left flank of Early's army. When Union infantry stormed into the flank, Lomax's command dissolved and fled from the field, exposing the entire Confederate line. The final ignominy came at Tom's Brook on October 9 when Sheridan's troopers routed the Southerners in the so-called "Woodstock Races." During the rout Lomax was captured but managed to escape.

Despite his units' performances Lomax was assigned to command of Early's cavalry on October 31. On August 10 he received promotion to major general, effective the same day. His command remained in the Shenandoah Valley during the winter of 1865. When he learned of the fall of Richmond several days later, he marched his troops southward toward North Carolina, where he surrendered his troops.

After the war Lomax settled on a farm near Warrenton, Virginia. In 1885 he accepted the presidency of Virginia Polytechnic Institute, serving until 1899. For the next six years he assisted in the compilation of the *Official Records*. Lomax then served as commissioner of the Gettysburg National Military Park. He died in Washington, D.C., on May 28, 1913, and was buried in Warrenton.

Lomax's Confederate career reflected the fortunes of the Southern cavalry during the war. He proved an able brigadier general when his troopers matched the Union horsemen. But in the war's final year as Federal superiority in armaments, horseflesh, and numerical strength proved decisive, Lomax's record, notably in the Shenandoah Valley, was one of defeat and rout.

Jeffry D. Wert

Freeman, Douglas Southall, *Lee's Lieutenants: A Study in Command* (New York, 1942–44).

Wert, Jeffry D., *From Winchester to Cedar Creek: The Shenandoah Campaign of 1864* (Carlisle, Pa., 1987).

Lomax's insignia cannot be accurately read in this damaged portrait, but it shows him either as a lieutenant in the old U.S. cavalry, or else as a Virginia captain early in the war. (William A. Turner Collection)

One of a brace of portraits from a late war sitting. (Museum of the Confederacy, Richmond, Va.)

A variant taken at the same sitting. (Albert G. Shaw Collection, Virginia Historical Society, Richmond, Va.)

✯ *Armistead Lindsay Long* ✯

The only known uniformed portrait of General Long, taken between September 1863 and the end of the war. (Library of Congress)

Armistead L. Long was born in Campbell County, Virginia, on September 3, 1825. An 1850 graduate of the United States Military Academy, ranking seventeenth in the class, Long was brevetted a 2d lieutenant of artillery. For the next decade the artillery officer served at various garrisons and posts throughout the country, including Forts Moultrie, McHenry, and Monroe; in New Mexico, Kansas, and Nebraska; and at the Augusta Arsenal in Georgia. During part of his service Long trained under Henry Hunt, the future artillery commander of the Army of the Potomac. On May 20, 1861, Long was appointed to the staff of his father-in-law, regular army Brigadier General Edwin V. Sumner. But he held his post for less than a month, resigning his commission on June 10 and accepting the rank of major of artillery in the Confederate forces.

Long served initially on the staff of Brigadier General William W. Loring as chief of artillery and as acting inspector general during that general's operations in western Virginia. In the autumn of 1861 Long accepted a staff position with Robert E. Lee in South Carolina. Lee had known Long during the general's duties in western Virginia. When Lee was appointed military advisor to President Jefferson Davis in early 1862, Long went with him to Richmond. By mid-May Long was signing Lee's correspondence as his military secretary.

On June 1, 1862, Lee assumed command of the Army of Northern Virginia. Long, Charles Marshall, Walter H. Taylor, and Charles Venable came to form Lee's personal staff, his inner circle of aides. Long retained the position of military secretary, sharing the paperwork duties with Marshall. It was an onerous task for the two aides, as Lee detested such work and left it in the hands of Long and Marshall.

The elegant and highly intelligent Long served as Lee's military secretary until September 1863. Increasingly during these months Lee utilized Long's experience as an artillery officer. He examined terrain and assisted in the placement of batteries. For his efforts at Fredericksburg Lee praised Long for "posting and securing the artillery." Finally, in the summer of 1863 Lee recommended Long for the post of chief of artillery of the II Corps. On September 21, 1863, Long was assigned to the command and promoted to brigadier general, to rank from the same day.

Long directed the batteries of the II Corps throughout the bloody battles of the Wilderness, Spotsylvania, and Second Cold Harbor during May and June 1864.

He also participated in Lieutenant General Jubal A. Early's raid against Washington, D.C., in July and in the early operations of the 1864 Shenandoah Valley Campaign. But Long became ill during August and relinquished his command. His convalescence lasted into the winter of 1865. He returned to duty with Early to share in the debacle at Waynesborough on March 2. Long was paroled weeks later following Lee's surrender at Appomattox.

Long settled at Charlottesville after the war, accepting a position as chief engineer of the James River & Kanawha Canal Company. In 1870 he became totally blind. The Confederacy's old foe, Ulysses S. Grant, however, appointed Long's wife postmistress of Charlottesville, which provided the family with an income. Despite the blindness and by use of a slate, Long spent his remaining years writing numerous articles on the operations of the Army of Northern Virginia and a biography of Lee. In 1886 his *Memoirs of Robert E. Lee, His Military and Personal History* appeared. Long provided readers and future historians with a valuable, intimate portrait of Lee's headquarters and campaigns. Long died in Charlottesville on April 29, 1891, and was buried there.

Jeffry D. Wert

Dowdey, Clifford, *Lee* (Boston, 1965).

Freeman, Douglas Southall, *R. E. Lee* (New York, 1934–35).

Wert, Jeffry D., "The Tycoon: Lee and His Staff," *Civil War Times Illustrated*, Volume XI, No. 4 (July 1972), pp. 10–19.

Longstreet posed probably as a brigadier for this, his only full-length portrait from the war to survive. (University of Georgia Press)

✴ *James Longstreet* ✴

James Longstreet, nicknamed "Old Pete" and "Lee's War Horse," ranks among the top corps commanders of the Confederate army. His performance as lieutenant general of the I Corps of the Army of Northern Virginia rivals that of "Stonewall" Jackson, yet his reputation lags because of his postwar political affiliations and criticism of Robert E. Lee.

Born on his grandparents' cotton plantation in the Edgefield District, South Carolina, January 8, 1821, Longstreet spent his boyhood outside Gainesville, Georgia. When his father died in 1833, Longstreet's mother moved to Alabama, sending James to live with his uncle, humorist Augustus Baldwin Longstreet. James attended preparatory school near Augusta, Georgia; won appointment to West Point from Alabama (Georgia's positions were filled); and entered the U.S. Military Academy in 1838 with such future generals in the Union and Confederate armies as Richard S. Ewell, William Tecumseh Sherman, and William S. Rosecrans, who was his roommate. He graduated fifty-fourth of sixty-two in the class of 1842.

Assigned as brevet 2d lieutenant of the 4th U.S. Infantry at Jefferson Barracks in Missouri, Longstreet accompanied his unit to Louisiana in May 1844 to join General Zachary Taylor's "Army of Observation." He became brevet 2d lieutenant of the 8th Infantry on March 4, 1845, serving in Florida until the war with Mexico. As regimental adjutant from June 8, 1847, to July 1, 1849, Longstreet fought under Generals Taylor and Winfield Scott and was wounded assaulting Mexican positions at Chapultepec. His bravery and ability earned him brevets as captain on August 20 and major on September 8, 1847. After the war he married Maria Louisa Garland, cousin to Julia Dent, who became Mrs. Ulysses S. Grant. Promoted captain December 7, 1852, Longstreet performed various duties in Texas, including fighting Indians. On July 19, 1858, he accepted the position of major in the paymaster's department; was at Albuquerque, New Mexico Territory, when the South seceded; and resigned from United States service on June 1, 1861.

Commissioned brigadier general on June 17, 1861, to rank from the same day, Longstreet guarded Blackburn's Ford near Manassas with his 4th Brigade of Virginians. Although Federal soldiers pushed their way across on July 18, Longstreet displayed a coolness under fire that became a hallmark of his style. An aide later observed that during his career Longstreet was "like a rock in steadiness when sometimes in battle the world seemed flying to pieces." He was promoted to major general on October 7, to rank from the same day.

A new year brought both tragedy and triumph to the division commander. In January 1862 three of Longstreet's children died when scarlet fever swept Richmond. Generally affable, although moody, he grew more reserved because of the loss. At the Battle of Williamsburg on May 5 he distinguished himself in rear-guard action, but at Seven Pines on May 31 his confusion over verbal orders contributed to delays and poor coordination in the Confederate attacks. He redeemed himself during the Seven Days' battles, June 25–July 1, winning praise from Lee, who called him "the staff of my right hand."

Longstreet led what was then termed the right wing of the recently christened Army of Northern Virginia. His men delivered a crushing counterattack against the Federals at Second Manassas on August 30 and provided stiff defense on the Confederate right September 17 at Sharpsburg, where he presented an unforgettable sight by casually sitting sidesaddle and wearing carpet slippers because of a foot injury. After the Battle of Sharpsburg, Lee greeted his principal lieutenant with the famous phrase: "Ah! here is Longstreet; here is my old war-horse!" Lee recommended Longstreet's promotion to lieutenant general—made on October 11, to date from October 9, 1862—solidifying the corps system and giving his war horse command of the I Corps.

Longstreet's appreciation of the power of the defensive probably matured at Fredericksburg on December 13, 1862, when his soldiers repulsed numerous Federal

Longstreet's best-known portrait probably dates from 1863 and shows the aging and strain caused by the war. (Lee-Fendall House, Alexandria, Va.)

assaults while losing only eight hundred men behind strongly fortified positions on Marye's Heights. Scholars credit Longstreet with encouraging the use of entrenchments, thus contributing a tactical innovation to the army. During that winter he ordered widespread use of traverses, short earthen walls cutting across a trench to protect the flanks of men inside. The works impressed Lee, who reportedly said the army was "as much stronger for these new entrenchments as if I had received reinforcements of 20,000 men."

In early 1863 Lee sent Longstreet and two divisions south of the James River to gather provisions. There he conducted an abortive siege at Suffolk, which detractors cite as proof of his lack of aggressiveness, while supporters claim he exercised due caution. Because of the assignment he missed the Battle of Chancellorsville (May 1–4) but marched north with the Army of Northern Virginia toward Gettysburg in June 1863.

Disagreement with Lee over strategy for the Gettysburg Campaign cast a shadow over Longstreet's reputation that stretches to today. Scholars have disproved the charge that Longstreet ignored orders to attack early on the morning of July 2, 1863, but the impression persists that he was sluggish and sulky because Lee rejected his advice to move around the Federals to seek another position from which to force an attack. According to an aide, Longstreet did have "apparent apathy in his movements. They lacked the fire and point of his usual bearing on the battlefield." Yet his I Corps mounted a savage attack through the Peach Orchard and the Wheatfield, nearly capturing Little Round Top and turning the Union left. Even though Longstreet opposed the frontal assault on July 3 against Union positions on Cemetery Ridge, the lieutenant general's tenacity once fighting began impressed an English observer: "I could now thoroughly appreciate the term bulldog, which I had heard applied to him by the soldiers. Difficulties seem to make no other impression upon him than to make him a little more savage."

After Gettysburg the I Corps was detached to the Western theater, where Longstreet gave a mixed performance. Chickamauga earned him another nickname—"Bull of the Woods"—for routing Federal soldiers on September 20, 1863. From then until his corps rejoined Lee's army the following spring, Longstreet revealed limitations as an independent commander in East Tennessee. He quarreled with subordinates, bringing Major General Lafayette McLaws up on court-martial charges for the unsuccessful assault on

Longstreet continued to age, as this 1863 or 1864 portrait clearly shows. (Library of Congress)

An indistinct portrait made probably at the same sitting as the previous image. (Museum of the Confederacy, Richmond, Va.)

Fort Sanders at Knoxville on November 29. Back with Lee in Virginia, Longstreet pushed his men on a forced march to the Wilderness in time to stem the rout of May 6, 1864. In an eerie repetition of the shooting of Stonewall Jackson the year before, Confederate soldiers fired on the general and his staff, wounding Longstreet in the throat and leaving his right arm useless. He returned to the army on October 19, 1864, remaining through the surrender at Appomattox.

Had Longstreet died of his wound, his reputation may not have suffered. Pardoned on June 19, 1867, he became a Republican and endorsed his kinsman, General U. S. Grant, as president. After a stint in Louisiana as a cotton factor and officer of an insurance corporation, Longstreet accepted a number of governmental appointments, including surveyor of the Port of New Orleans in 1869; postmaster at Gainesville, Georgia, in 1879; United States Minister to Turkey in 1880; and Federal marshal for northern Georgia in 1881. President William McKinley appointed him United States Commissioner of Railroads in 1897.

That he was a scalawag might have been forgiven, but Longstreet compounded these sins with a defense of his actions at Gettysburg that included criticism of Lee. Published in the *Philadelphia Weekly Times* of November 3, 1877, and February 28, 1878, the articles sparked immediate reactions from former Confederate officers who counterattacked through the *Southern Historical Society Papers*. They found Longstreet a convenient scapegoat for the South's loss at Gettysburg, branding him as slow, sulky, and insubordinate. Their effort has affected even the way later generations remembered him physically: Douglas Southall Freeman trimmed the six-foot-two general down to five-foot-ten.

Longstreet respected and admired Lee but did not always agree with his commander. Old Pete argued for defensive actions during the Gettysburg Campaign and favored—along with a number of Confederate officers whom scholars have termed the "western concentration bloc"—a greater commitment of arms and men in the western Confederacy. Though Longstreet hoped for a command in the West, his relations with Lee remained cordial. The two often traveled together and pitched their tents near one another. When officers approached the lieutenant general on April 8, 1865, to suggest he stress to Lee the necessity of surrender, Longstreet refused, reportedly saying he was there to support Lee, not to pull him down. Longstreet had limitations, particularly as an independent commander. His vanity and defensiveness in postwar writings certainly contributed to his loss of reputation. Yet, even many critics concede that none surpassed his ability to direct troops once battle had begun.

Longstreet began shifting his political base from Louisiana to Georgia in 1875 when he bought property near Gainesville, where he had spent his youth. He married thirty-four-year-old Helen Dortch on September 8, 1897 (Louise had died December 29, 1889), and passed away in Georgia on January 2, 1904. He was buried in Alta Vista Cemetery, Gainesville.

William Alan Blair

Longstreet, James, *From Manassas to Appomattox* (Philadelphia, 1896).

Piston, William Garrett, *Lee's Tarnished Lieutenant: James Longstreet and His Place in Southern History* (Athens, Georgia, 1987).

Probably Longstreet's latest wartime pose or else an early postwar image for which he put on his old uniform. (William A. Turner Collection)

A little-known standing portrait of General Loring in full uniform. (Museum of the Confederacy, Richmond, Va.)

⭐ *William Wing Loring* ⭐

William W. Loring was born in Wilmington, North Carolina, on December 4, 1818. His family moved to Florida when the boy was only four years old and settled in St. Augustine. Young Loring began his military career at the tender age of fourteen with a state unit fighting Seminoles and held a Florida commission as a lieutenant when he was eighteen.

Loring attended a preparatory school in Alexandria, Virginia, then studied for a time at Georgetown College. He read law in Florida and passed that state's bar in 1842. Despite his youth Loring served in the Florida legislature from 1842 to 1845.

When the United States Army organized its Regiment of Mounted Rifles early in the Mexican War, Loring received a commission as captain, to rank from May 27, 1846. He participated in General Winfield Scott's campaign from Vera Cruz to Mexico City with as much high distinction as any officer in the army. Loring's commission as major, dated February 16, 1847, put him in command of the regiment during the extended absences of the other two field-grade officers. Gallant and meritorious conduct at Contreras and Churubusco earned Loring a brevet as lieutenant colonel. Chapultepec resulted in another brevet, to full colonel; it also cost him an arm. Loring bore the amputation stolidly without anesthetic and smoked a cigar during the operation. He later told a subordinate that the loss of his arm in battle "was the proudest moment of his life," since it bestowed a permanent and visible badge of honor.

Colonel Loring commanded the Mounted Rifles for the rest of the prewar period, rising to permanent rank of lieutenant colonel on March 15, 1848, and to colonel on December 30, 1856. He led the rifles on an epic cross-country march in 1849 and commanded the regiment in Oregon until 1851. E. Kirby Smith wrote of Loring during this period that he was "an excellent fellow" who had "won the esteem and respect of all." Loring and his regiment spent some years in Texas, then in 1857 pursued Apaches in New Mexico. The following year Loring and the rifles marched into Utah, then back overland to New Mexico. Late in the decade the colonel visited Europe to examine military systems there. He returned to command of a district in New Mexico in March 1861. Three months later he began a long trip to Virginia in company with H. H. Sibley, leaving his colleagues in the Federal army attesting to his "unflinching honor and integrity." At his resignation Loring was the youngest colonel in the U.S. Army by a very wide margin and more than twenty years younger than the average.

Loring's Confederate career began at the rank of colonel, to date (with most other early war commissions) from March 16, 1861. His promotion to brigadier general on May 20, 1861, ranked from the same day; Loring accepted both commissions on August 5. He was posted to northwestern Virginia and participated in the difficult operations there. One of his subordinates described the new general as "a most pleasant gentleman [and]…a most efficient officer…very handsome and talkative." A Northern newspaper reported that Loring was a "jovial, good-hearted fellow," who "dresses magnificently." Loring's striking attire included "a velveteen coat" instead of a uniform in late 1861.

Early in 1862 Loring and his force were ordered to collaborate with Major General "Stonewall" Jackson in the mountains west of Winchester. The resulting winter campaign left the two generals starkly at odds. Loring circumvented military channels with complaints to Richmond; Jackson countered by filing charges against Loring. The president and the secretary of war sided with Loring, promoting him to major general on February 15, 1862, to rank from the same day, and assigning him to operations in another theater. Loring led troops to the vicinity of Charleston, Virginia, during the fall of 1862. In November he was transferred to Lieutenant General John C. Pemberton's command in Mississippi.

General Loring spent the rest of the war with the Confederacy's western armies. He escaped with his division from entrapment at Vicksburg in 1863 and joined General Joseph E. Johnston. Loring led his division during the 1864 Georgia campaign under Johnston and then under General John B. Hood. He participated in Hood's disasters at Franklin and Knoxville, then followed Johnston to the bitter end in April 1865 in North Carolina.

For four years after the war Loring engaged in banking in New York as a consultant on Southern investments. In 1869 he went to Egypt in company with several other Civil War veterans from both sides and accepted a commission as brigadier general under the khedive of Egypt. Loring overcame considerable cultural frustration to achieve some success as an inspector-general, reporting directly to the khedive. He participated in a major Abyssinian campaign from 1875 to 1876, winning promotion, several decorations, and designation as pasha.

In 1879 Loring Pasha returned to the United States, where he split time between New York City and St. Augustine. He was active in Florida political campaigns and railroad ventures and lectured widely on his Egyptian experiences. Loring busily collected material for a projected autobiography, "Fifty Years a Soldier," but unfortunately had not made any progress on it when he died suddenly of pneumonia in New York on December 30, 1886. An obituary described the general as "a short, thickset man, weighing about 200 pounds," and standing about five feet seven inches high (in 1863 a reporter had guessed his height as two inches taller). Loring's remains were buried at Grace Episcopal Church in New York City, then removed to Woodlawn Cemetery in St. Augustine a few months later with much pageantry.

Robert K. Krick

Wessels, William L. *Born to be a Soldier* (Fort Worth, 1971)

Loring, William W. *A Confederate Soldier in Egypt* (New York, 1884)

New York *Times*, December 31, 1886.

A seated portrait made probably at a different sitting, since he is wearing his cross belt on the opposite side. (Museum of the Confederacy, Richmond, Va.)

Major General Mansfield Lovell in an image that cannot be dated but which is probably from early in the war. (Museum of the Confederacy, Richmond, Va.)

⭐ *Mansfield Lovell* ⭐

Lovell was born in Washington, D.C., on October 20, 1822, the son of the first surgeon general of the United States Army Medical Department. He grew up there and, after his parents' deaths in 1836, in New York State. He graduated ninth in a class of fifty-six at West Point in 1842. After graduation Lovell became a 2d lieutenant in the 4th United States Artillery. He fought in the Mexican War, during which he was wounded twice and brevetted as captain for gallantry. During part of the conflict he served on the staff of Brigadier General John A. Quitman. Lovell and Quitman soon became very good friends, a relationship that probably became like that between a father and son. Lovell's friendship with Quitman continued after the Mexican War ended. The long and close relationship between them explains in large part Lovell's support of the South and Southern rights.

Lovell resigned his commission in 1854 and took employment with an iron works in Trenton, New Jersey. In 1858 Lovell became superintendent of street improvements for New York City. Later that year his old friend Gustavus W. Smith named him to the position of deputy street commissioner shortly after Smith assumed the duties as street commissioner.

At the start of the Civil War Lovell and Smith left New York and arrived in Smith's native Kentucky in July or August 1861. General Joseph E. Johnston on August 19 recommended them to President Jefferson Davis as division commanders in his army around Manassas. Johnston called them two "of the best officers whose services we can command" and pronounced them "as fit to command a division as any men in our service." The two did not get to Richmond until September 11. On September 25 Lovell was made a brigadier general and ordered to report to Major General David E. Twiggs at New Orleans. He would have charge of the coastal defenses of Department No. 1.

Before Lovell left for his new assignment, Twiggs asked to be relieved of command. On October 7 the president promoted Lovell to the rank of major general effective the same day and named him as Twiggs' replacement. Lovell did everything he could to improve the defensive posture of New Orleans and the lower Mississippi River but had his hands tied because Jefferson Davis would not allow him to exercise any control over the naval forces in his department. Several historians have noted that "the divided command at New Orleans was a vital factor in its fall."

In early February 1862 Davis and the War Department began stripping New Orleans of men, material, and naval vessels for the defense of Tennessee and the upper Mississippi River. Early on April 24 Flag Officer David G. Farragut's fleet ran past the forts below New Orleans. Lovell quickly ordered an evacuation of the city rather than subject the civilian populace to a bombardment. Union warships reached New Orleans the next day. Davis quickly made Lovell the scapegoat for the fall of the Crescent City to cover his own mistakes and those of his advisors. Nevertheless Lovell rushed men, artillery, and supplies to Vicksburg, Mississippi, to prevent the enemy fleet from ascending the river any farther than that point. His quick actions in May 1862 prevented Union forces from capturing that strategically important place at that time.

On June 27 under orders from Davis, Major General Earl Van Dorn replaced Lovell in command in Mississippi. Van Dorn later assigned Lovell to command of a division in his army that he was organizing for an offensive into northern Mississippi and western Tennessee. Lovell led his division at the Battle of Corinth October 3–4, and his men acted as the army's rear guard in its retreat. Van Dorn praised Lovell's conduct during the battle, writing Davis: "General Lovell has now the entire confidence of the troops and gained reputation in the late battle."

The Corinth campaign was Lovell's last real active service in the Confederate army. Van Dorn reorganized his command after the battle and assigned Lovell to command one of his corps. Lovell remained with the army during its operations in northern Mississippi in October and November, but his men did no serious fighting. Lieutenant General John C. Pemberton assumed command of the Department of Mississippi and East Louisiana in October, and when the War Department reorganized the department in December, Lovell was relieved of duty and told to "await further

A later war image, for which Lovell has grown full mutton-chop whiskers. (Library of Congress)

orders." A court of inquiry to investigate the fall of New Orleans began meeting in April 1863 and issued its findings in July. Though cleared by the court, Lovell still did not receive any orders to return to active duty.

Johnston asked the War Department in January 1864 to assign Lovell to the Army of Tennessee so he could command one of the three corps Johnston hoped to organize. Davis informed the general that he would not receive Lovell's services. Shortly afterwards General Braxton Bragg suggested several names, including Lovell's, as possible chiefs of artillery for Johnston's army. Bragg said, "Lovell was one of the best artillery officers in the old service, a good judge and fond of good horses." Johnston asked for Lovell's assignment as chief of artillery, but again Davis refused the request.

Lovell served as a volunteer aide to Johnston during the Atlanta Campaign. When Lieutenant General Alexander P. Stewart succeeded to the command of Lieutenant General Leonidas Polk's corps in late June, Johnston recommended Lovell as the new commander for Stewart's division. The War Department rejected the request. General John B. Hood replaced Johnston on July 17 and asked for Lovell's assignment to command his old corps. Hood had no better luck than had Johnston. Lovell then moved with his family to Columbia, South Carolina. After Johnston took command in the Carolinas in March 1865, he asked General Robert E. Lee to order Lovell to report to him for duty. On April 7 Lovell received assignment to command of Confederate forces in South Carolina. The war was practically over, but Lovell remained on duty until late May, when he finally surrendered to Union forces.

Lovell remained in the South after the end of the war and operated a rice plantation near Savannah. A tidal wave destroyed his first crop, and he was forced to return to New York City with his family. There he became a civil engineer and surveyor. Lovell served as assistant engineer under former Union general John Newton when the latter supervised the removal of obstructions in the East River at Hell's Gate. After a short illness Lovell died on June 1, 1884, and was buried in Woodlawn Cemetery.

Arthur W. Bergeron, Jr.

Bergeron, Arthur W., Jr., "Mansfield Lovell," in *The 1989 Deep Delta Civil War Symposium: Leadership During the Civil War*, ed. by Roman J. Heleniak and Lawrence L. Hewitt (Shippensburg, Pa., 1991).

Sutherland, Daniel E., "Mansfield Lovell's Quest for Justice: Another Look at the Fall of New Orleans," *Louisiana History*, XXIV (1983), pp. 233–59.

At the same sitting as Lovell's standing portrait. (Medford Historical Society, Medford, Mass.)

✶ *Mark Perrin Lowrey* ✶

Mark Lowrey was born on December 30, 1828, in McNairy County, Tennessee. His father died when he was very young, and he never received much education. When Lowrey was fifteen, his mother moved the family to Farmington in Tishomingo County, Mississippi. He volunteered for duty in the 2d Mississippi Volunteers in 1847 and went to Mexico, but the war there ended before he saw any fighting. In later life Lowrey wrote that he "formed a taste for military discipline and tactics" during his service with the Mississippi regiment.

Lowrey became a brick mason after he returned to Mississippi but in 1853 became a minister in the Baptist church. By 1861 he had become pastor of a church in Kossuth. He had improved his education by taking in the local school teacher as a boarder.

In the fall of 1861 the Mississippi legislature issued a call for sixty-day volunteers. Lowrey was elected captain of a company nicknamed "the Lowrey Guards," which was mustered in on December 6. This unit became Company H, 4th Mississippi State Troops of General Reuben Davis' brigade, and Lowrey was elected colonel of the regiment. The 4th Mississippi received orders to go to Bowling Green, Kentucky, to reinforce General Albert Sidney Johnston's army and arrived there on December 16. Lowrey's men helped garrison the entrenchments around the town and suffered severely from disease. Davis' regiments were discharged at the expiration of their enlistment, and his troops were back in Mississippi by February 1862.

Following the fall of Fort Donelson Lowrey began raising a new regiment in the counties around Tishomingo. He was elected colonel of the 32d Mississippi Infantry on April 3 when it was mustered in at Corinth. The regiment

in the Battle of Shiloh April 6–7. After its assignment to the brigade of Sterling A. M. Wood the regiment occupied part of the fortifications around Corinth but saw little action except in a few of the skirmishes around that town. Lowrey and his men accompanied the Army of Mississippi to Chattanooga in July.

From time to time during the early stages of the invasion of Kentucky (August–October), Lowrey exercised command of his brigade. He led his regiment in the Battle of Perryville on October 8 and succeeded Wood when that officer was wounded by a shell fragment. During an attack Lowrey received a painful wound in his left arm, which disabled him for nearly eight weeks. The 32d Mississippi was on detached duty during the first day of fighting at the Battle of Murfreesboro December 31, 1862–January 2, 1863, but Lowrey wrote after the war that his men saw some skirmishing in succeeding days. He also claimed that he had led the brigade during the army's retreat.

Major General Patrick R. Cleburne had taken over the division in which Wood's brigade served, and he worked closely with his generals and colonels in drilling the men during the months spent around Tullahoma and Shelbyville. Then and later Lowrey took the opportunity to minister to the troops. One of his soldiers recalled that "during seasons of rest from active campaigning [he] would preach to his command with zeal and power."

The 32d Mississippi took part in several skirmishes with the enemy in the army's retreat toward Chattanooga in July 1863. Again Lowrey exercised temporary brigade command. By July 31 the 45th

Believed to be a uniformed photograph of Mark Perrin Lowrey. (Museum of the Confederacy, Richmond, Va.)

Mississippi had been consolidated with the 32d under Lowrey. He led this regiment September 19–20, 1863, in the Battle of Chickamauga where he lost about one-fourth of his men in one attack. Both Cleburne and Lieutenant General Daniel H. Hill praised Lowrey for his gallantry and coolness in the battle. Shortly afterward Wood resigned his commission and Lowrey was promoted to brigadier general on October 6, effective October 4, 1863. Hill commented that "a worthier object of advancement could not have been selected."

At Missionary Ridge on November 25 Lowrey's brigade held a position south of the tunnel at Tunnel Hill. He moved his men to Cleburne's right flank as Union attacks threatened it, and they held their position against all enemy assaults. Lowrey played an important role in the fighting at Ringgold Gap, or Taylor's Ridge, on November 27 when Cleburne's division checked the Federal pursuit of the Army of Tennessee. Lowrey's brigade was in reserve when the battle began, but he reinforced the right wing at a critical moment, stopping the enemy from overrunning the position. He recalled later, "This was the most glorious triumph I ever witnessed on a battlefield."

Lowrey was one of the signers of Cleburne's January 2, 1864, proposal to free and arm the slaves to help defend the Confederacy. A few months later Lowrey and his men participated in all of the engagements of Cleburne's division during the Atlanta Campaign May 1–September 2, and the general added new laurels to his growing reputation as a fighter. Cleburne credited him with saving the army's right flank at New Hope Church on May 27. Lowrey led a counterattack under heavy fire and over difficult, unfamiliar ground, and his men pushed the Federals back. In one of the battles around Marietta in June, he was said to have temporarily halted the fighting and urged the Union commanders opposite him to put out a fire that threatened to engulf wounded soldiers lying between the lines. Lowrey's brigade supported that of Brigadier General Clement H. Stevens during the Battle of Peachtree Creek on July 20 and saw little action. In the Battle of Atlanta on July 22 Lowrey was moving his brigade to the front when he noticed a gap between two divisions. He quickly pushed his men into the area and saw Federal troops about to exploit the gap. Lowrey ordered an attack and prevented the enemy from penetrating the Confederate line. Captain Irving A. Buck, Cleburne's adjutant general, later wrote that if Lowrey had not acted as he did, the Union assault would have "imperiled one or both of the two divisions." On August 30 Lowrey assumed command of Cleburne's division when that officer temporarily took over direction of Lieutenant General William J. Hardee's corps. Lowrey led the division in the Battle of Jonesboro August 31–September 1 and for about a week afterward.

Resuming command of his brigade, Lowrey led it into Tennessee with the rest of the army. His and Brigadier General Daniel C. Govan's brigades were the only troops to engage the Federals at Spring Hill on November 29. When General John B. Hood decided to engage the enemy at Franklin the next day, Lowrey clasped hands with his commander as he declared, "We will make the fight." Lowrey's men lost about half their number in the bloody charge. They reached the Union entrenchments but could not advance beyond the ditch. Cleburne's death left Lowrey in command of the division for several days until Brigadier General James A. Smith could take over. During the first day of fighting in the Battle of Nashville on December 15 Lowrey led his brigade on the army's extreme right. The next day he commanded Major General Benjamin F. Cheatham's old division on the army's left flank. Lowrey's horse, which had been wounded at Franklin, was killed under him about the time the army was driven back.

The general continued to lead Cheatham's division into the early stages of the Carolinas Campaign (February–April 1865). He resigned from the army on March 14 and returned to Mississippi. Lowrey resumed his ministry in Tippah County. He founded Blue Mountain Female Institute (later renamed Blue Mountain College) in 1873. He served as president and professor of history and moral science at the school until he died; was president of the Mississippi Baptist Convention from 1868 to 1877; and served on the University of Mississippi board of trustees from 1872 to 1876. Lowrey died suddenly in the railway station at Middleton, Tennessee, on February 27, 1885, and his body was buried at Blue Mountain.

Though he had little formal education and only rudimentary military experience before the war, Lowrey became one of the Confederacy's most able brigadiers and was deeply loved by his men.

Arthur W. Bergeron, Jr.

Lowrey, Mark P., "General M. P. Lowrey, An Autobiography," *Southern Historical Society Papers*, XVI (1888).

Rowland, Dunbar, *Military History of Mississippi 1803–1898* (Spartanburg, S.C., 1978).

⋆ *Robert Lowry* ⋆

No uniformed photo of Robert Lowry is known. This one probably dates from the 1870s. (Virginia Historical Society)

Born in the Chesterfield District of South Carolina on March 10, 1830, Robert Lowry moved with his parents to Tennessee as a young boy. In 1840 the family again moved, this time to Tishomingo County, Mississippi. An uncle who served as a judge in Raleigh, Mississippi, raised Lowry, who joined him as a partner in the mercantile business. After marrying, Lowry moved to Arkansas, where he read law. He returned to Mississippi five years later, entered politics, and was elected to the state legislature and senate.

Lowry was a practicing lawyer and avid secessionist in 1861. When war came, he joined the Rankin Guards as a private and entered the 6th Mississippi Regiment with his company. When the regiment was reorganized, Lowry was elected major. He was wounded twice at Shiloh (April 6–7, 1862), and his regiment suffered heavy losses. On May 23 he was elected colonel of the 6th Mississippi when the previous commander resigned because of wounds received at Shiloh. Colonel Lowry served at Corinth in October and was assigned to General Joseph Johnston's force during the 1863 Vicksburg Campaign. At the Battle of Port Gibson, General Martin Green wrote that Lowry "deserves the highest commendation for his coolness and promptness in executing every order." Lowry also participated in the Battle of Champion's Hill, but there is no record of his actions there.

During the 1864 Atlanta Campaign Lowry's regiment was a part of John Adams' brigade, but he sometimes temporarily commanded Winfield Scott Featherston's brigade. Lowry served throughout the campaign, and June 27 at Kennesaw Mountain he commanded a skirmish line that managed to repulse two separate Union attacks. When General John Bell Hood invaded Tennessee in the autumn of 1864, Lowry accompanied the Army of Tennessee northward. At Franklin, Adams was killed and Lowry took command of the brigade. He led the Mississippians at the Battle of Nashville December 15–16 and on the subsequent retreat.

On February 13, 1865, Lowry was promoted to brigadier general, to rank from February 4. He participated in the Carolinas Campaign with Johnston that spring and was at the Battle of Bentonville March 19–21. Lowry was with Johnston at the surrender and was paroled at Greensboro, North Carolina, in May 1865.

After the war Lowry returned to Mississippi and served as a state senator from 1865 to 1866. In 1869 the Democratic party nominated him for attorney general against his wishes, and he lost the election. During Reconstruction Lowry helped oust the Republican carpetbagger government and was elected governor in 1881 as a compromise candidate. A popular governor, he was reelected in 1885 without opposition. In 1898 he was defeated for the United States Senate in his last bid for political office. Lowry served as commander of the Mississippi United Confederate Veterans from 1903 to 1910 and coauthored a history of the state. He died on January 19, 1910, and was buried in Brandon.

Terry L. Jones

Hooker, Charles E., *Mississippii*, Vol VII in Evans, *Confederate Military History*.

⭐ *Hylan Benton Lyon* ⭐

The only known uniformed pose of Kentuckian Hylan B. Lyon, taken in the last year of the war. (U.S. Army Military History Institute, Carlisle, Pa.)

Born at "River View" in Caldwell (now Lyon) County, Kentucky, on February 22, 1836, Hylan Benton Lyon was orphaned at the age of eight. After being educated in local schools, he won an appointment to West Point in 1852 and graduated nineteenth in the class of 1856. Brevetted a 2d lieutenant of artillery, Lyon served against the Seminoles in Florida 1856–57 before being assigned to California. In 1858 he saw action against Indians in the Washington Territory. Promoted to 1st lieutenant of the 3d Artillery, Lyon took a leave of absence from his unit during the secession crisis and resigned his commission on April 30, 1861.

First entering Confederate service as a captain of artillery, Lyon was elected lieutenant colonel of the 8th Kentucky Infantry on February 3, 1862, and served as commanding officer during the Battle of Fort Donelson February 13–16. The regiment lost approximately one hundred men during the bitter fighting around the fort, and Lyon's brigade commander described him as a "gallant officer." Taken prisoner when the fort surrendered, Lyon was held at Johnson's Island until exchanged seven months later.

Upon being exchanged, Lyon was promoted to colonel of the 8th Kentucky and was assigned to Brigadier General Lloyd Tilghman's division at Holly Springs, Mississippi. In a small fight at Coffeeville on December 5, 1862, Lyon was praised by Tilghman for his role in the Confederate victory. In 1863 he was given command of a brigade and saw service during the Vicksburg Campaign. In May his men patrolled the Big Black River region and skirmished with the Yankees. One of his antagonists, Union Brigadier

General P. J. Osterhaus, wrote that Lyon was "described as overbearing, and towards our wounded at Champion's Hill a very rude character." On June 2 General Joseph E. Johnston placed Lyon in command of all the cavalry in the Clinton area but on June 11 ordered him to assume command of all Confederate troops around Port Hudson, Louisiana. Lyon was to harass the enemy besieging the Confederate garrison there. His orders stated, "General Johnston has selected you for this very important duty because of his confidence in your skill and judgement...."

Later Lyon requested permanent cavalry duty, and General Braxton Bragg sent him to Major General Joseph Wheeler with instructions for Wheeler to start Lyon out with small commands until his ability could be judged. Joining Wheeler in November 1863, Lyon was given command of 320 cavalrymen at Kingston, Tennessee, with orders to keep an eye on Union activity. When Bragg's army was routed on Missionary Ridge on the 25th, Lyon was put in temporary charge of the artillery and managed to remove most of the guns to safety.

Lyon next was given a brigade of Kentucky cavalry in Brigadier General Abraham Buford's division of Major General Nathan Bedford Forrest's cavalry command. He opened the Battle of Brice's Cross Roads on June 10, 1864, by advancing against Union cavalry. His troopers fought for an hour unsupported and continued to perform well in the fight. Lyon lost twenty percent of his command and was praised by Forrest for being cool and courageous throughout the battle. Some of Lyon's best service was with Forrest. He was described by Forrest's biographer, John Allan Wyeth, as "one of Forrest's most devoted followers, a stubborn fighter, exhibiting at times a recklessness akin to desperation."

Promoted to brigadier general June 14, 1864, effective the same day, Lyon was put on detached service from Forrest and tried unsuccessfully to gather recruits behind enemy lines. He rejoined the cavalry in time for Forrest's raid into north Alabama and central Tennessee that September and October and according to Forrest, "rendered much valuable service" during the Johnsonville Raid in November. Returning to Corinth, Mississippi, after the raid to collect arms for his men, Lyon was ordered by General John Bell Hood to raid Clarksville, Tennessee, in order to cut Union communications with Nashville. In early December his eight hundred men captured and destroyed several Union steamers on the Cumberland River. Bypassing strongly defended Clarksville, Lyon entered Kentucky, burning courthouses, bridges, and railroads along his path. Unfortunately, when his brigade received word of Hood's defeat at Nashville and retreat from Tennessee, five hundred of Lyon's men deserted. His long raid ended when his weakened brigade returned to north Alabama. On the night of January 15, 1865, at Red Hill, Alabama, Lyon was surprised and captured by Federal cavalry in a citizen's house. While he got dressed in a dark room, a warning cry outside the house of approaching cavalry distracted his guards. Lyon pulled two pistols from beneath his pillow, shot one Yankee dead, and escaped half-dressed out the rear of the house. Lyon ended the war in command of a Union-occupied district in western Kentucky, apparently placed there as part of an attempt to reduce the surplus number of officers in Forrest's small command.

Lyon briefly went into exile in Mexico after the war but returned to Kentucky in 1866 to farm near Eddyville. He became active in veterans' affairs, a lessee of the state penitentiary, and a member of Kentucky's prisons commission. He died at Eddyville on April 25, 1907, and was buried there.

Terry L. Jones

Lyon, Hylan Benton, "Memoirs of Hylan B. Lyon, Brigadier General, C.S.A." Edited by Edward M. Coffman, *Tennessee Historical Quarterly*, 18 (March 1959), 35–53.

Wyeth, John Allen, *That Devil Forrest: Life of General Nathan Bedford Forrest* (Baton Rouge, 1989).

✯ *John McCausland* ✯

Brigadier General John McCausland, photographed during the last year of the war. (*Civil War Times Illustrated* Collection, Harrisburg, Pa.)

John McCausland was born on September 13, 1836, in St. Louis, Missouri. The son of an Irish immigrant, McCausland received an education in the schools of Point Pleasant in western Virginia where his parents had relocated. Entering the Virginia Military Institute, he was graduated first in the class of 1857. McCausland then spent a year at the University of Virginia before returning to VMI and accepting a position of assistant professor of mathematics.

When Virginia seceded in April 1861, McCausland organized the Rockbridge Artillery from recruits in the Lexington area and was elected its commander. He declined the command, however, when Virginia Governor John Letcher offered him a commission of lieutenant colonel and assigned him to recruiting duties in the Kanawha Valley of western Virginia. McCausland returned to his native section of the state, established headquarters at Charleston, and worked tirelessly to enlist volunteers in the Union-sympathizing region. By summer's end he had organized the 36th Virginia and was commissioned its colonel.

The new regiment joined John B. Floyd's Confederate command, participating in the operations in the region during the fall. McCausland's troops' initial combat occurred on September 10 at the Battle of Carnifix Ferry. Confederate authorities subsequently transferred the regiment to the Western theater, assigned to Southern forces in the Bowling Green, Kentucky, area. In February 1862 McCausland commanded a brigade in Floyd's division at Fort Donelson. A fiery, determined man, McCausland was one of the few officers who led his men out of the doomed works before the Federals sealed the escape routes.

McCausland's troops remained in Tennessee for a few months but did not participate in the Battle of

Shiloh in April. After that engagement he returned to Virginia where his regiment was assigned to the command of William Loring in western Virginia. From the spring of 1862 until the spring of 1864 McCausland served in this region under Loring, Brigadier General John Echols, and Major General Samuel Jones. When Brigadier General Albert Jenkins was killed in the battle at Cloyd's Mountain on May 9, 1864, McCausland assumed command of Jenkins' scattered cavalry units. Nine days later on May 24, 1864, he was promoted to brigadier general, to rank from May 18.

McCausland's initial cavalry service followed the next month when he ably opposed the advance of Major General David Hunter's Union army on Lynchburg. But Hunter was stopped in the outskirts of the railroad center by troops from the Army of Northern Virginia under Lieutenant General Jubal Early. For his role in the defense, the grateful citizens of Lynchburg gave McCausland an address of congratulations, a cavalry officer's uniform, sword, spurs, and a horse.

With Hunter swept from the Shenandoah Valley, Early marched northward in a raid into Maryland and against Washington, D.C. Early ordered McCausland to exact a two hundred thousand dollar ransom from the citizens of Hagerstown, Maryland, but McCausland erred in his demand and secured only twenty thousand and some clothing. On July 9 at the Battle of Monocacy McCausland crossed the river, securing a passage for Confederate infantry to advance on the Union lines. Early stated that McCausland's movement "was brilliantly executed." McCausland's thousand-man brigade then led the march on the Federal capital, but the Confederates could not overcome the miles of earthworks and cannon.

After the Confederate withdrawal into Virginia, Early ordered McCausland and Brigadier General Bradley Johnson to raid into Pennsylvania and demand one hundred thousand dollars in gold or five hundred thousand dollars in cash from the community of Chambersburg. If the citizens refused, Early directed that the town should be burned in retaliation for Hunter's devastation in the Shenandoah Valley.

McCausland and Johnson's cavalrymen reached Chambersburg on the morning of July 30. McCausland, nicknamed "Tiger John," was intensely devoted to the Confederate cause, and he demanded the tribute. When town officials refused to comply, his men began looting and burning. The flames engulfed eleven squares of Chambersburg, destroying over four hundred buildings, including 274 private dwellings. Damages amounted to over one and a half million dollars.

During the raiders' return march to Virginia, Union pursuers under William W. Averell surprised the Confederates on the morning of August 7 at Moorefield, West Virginia, and routed the Southerners. It was an embarrassing conclusion to a controversial operation. Johnson blamed McCausland for the defeat, but Confederate authorities took no formal action against either general.

McCausland then participated in the 1864 Shenandoah Valley Campaign that resulted in a string of defeats for Early's army. By the spring of 1865 McCausland's brigade was attached to the cavalry division of Major General Thomas Rosser at Petersburg. On April 1, 1865, McCausland fought under Rosser at Five Forks. Before Robert E. Lee surrendered at Appomattox on the 9th, McCausland led his veterans through the Federal lines and escaped, riding to Lynchburg where the cavalrymen restored civil order.

An unreconstructed Rebel who refused to accept Confederate defeat, McCausland fled the country, journeying for two years in Europe and Mexico. Returning to West Virginia, he bought six thousand acres of land, called his farm "McCausland," and resided there for six decades. The controversial but capable Southern officer died on January 22, 1927. Only one other Confederate general outlived him. McCausland was buried at Henderson, West Virginia.

Jeffry D. Wert

Cooling, Benjamin Franklin, *Jubal Early's Raid on Washington 1864* (Hamden, Conn., 1989).

Lowry, Terry, *The Battle of Scary Creek: Military Operations in the Kanawha Valley, April, July 1861*, (Charleston, 1982).

Lowry, Terry, *September Blood: The Battle of Carnifex Ferry*, (Charleston, 1985).

✳ *William McComb* ✳

William McComb was one of the small group of Northern-born men who served as general officers in the Confederate army. (Three of his brothers served in the Federal army.) McComb first saw the light of day in Mercer County, Pennsylvania—probably on November 21, 1831. The date of his birth is unknown, and there is even some question about the year. Different sources give his year of birth as anywhere from 1828 to 1832. In February 1865, however, McComb himself stated that he was then thirty-three years and three months of age.

Nothing is known of McComb's early life and education. He probably had some training or experience in civil engineering or business, and in the mid-1850s he went to Montgomery County, Tennessee, to superintend construction of a large flour mill at Price's Landing on the lower Cumberland River. Settling in the Volunteer State, McComb was living in the Clarksville area when the Civil War began. He enlisted as a private in a local unit that became Company L of the 14th Tennessee Infantry Regiment. He was soon (May 1861) elected 2d lieutenant.

After the regiment was organized at Camp Duncan, near Clarksville, Colonel William A. Forbes, the commander, appointed McComb as adjutant. In July 1861 the regiment was ordered to Virginia and brigaded with the 1st (Maney's) and 7th Tennessee regiments. The brigade—which from time to time included other units—became the Tennessee Brigade of the Army of Northern Virginia. The brigade was commanded by Brigadier Generals Samuel R. Anderson (July 1861–May 1862), Robert Hatton (May 1862), James J. Archer (June 1862–October 1864), and William McComb (October 1864–April 1865).

McComb served with his unit in western Virginia during the last part of 1861 and the early months of 1862. The brigade was then transferred to the Army of Northern Virginia and assigned to Major General Ambrose P. Hill's Light Division. Meanwhile in May 1862 at the expiration of its first year of service the regiment had been reorganized. As part of this process McComb was elected major.

In the battle of Cedar Mountain August 9, 1862, the regiment's lieutenant colonel, G. A. Harrell, was mortally wounded. McComb was promoted to succeed him. Three weeks later at Second Manassas Colonel Forbes was mortally wounded. He died on September 2, and McComb was moved up another grade to colonel. At Antietam on September 17 McComb won praise for gallantry and was himself seriously wounded. He was back in command of his regiment in early 1863 and was again wounded on May 3 at Chancellorsville. This second wound was also serious. It kept McComb away from the army for several months, and as a result he was not with his regiment at Gettysburg.

The army had been reorganized after Chancellorsville, and Archer's Brigade had been assigned to Major General Henry Heth's division in the III Corps. General Archer was captured at Gettysburg and was not exchanged until the summer of 1864. After his exchange illness often kept Archer away from the army, and McComb, as the senior colonel, was therefore often in command of the brigade.

A previously unpublished portrait of William McComb as colonel of the 14th Tennessee Infantry, and his only known uniformed portrait. (William A. Turner Collection)

Archer died on October 24, 1864. Soon afterward the Tennessee officers submitted a petition to have McComb named as his replacement. Heth, commanding the division, also urged McComb's promotion, calling him "a good disciplinarian, a gallant and deserving officer." Meanwhile the brigade had been expanded by the addition of the 2d Maryland Battalion (also called the 1st Maryland Battalion and the 2d Maryland Regiment). It had also been consolidated with the remnants of six other Tennessee regiments that had come to Virginia earlier in 1864.

In commenting on the recommendation for McComb's promotion, commanding general Robert E. Lee noted that John M. Hughes, commander of the 25th Tennessee, was the senior colonel with the consolidated units but that McComb "is the best officer to command...[the united brigades]." Hughes, pronounced incompetent by a board of officers, soon resigned. McComb was promoted into the vacant brigadier's slot on February 13, 1865, with his date of rank set at January 20.

During McComb's brief tenure as a general he and his men were posted in the Rebel lines below Petersburg in the Hatcher's Run area. There they fought gallantly in the closing weeks of the war. When the Federals broke through the Southern lines on April 2, 1865, survivors of the Tennessee Brigade joined the retreating Rebel forces. McComb and those of his men who were able to make the march westward to Appomattox Court House surrendered there with the rest of the army on April 9, 1865.

Immediately after the war McComb went to "Ingleside," the Louisa County, Virginia, home of Dr. Charles Quarles. There he spent some time recuperating from his wartime injuries. (There are unverified reports of a third wound—perhaps received in the closing days of the conflict.) He then lived in Alabama and Mississippi for a few years. In 1868 he married Quarles' daughter Annie and settled in Louisa County near Gordonsville. After his wife's death in 1895 McComb lived on his Louisa County plantation, often spending time with a married daughter and her family in Richmond.

McComb took part in many veterans' activities. In 1890, for example, he served on the nominating committee of the Association of the Army of Northern Virginia. He also attended some of the reunions of various veterans' groups, and he frequently participated in the massive parades and other ceremonies that often accompanied the dedication of one or another of the great Confederate monuments in Richmond.

After a two-week illness McComb died at the Gordonsville home of a married daughter on July 21, 1918 (twenty-three years to the day after his wife's death). He was a "staunch Democrat" and for more than fifty years an active member of the Mechanicsville Baptist Church, serving as a deacon and as the superintendent of its Sunday school. He was buried in the church cemetery, on state highway 22, southeast of Gordonsville. After his death only nine former Confederate generals—all brigadiers—survived.

Richard M. McMurry

Porter, James D., *Tennessee*, Vol. VIII in Evans, *Confederate Military History*.

⋆ *John Porter McCown* ⋆

Born near Sevierville, Tennessee, on August 19, 1815, John Porter McCown ranked tenth among the forty-two graduates in the West Point class of 1840. Entering the 4th Artillery as a 2d lieutenant on July 1, McCown immediately began moving Indians west of the Mississippi River. Later that year he was assigned to the U.S.–Canadian boundary, where he remained until the border disturbances ended in 1841. Promoted to 1st lieutenant on September 30, 1843, McCown served along the Rio Grande (1845–46) and distinguished himself during the Mexican War at Palo Alto, Resaca de la Palma, Monterrey, Vera Cruz, Cerro Gordo, and Mexico City. His heroism at Cerro Gordo earned him a brevet captaincy on April 18, 1847. McCown also served as quartermaster from March 29, 1847, to January 12, 1849. Stationed on the Rio Grande after the war, he was promoted to captain on January 9, 1851. He fought the Seminoles in Florida (1856–57), participated in the Utah Expedition of 1858, and served in Nebraska and in the Dakotas until he resigned on May 17, 1861, to enter Confederate service.

McCown had already accepted a lieutenant colonel's commission from the Confederate government on March 16, and on May 9, when Tennessee Governor Isham G. Harris created the Artillery Corps of the Provisional Army of Tennessee, Harris nominated McCown to command it. On May 17 Harris successfully nominated McCown for promotion to colonel. Commissioned a brigadier general on October 12, McCown left what was commonly referred to as McCown's Artillery Corps. Of the nineteen companies that had been authorized while McCown commanded that corps, seventeen had successfully completed their

organization. When Federal forces attacked Belmont, Missouri, on November 7, McCown led a column northward from Columbus, Kentucky, on the opposite bank of the Mississippi River. He quickly ascertained that no enemy troops threatened Columbus, and this information enabled Major General Leonidas Polk to transfer troops to the west bank in time to drive the Federals from the field.

When Polk abandoned Columbus (February 29–March 2, 1862), he ordered McCown to reinforce the garrison at New Madrid, Missouri, and Island No. 10 with five thousand soldiers and several cannon. Opposing McCown were eighteen thousand troops under Major General John Pope and a flotilla of six gunboats and eleven mortar boats under Flag Officer Andrew H. Foote. On March 3 Pope surrounded New Madrid, but McCown's heavy cannons ashore, supported by four gunboats, necessitated a siege. While Pope waited for his siege artillery to arrive, McCown received his major general's commission on March 14, effective March 10. Three days later Pope opened a massive bombardment which quickly convinced Confederate Navy Captain George N. Hollins to withdraw his fleet. Hollins' action convinced McCown to follow suit, and that night he ordered the garrison to the peninsula across the river to avoid being trapped on the north shore. McCown's evacuation of New Madrid effectively trapped his troops if they remained on the peninsula and island—which McCown chose to do. Relieved on March 31 for

The only known genuine uniformed portrait of General John McCown, this previously unpublished portrait dates probably from late in the war. (Museum of the Confederacy, Richmond, Va.)

his abandonment of New Madrid, McCown's successor, Brigadier General William W. Mackall, also chose to remain on the peninsula. Although it was Mackall who surrendered the garrison on April 8, the blame fell upon McCown. General Pierre G. T. Beauregard termed McCown's evacuation of New Madrid as "the poorest defense made by any fortified post during the whole course of the war."

Reporting to Corinth, McCown commanded a division under Major General Earl Van Dorn in late April. When Van Dorn departed for Vicksburg on June 20, McCown succeeded him as commander of the Army of the West. On July 3 when General Braxton Bragg felt compelled to send reinforcements to Major General Edmund Kirby Smith in East Tennessee, he sent a division under McCown. When Kirby Smith placed McCown in command of Chattanooga, Bragg wrote Kirby Smith: "The officer I sent you, I regret to say, cannot be trusted with such a command, and I implore you not to intrust him indeed with any important position. New Madrid fell by his errors and want of decision and firmness, as is supposed, while other prominent instances and evidences of his want of capacity and nerve for a separate, responsible command have just been brought to my notice. His high rank constraining me to send him with his division, I had no alternative at the time."

Indeed, only Bragg, Polk, and Major General William J. Hardee outranked McCown at Tupelo, and Bragg wanted a more capable officer in command of what amounted to one-fourth of his army. Left behind to command the Department of East Tennessee when Kirby Smith invaded Kentucky in August, McCown joined Bragg in Kentucky in October and commanded a division during the retreat.

Although Bragg believed McCown to be his worst division commander, he selected him to open the attack at Murfreesboro on December 31, 1862; when it went badly, Bragg blamed McCown. In February 1863 Bragg preferred charges against McCown for disobedience of orders; he had previously reported to the War Department that McCown was unfit for responsible command. McCown, on the other hand, believed that Bragg should be relieved, and he promised to resign from the army and grow potatoes if Bragg remained in command. At Shelbyville, Tennessee, on March 16, 1863, a court-martial found McCown guilty and sentenced him to be suspended from rank, pay, and emoluments for six months. Embittered by the court's ruling, McCown wrote that the Confederacy was "a *damned* stinking cotton oligarchy...gotten up for the benefit of Isham G. Harris and Jeff Davis and their damned corrupt cliques." Public utterances along this line relegated him to military obscurity until April 1865, when he defended a crossing on the Catawba River near Morganton, North Carolina, with a single piece of artillery and three hundred men against a division of Federal cavalry.

After the war McCown taught school in Knoxville. He later took up farming near Magnolia, Arkansas. He died in Little Rock on January 22, 1879, while attending a meeting of the Masonic Lodge. He was buried in Magnolia.

Lawrence L. Hewitt

Heitman, Francis B., *Historical Register and Dictionary of the United States Army, From Its Organization, September 29, 1789, to March 2, 1903* (Washington, 1903).

Hewitt, Lawrence L., "Braxton Bragg and the Confederate Invasion of Kentucky in 1862," in Roman J. Heleniak and Lawrence L. Hewitt, eds., *The 1989 Deep Delta Civil War Symposium: Leadership During the Civil War* (Shippensburg, 1991).

Porter, James D., *Tennessee*, Vol. VIII in Evans, *Confederate Military History*.

[Tennessee] Civil War Centennial Commission. *Tennesseans in the Civil War: A Military History of Confederate and Union Units with Available Rosters of Personnel* (Nashville, 1964).

Ben McCulloch never lived long enough to wear a uniform, and perhaps would not have in any case. Friends later asserted that in this image he is wearing the civilian suit in which he was killed at Elkhorn Tavern. (University of Texas at Austin)

✶ *Ben McCulloch* ✶

Ben McCulloch was born in Rutherford County, Tennessee, on November 11, 1811. He was the fourth son of Frances F. LeNoir, the daughter of a prominent Virginia planter and slaveholder, and Alexander McCulloch, a graduate of Yale College and a major on Brigadier General John Coffee's staff during Andrew Jackson's campaign against the Creeks in Alabama. He was also the elder brother of Henry Eustace McCulloch, who followed in Ben's footsteps as Indian fighter, Texas Ranger, United States marshal, and brigadier general in the army of the Confederate States of America.

The McCullochs had been a prosperous and influential colonial North Carolina family but had lost much of their wealth as a result of the revolutionary war and the improvidence of Ben's father. Alexander McCulloch so wasted his inheritance that he was unable to educate his younger sons, although two of Ben's older brothers briefly attended school taught by a close neighbor and family friend in Tennessee, Sam Houston. Typical of many families on the western frontier, the McCullochs moved from North Carolina to East Tennessee to Alabama and back to West Tennessee between 1812 and 1830, settling at last near Dyersburg, where David Crockett was among their closest neighbors and most influential friends. After five years of farming, hunting, and rafting, but virtually no formal schooling, Ben agreed to follow his mentor Crockett to Texas, planning to meet him in Nacogdoches on Christmas Day 1835.

Ben and Henry arrived too late, however, and Ben alone followed Crockett toward San Antonio. When a case of measles prevented him from reaching the Alamo before its fall, McCulloch joined Sam Houston's army on its retreat into east Texas. At the Battle of San Jacinto he commanded one of the pieces of Texan artillery—the famed "Twin Sisters"—and won from Houston a battlefield commission as 1st lieutenant. He soon left the army, however, to earn his living as a surveyor in the Texas frontier communities of Gonzales and Seguin. There he joined the Texas Rangers and served as 1st lieutenant under John Coffee Hays, winning a considerable reputation as an Indian fighter.

In 1839 McCulloch was elected to the house of representatives of the Republic of Texas in a campaign marred by a rifle duel with Ruben Ross, a political rival. In the affray McCulloch received a wound that partially crippled his right arm for the rest of his life. On Christmas Day of that year Henry McCulloch killed Ross in a pistol duel in Gonzales.

Ben chose not to stand for reelection in 1841 but returned to surveying and the pursuit of a quasi-military career. At the Battle of Plum Creek on August 12, 1840—the engagement that broke the power of the Comanches in central Texas—McCulloch distinguished himself as a scout and as commander of the right wing of the Anglo-Texan army. When in February 1842 the Mexican government launched a raid against Texas that seized the strategic town of San Antonio, McCulloch rendered invaluable service as a scout and took a prominent role in the fighting that harried the invaders back below the Rio Grande. On September 11, 1842, a second Mexican expedition captured San Antonio. McCulloch again rendered valuable scouting service and joined in the pursuit of the Mexicans to the Hondo River, where Hays' rangers engaged them on September 21. After the repulse of the second Mexican invasion in six months McCulloch remained with the ranger company that formed the nucleus of an army with which the Texans planned to invade Mexico. The so-called Somervell expedition was poorly managed, however, and Ben and Henry left it on the Rio Grande only hours before the remainder of the Texans were captured at Mier, Mexico, on December 25, 1842.

With the outbreak of the Mexican War McCulloch raised a command of Texas Rangers which became Company A of Colonel Jack Hays' 1st Regiment, Texas Mounted Volunteers. Ordered to report to the United States army on the Rio Grande, McCulloch was soon named Zachary Taylor's chief of scouts and won his commander's praise and the admiration of the nation with his exciting reconnaissance expeditions into northern Mexico. The presence in his company of George Wilkins Kendall, editor of the New Orleans

Picayune, and Samuel Reid, who was to write a popular history of the campaign, *The Scouting Expeditions of McCulloch's Texas Rangers*, propelled McCulloch's name into national prominence. Leading his company as mounted infantry at the Battle of Monterrey, McCulloch further distinguished himself, and before the Battle of Buena Vista his astute and daring reconnaissance work saved Taylor's army from disaster and won him a promotion to the rank of major of United States volunteers.

Returning to Texas at the end of the war, McCulloch served for a time as a scout under Brevet Major General David E. Twiggs and then set out from Austin on September 9, 1849, for the gold fields of California. Although he failed to strike it rich, he was elected sheriff of Sacramento. Hoping to return him to the army, however, McCulloch's friends in the senate, Sam Houston and Thomas Jefferson Rusk, mounted a campaign to put the former ranger in command of a regiment of regular United States cavalry for duty on the Texas frontier. Largely due to McCulloch's lack of formal education, however, the attempt was frustrated. In 1852 President Franklin Pierce promised him the command of the elite 2d United States Cavalry, but Secretary of War Jefferson Davis bestowed the command instead on his personal favorite, Albert Sidney Johnston. McCulloch was, however, appointed as the United States marshal for Texas and served under Pierce and James Buchanan. In 1858 he was appointed as one of two peace commissioners to treat with Brigham Young and the elders of the Mormon church and is credited with helping to prevent armed hostilities between the United States government and the Latter-day Saints in Utah.

With his state's secession from the Union McCulloch was commissioned a colonel in the Texas army and authorized to demand the surrender of all Federal posts in the Military District of Texas. After a bloodless confrontation at the Alamo on February 16, 1861, David Twiggs turned over to McCulloch the Federal arsenal and all other United States property in San Antonio. On May 14, 1861, Jefferson Davis appointed McCulloch a brigadier general, to rank from May 1, the second ranking brigadier general in the Confederate provisional army and the first general grade officer to be commissioned from the civilian community. Assigned to the command of the Indian Territory, he established his headquarters at Little Rock, Arkansas, where he began to build the Army of the West with regiments from Arkansas, Louisiana, and Texas. Although hampered by logistical nightmares and a total disagreement over strategic objectives with Missouri general Sterling Price, with whom he had been ordered to cooperate, McCulloch with the assistance of Albert Pike established vital alliances with the Cherokees, Choctaws, Creeks, and other tribes of what is now eastern Oklahoma. On August 10, 1861, McCulloch won an impressive victory over the army of Nathaniel Lyon at Wilson's Creek, or Oak Hills, in southwest Missouri.

McCulloch's continuing inability to come to personal or strategic accord with Price, however, caused Jefferson Davis on January 10, 1862, to appoint Earl Van Dorn to the command of both McCulloch's and Price's armies. Van Dorn immediately launched the Army of the West on an expedition to capture St. Louis, a plan that McCulloch bitterly resisted. Due largely to McCulloch's remarkable knowledge of the terrain Van Dorn's army was able to flank the army of Union Major General Samuel R. Curtis out of a strong position along Little Sugar Creek in northwest Arkansas and cut his line of communication to the north. McCulloch, commanding the Confederate right wing in the ensuing Battle of Pea Ridge, or Elkhorn Tavern, March 7, 1862, enjoyed early success, overrunning a battery of artillery and driving the enemy back from his original position. As Federal resistance stiffed around 10:30 A.M., however, McCulloch rode forward through the thick underbrush to determine the location of the enemy line and was shot from his horse, dying instantly. His command devolved upon Brigadier General James McIntosh, who was killed but a few minutes later leading a charge to recover McCulloch's body. Colonel Louis Hébert, the division's senior regimental commander, was captured in the same charge and soon McCulloch's leaderless division began to fall apart and drift toward the rear. Most participants and later historians attribute to McCulloch's untimely death the disaster at Pea Ridge and the subsequent loss of Arkansas to the Union.

He was first buried on the field, but his body was removed to the cemetery at Little Rock and then to the Texas State Cemetery in Austin. McCulloch never owned a uniform and at the time of his death was wearing a black velvet suit.

Thomas W. Cutrer

Reid, Samuel C., *Scouting Expedition of McCulloch's Texas Rangers* (Philadelphia, 1847).

Rose, Victor M., *The Life and Services of Gen. Ben McCulloch* (Philadelphia, 1888).

☆ *Henry Eustace McCulloch* ☆

No uniformed portrait of Henry McCulloch is known to exist. This portrait is quite clearly postwar. (University of Texas at Austin)

Henry Eustace McCulloch was born on December 6, 1816, in Rutherford County, Tennessee, the son of Frances F. LeNoir and Major Alexander McCulloch. Major McCulloch, a native Virginian, was raised in North Carolina and served as an aide-de-camp to General James Coffee under General Andrew Jackson from 1812 until 1815.

Henry McCulloch was raised on a farm in West Tennessee but followed his brother Ben to Texas in the fall of 1837. In 1838 he joined Ben at Gonzales; two years later he was elected assessor of Gonzales County and in 1843 became the sheriff. He participated in numerous Indian campaigns and fought in the Mexican War, during which he commanded a company of Texas Rangers. In 1850 he served as captain of a body of rangers, being mustered out of service by Captain James Longstreet in November of the following year.

He also served in the Texas legislature from Guadalupe County in 1853. In 1855 he was elected to the Texas Senate and served four years. At the end of his term in office he was appointed United States marshal for the eastern district of Texas by President James Buchanan and was holding that position when the Civil War began.

On February 5, 1861, he was appointed colonel of cavalry by the Committee of Public Safety at Austin and directed to raise troops and demand the surrender of United States forts on the Texas northwestern frontier. Under these orders Forts Mason, Chadbourne, and Camp Colorado surrendered without resistance after an agreement was reached between McCulloch and Captain Edmund Kirby Smith of the 2d U.S.

Cavalry. Smith had originally refused to relinquish the posts, but upon learning that U.S. Brevet Major General David E. Twiggs had surrendered to Ben McCulloch, decided to evacuate the Federal troops.

In March 1861 Colonel Earl Van Dorn ordered Henry McCulloch to take command of the Texas state troops on the Red River. In April McCulloch was colonel of the 1st Texas Mounted Rifles, Confederate States Provisional Army. In May he was instructed by the War Department to raise a volunteer regiment for the protection of the Texas frontier. In August he was recalled to San Antonio and ordered by Van Dorn to take command of the Department of Texas, which he officially headed from September 4 through September 18.

In mid-October he claimed that although Brigadier General Paul O. Hébert had arrived to relieve him and had been in Galveston for several weeks, Hébert had not published any order assuming command. This disregard for Hébert's authority caused some hard feelings and a court of inquiry in January 1862. However, nothing came of this, and the next month McCulloch was in command of the Sub-military District of the Rio Grande with headquarters at San Antonio.

McCulloch was promoted to brigadier general shortly after his brother Ben died March 7 at Pea Ridge. His date of appointment was March 18, 1862, to rank from March 14. Now a brigadier, Henry planned to cross the Mississippi River and join Ben's old command near Corinth. Delayed in Louisiana, however, he realized his service would be more useful in Texas; he requested and was granted permission to return. His orders instructed him to coordinate troop movement in eastern Texas, and he established his headquarters at Tyler. From there he forwarded over twenty thousand Confederates toward Little Rock. McCulloch had a talent for administration and did an excellent job of sending men to Arkansas. In September he joined the Texans, where Lieutenant General Theophilus H. Holmes placed him in command of a division of Texas infantry at Camp Nelson, north of Little Rock.

McCulloch remained in command until December, when he was replaced by Major General John G. Walker. McCulloch was relegated to the command of a brigade in Walker's division. He fought under Walker at Milliken's Bend on June 7, 1863, but his performance was so unsatisfactory that he was ordered by General E. Kirby Smith to report to Major General J. B. Magruder, who commanded the District of Texas, at Houston. Major General Richard Taylor said of McCulloch's leadership qualities at Milliken's Bend: "In this affair General McCulloch appears to have shown great personal bravery, but no capacity for handling masses." Furthermore, the "injudicious handling of the troops prevented the attainment of the results which were anticipated."

McCulloch returned home to Seguin, Texas, but on Smith's suggestion he was placed in command of the Northern Sub-district of Texas; on September 5, 1863, he was ordered by Magruder to make his headquarters at Bonham. In December he requested a transfer from his administrative duties to an active field command, but this was not forthcoming. In Bonham McCulloch was plagued by many problems, including what to do with the notorious William Quantrill. In addition, the frontier was full of Indian war parties and roving gangs of deserters and draft dodgers, and McCulloch never had enough men to assure the safety of Texans. By the end of 1864 McCulloch had 1,330 effectives, but this was still not enough and the government of Texas finally closed the frontier until the war's end. In late 1864 McCulloch was still petitioning for an active field command, but he remained in charge at Bonham until the end of the war. He was paroled at San Antonio on August 19, 1865.

After the war he engaged in various pursuits; one was shipping Texas cattle to Havana. He worked for the railroad until he was appointed superintendent of the Asylum for the Deaf and Dumb, a position he held until 1879 when he retired to his farm at Seguin. He died in Rockport, Texas, on March 12, 1895, and was buried at Seguin.

Anne Bailey

Roberts, O. M., *Texas*, Vol. XI in Evans, *Confederate Military History*.

Samuel McGowan

General Samuel McGowan taken sometime between 1863 and 1865. (Albert G. Shaw Collection, Virginia Historical Society, Richmond, Va.)

Samuel McGowan was born in the Laurens District, South Carolina, on October 9, 1819. The son of Irish immigrants, McGowan was graduated from South Carolina College in 1841. He then studied law in the offices of T. C. Perrin in Abbeville and was admitted to the bar the following year. A skillful attorney and gifted speaker, McGowan soon had a flourishing legal practice and was elected to the state house of representatives. When the Mexican War began, McGowan volunteered, serving as captain in the quartermaster department. At the Battle of Chapultepec he was a volunteer aide-de-camp to General John Quitman, whose division stormed the gateway. McGowan earned a commendation for his service.

When South Carolina seceded in December 1860, McGowan was a major general in the state's militia. During the bombardment of Fort Sumter in April 1861 he commanded a militia brigade. He then volunteered for service, acting as an aide-de-camp to Brigadier General Milledge Bonham at First Manassas. Returning to South Carolina, he was appointed lieutenant colonel of the 14th South Carolina. In the spring of 1862 upon the resignation of Colonel James Jones, McGowan assumed command of the regiment with the rank of colonel.

The 14th South Carolina, along with the 1st, 12th, 13th, and Orr's Rifles, comprised the famous South Carolina brigade of Maxcy Gregg. As part of Major General A. P. Hill's Light Division Gregg's brigade fought valiantly in the Seven Days' Campaign of June 25—July 1. At Gaines' Mill on June 27 McGowan suffered a wound but remained with the regiment throughout the campaign. Hill cited the colonel and the 14th for its performances at Gaines' Mill and Frayser's Farm.

At Second Manassas August 29—30 Gregg's brigade held the left of Major General "Stonewall" Jackson's line. At a crucial point in the struggle on the 29th McGowan led the regiment in a counterattack that stabilized Gregg's line and secured the position. McGowan, however, fell severely wounded and missed the Sharpsburg campaign. He returned to duty before the Battle of Fredericksburg in December. Gregg was killed in the fighting of the 13th, and a month later McGowan was promoted over two senior colonels of the brigade to command of the brigade. His brigadier-generalcy was appointed on April 23 and took effect January 17, 1863.

McGowan was the popular choice of the brigade. He had not been a stern disciplinarian but proved to be an efficient officer and excellent drillmaster. In combat he had demonstrated vigilance and perception and inspired confidence. His record as a regimental commander earned him promotion.

McGowan's initial action as brigade commander came at Chancellorsville in May. On the 3d his South Carolinians attacked a Union line of fieldworks. They captured one line before retiring when a brigade on their right failed to advance. McGowan, however, suffered another wound, hit in a leg below the knee by a bullet. This serious wound kept him out of field service until February 1864. When he returned, the leg had not fully healed and he required the use of a cane.

McGowan led the brigade at the Wilderness where on May 6 his command and other Confederate brigades were broken under a massive Union attack at daylight. As his men were fleeing, they passed General Robert E. Lee, who exclaimed: "My God, General McGowan, is this splendid brigade of yours running like a flock of geese?"

"General Lee," responded McGowan, "the men are not whipped. They only want a place to form, and they will fight as well as ever they did."

Confederate reserves counterattacked, stopping the Federal onslaught and giving the South Carolinians and others a place to rally, and they did as McGowan had promised.

Six days later at Spotsylvania the brigade redeemed itself in the bloody combat at the "Mule Shoe," or "Bloody Angle." Still using a walking stick, McGowan led his veterans in a splendid counterattack, earning the praise of Major General Robert E. Rodes. McGowan took a bullet in the right arm and had to relinquish command of the brigade. The South Carolina brigadier returned to duty in August, rejoining his troops in the Petersburg trenches. For the next seven or eight months he and his brigade endured the deadly combat of the siege. The South Carolinians were paroled together at Appomattox. From the Seven Days' to the end, McGowan was one of the finest regimental and brigade commanders in the Army of Northern Virginia.

Soon after his return to Abbeville McGowan was elected to the U.S. House of Representatives. The members of the chamber, however, refused him the seat, and he returned home. During the subsequent decade he became an outspoken opponent of Radical Republican rule. In 1878 he secured a seat in the state legislature and a year later was elected associate justice of the state supreme court. He held his judicial post for fourteen years until defeated for reelection in 1893. McGowan died at his home in Abbeville on August 9, 1897, and was buried in Long Cane Cemetery in the community.

Jeffry D. Wert

Coldwell, J. F. J., *The History of A Brigade of South Carolinians Known First as "Gregg's," And Subsequently as "McGowan's Brigade"* (Philadelphia, 1866).

Freeman, Douglas Southall, *Lee's Lieutenants: A Study in Command* (New York, 1942–44).

Schenck, Martin, *Up Came Hill: The Story of the Light Division and Its Leaders* (Harrisburg, 1958).

The clothing on McGowan is very indistinct, but there are hints that this may be a uniform coat, with no signs of rank visible. (William A. Turner Collection)

★ *James McQueen McIntosh* ★

A view of James McIntosh probably taken in 1861 before his promotion to brigadier. (University of Arkansas Archives, Little Rock)

James McQueen McIntosh was born in the Florida Territory in 1828 while his father was stationed at Fort Brooke (now the site of Tampa). He was the son of army officer Colonel James S. McIntosh; the elder McIntosh died during the Mexican War in the Battle of Molina del Rey. He was also the great-grandnephew of Lachlan McIntosh, the revolutionary war general remembered for killing Button Gwinnett, a signer of the Declaration of Independence.

In 1849 James McIntosh graduated from West Point last in his class of forty-three. Because of his low standing he was assigned to the infantry, but in 1855 he transferred to the cavalry when that branch of the service expanded. In 1857 he was promoted to captain in the 1st Cavalry and spent his time on the frontier.

He resigned from the army on May 7, 1861. James' younger brother John Baillie McIntosh, who had been a midshipman during the Mexican War, believed it was "a blot on his family honor" when his older brother joined the Confederacy. (John remained loyal to the Union, lost a leg in combat, and rose to the rank of brevet major general of volunteers.) On May 11 Albert Pike wrote R. W. Johnson that Captain McIntosh, who was at that time in Georgia, "desires to go into the service in the Indian country, and I should if I were to command here, much desire to have him." Two days later McIntosh was ordered to report to Brigadier General Ben McCulloch at Little Rock for duty and by late May was on Governor H. M. Rector's staff.

On July 5 he was part of a force that planned to assault Neosho, Missouri, but the Federal troops surrendered before there was a fight. He took part in the skirmish at Dug Springs, Missouri, on August 2. At Wilson's Creek he commanded the 2d Regiment, Arkansas Mounted Riflemen, and served also as brigade adjutant general. McIntosh reported that he led his dismounted command through a "dense thicket to a fence surrounding a corn field, where we became closely engaged with the enemy." He personally rode forward encouraging the men to charge and successfully drove the Federals back. Colonel Louis Hébert reported that the men were "led gallantly and bravely by Captain McIntosh, to whom I owe all thanks for assistance…. I cannot conclude without saying that the conduct of Capt. James McIntosh, in throwing himself with my regiment in our first fight and in the attack on [Franz] Sigel's battery, greatly contributed to the success of our arms, and deserves unlimited praise." A lieutenant colonel in the 3d Regiment Louisiana Volunteers noted that he wanted to call attention to the "gallantry and bravery of Colonel McIntosh who conducted us to the point of attack." Brigadier General N. B. Pearce, commanding the 1st Division, reported: "I deem it lost time for me to attempt to sound the praises of the brave and chivalrous McIntosh. Always in the midst of the fight cheering and leading his men forward to victory, his name and conduct were a host in our behalf."

On September 30, 1861, he was listed as the colonel of the 2d Arkansas Cavalry on duty with McCulloch in Arkansas. In December McIntosh told Douglas Cooper, another future brigadier general, that he had been left in command of his division by McCulloch and had established his headquarters at Van Buren because of a smallpox outbreak at Fort Smith. Cooper asked McIntosh to bring troops to the Cherokee Nation because of the "hostile stand taken by the Creek chief Hopoeithleyohola [Opothleyahola] and the disaffection which has sprung up in one of the Cherokee regiments." McIntosh headed to Fort Gibson with sixteen hundred men and participated in the Battle of Chustenahlah on December 26, 1861; the next day he skirmished with Creeks and Seminoles.

On January 1, 1862, McIntosh's division was stationed in western Arkansas and consisted of the 1st Brigade commanded by McIntosh and the 2d Brigade under Hébert. He was commissioned a brigadier general in the Provisional Army on March 16, 1861, to rank from December 13, 1861, and on January 31 had his brigade near Fort Smith, while Hébert's brigade was spread out at Fayetteville, Bentonville, and Caneville.

In the spring of 1862 Major General Earl Van Dorn, who took command of the Confederates in Arkansas, wrote that McIntosh had been "very much distinguished all through the operations which have taken place in this region." When the Confederates advanced from the Boston Mountains, Van Dorn placed McIntosh in command of the cavalry brigade and in charge of the pickets. He was killed while leading a cavalry charge at Pea Ridge (Elkhorn Tavern) on March 7, 1862, shortly after the death of Ben McCulloch. "He was alert, daring, and devoted to his duty," wrote Van Dorn. "His kindness of disposition, with his reckless bravery, had attached the troops strongly to him," so that after McCulloch died in the battle, Van Dorn believed that had McIntosh remained alive, "all would have been well with my right wing." But after leading a "brilliant charge of cavalry and carrying the enemy's batter he rushed into the thickest of the fight again at the head of his old regiment and was shot through the heart." One of McIntosh's regimental commanders reported that the men had such "implicit confidence" in his courage that he hoped history would do justice to his character and that future generations would appreciate his loss as "we felt it on that day."

The bodies of both McIntosh and McCulloch were carried to Fort Smith, Arkansas, where McIntosh was buried in the National Cemetery. McCulloch was removed to the Texas State Cemetery at Austin. James McIntosh's brother continued his distinguished career in the Union army and in 1866 became lieutenant colonel of the 42d Infantry. He retired as a brigadier general in 1870 and died in 1888.

Anne Bailey

Perry, Joseph, *Georgia*, Vol. VI in Evans, *Confederate Military History*.

⋆ *William Whann Mackall* ⋆

One of nine Marylanders to wear the three stars and wreath of a Confederate general officer, William Whann Mackall was born on January 18, 1817, in Cecil County (many sources state that he was born in the District of Columbia) into a family that had connections all along the Atlantic coast. He entered West Point in 1833 and graduated four years later, standing eighth in a fifty-man class.

Mackall was commissioned 2d lieutenant in the 1st U.S. Artillery in 1837. He was promoted to 1st lieutenant in 1838 and to captain, then major in 1847. He was wounded in both the Seminole and Mexican wars—severely in the former—and was cited for bravery on two occasions in the latter conflict. Transferring to the Adjutant General's Department, he served as an assistant adjutant general on the staffs of several commanders before resigning on July 3, 1861, to join the Confederacy. By that time he had established a reputation as a solid, capable officer and was well regarded by most of his professional contemporaries. Meanwhile, in 1844 he had married Aminta Sorrell, of a prominent Savannah, Georgia, family.

In September 1861 Mackall was commissioned as a Confederate lieutenant colonel and assigned as an assistant adjutant general and chief of staff to General Albert Sidney Johnston, commander of the Western Department. On March 6, 1862, Mackall was promoted to brigadier general with date of rank February 27 and ordered to report to Major General Leonidas Polk for duty with the "1st Grand Division" of the Army of Mississippi (later the Army of Tennessee). He was sent to command the Rebel defenses at New Madrid, Missouri, and nearby Island No. 10 in the Mississippi River. A week after Mackall assumed command his force was overwhelmed by the Federals. Unable to extricate his troops, Mackall surrendered with some thirty-five hundred of his men on April 7 at Tiptonville, Tennessee.

Mackall spent the next six months as a prisoner of war. Exchanged in October 1862, he was ordered to report to Major General Samuel Jones to command an infantry brigade in East Tennessee. In the following month he was reassigned to Mobile, Alabama, to command the District of the Gulf. Soon, however, he was replaced by Major General Simon B. Buckner. Mackall was then given command of an infantry division in the western part of the District of the Gulf.

In April 1863 Mackall returned to staff duty. He was ordered to the Army of Tennessee and assigned as chief of staff to his West Point classmate General Braxton Bragg, commander of the army. On October 17 Mackall was relieved from that assignment and sent to Mississippi to take charge of a brigade in the forces there under the command of General Joseph E. Johnston. Johnston was transferred to Georgia in December to replace Bragg as commander of the Army of Tennessee, then defending Atlanta and the northern part of Georgia. Mackall soon followed him, and on January 27, 1864, he once again became chief of staff of the Army of Tennessee.

Mackall served as the army's chief of staff throughout the first part of the Atlanta Campaign (May 1—September 2).

An excellent previously unpublished print of the only known uniformed portrait of William Mackall. The collar suggests a colonel's rank, but the buttons are those of a brigadier, and the latter was probably his rank when he posed for this post-1861 image. (Alabama Department of Archives and History, Montgomery, Ala.)

Like his commander Johnston, he was becoming very unhappy with the policies of the Confederate government in general and with its handling of the war in Georgia in particular. As was the case with many of Johnston's close friends, Mackall had believed for a year or so that the Confederate government was not treating Johnston fairly and, indeed, that the government was scheming to disgrace him by bringing about his defeat on the battlefield.

After Johnston was removed from command on July 17, Mackall served briefly under his successor, General John Bell Hood. On July 24 Mackall too was relieved from duty with the army. He went south to Macon, Georgia, where he spent the next nine months in a military limbo. His requests for field duty were ignored by the authorities, and he surrendered to Federal troops at Macon on April 20, 1865.

Mackall spent much of his postwar life on his farms in Fairfax County, Virginia. For the most part he avoided the bitter quarrels that raged among the defeated Confederates. He died on one of his farms on August 12, 1891, and was buried at Lewinsburg Presbyterian Church near McLean, Virginia.

Mackall was a highly competent staff officer whose performance frequently won the praise of almost all of his superiors. Often they asked for his assignment to their commands, and they frequently recommended his promotion to major general. On March 15, 1863, for example, Buckner wrote the government urging Mackall's promotion, praising his ability and pointing out that he was then in command of a division of three brigades—a position that would normally be filled by a major general. In the following month when Buckner was reassigned away from the command at Mobile, the governor of Alabama and a committee of local citizens petitioned unsuccessfully to have Mackall named as his replacement.

Despite his widely acknowledged abilities, Mackall's usefulness to the Confederacy was limited by three factors. For one thing, as a Marylander, Mackall did not have a strong political base in a Southern republic that did not include his native state. He therefore had no powerful political friends in the Confederate Congress to advance his claims to promotion and protect his interests. Mackall was also hampered by the fact that Confederate President Jefferson Davis, who had been U.S. secretary of war in the mid-1850s, harbored a long-time distrust of him. Finally, Mackall's chances for promotion and better assignments were handicapped by his close personal and professional association with a group of generals—especially Pierre G. T. Beauregard and Joseph E. Johnston—who were publicly identified as political enemies of the Davis government. In October 1862 Mackall called himself "a general made by Beauregard"—referring to that officer's role in his promotion to brigadier—and pointed out that Jefferson Davis would not be likely to give a choice assignment to such a general.

Richard M. McMurry

Mackall, William W., *A Son's Recollection of His Father* (New York, 1930).

McMurry, Richard M., "'The Enemy at Richmond': Joseph E. Johnston and the Confederate Government," *Civil War History* (1981).

In September 1863, while on the road to join Bragg's army for the Battle of Chickamauga, Major General Lafayette McLaws had this photo taken in Augusta, Georgia, in September 1862. (Museum of the Confederacy, Richmond, Va.)

⋆ *Lafayette McLaws* ⋆

Lafayette McLaws was born in Augusta, Georgia, on January 15, 1821, of French Huguenot stock. He attended the University of Virginia in 1837, then matriculated the following year at the United States Military Academy. After a successful first year at West Point (twenty-fourth in general merit among eighty-five classmates) McLaws plummeted toward the bottom of his class and stayed there throughout his term at the academy. He graduated in 1842 standing forty-eighth out of fifty-six graduates. The handful of graduating cadets who performed more poorly than McLaws included Earl Van Dorn (fifty-second) and James Longstreet (fifty-fourth). The three young men also stood far down the rankings in conduct.

After commission into the 6th United States Infantry in 1842 as a brevet 2d lieutenant McLaws faced the same sluggish promotion system that bedeviled so many of his fellow officers in the Old Army. He received promotion to 2d lieutenant, sans brevet, on July 1, 1842; to 1st lieutenant on February 16, 1847; and to captain on August 24, 1851. McLaws languished in the decade-old rank of captain when the Civil War began. Before the Mexican War McLaws was posted at Fort Gibson, Indian Territory; Pass Christian, Mississippi; Baton Rouge; and Fort Pickens, Florida. Lieutenant McLaws went off to the Mexican War with his uncle, Zachary Taylor, then transferred to Winfield Scott's army and was present at Vera Cruz. He came home sick from Mexico City and took up a recruiting post. In 1849 McLaws married Emily Allison Taylor, a daughter of his general's brother, and thus became a first cousin by marriage of Richard Taylor.

After Mexico the now-veteran McLaws followed his orders around the frontier to Jefferson Barracks, Missouri; Santa Fe; Fort Gibson again; Fort Smith, Arkansas; Utah; and New Mexico. When his native state seceded in 1861, Captain McLaws was on an expedition against the Navajos. He returned to Georgia to a family he had not seen for three years and to a commission as a Confederate major of infantry, dated from March 16, 1861. During April and May the major performed quartermaster duties around Savannah and served as a departmental adjutant. With a commission as colonel to rank from June 17, 1861, McLaws assumed command of the newly formed 10th Georgia Infantry, which he organized and trained and led to Virginia.

Lafayette McLaws obviously attracted strong positive attention from his superiors, because he was promoted to brigadier general on September 25, 1861, and to major general on May 23, 1862. Because of that very early promotion date McLaws outranked as major general such familiar names as A. P. Hill, Hood, Pickett, Early, Stuart, Trimble, and R. H. Anderson. Only Ewell and D. H. Hill among the familiar division commanders in the Army of Northern Virginia outranked McLaws, and both of those officers were away from the army for extended periods.

The division that General McLaws led for more than two years consisted of two Georgia brigades and one each from South Carolina and Mississippi. None of the brigadiers who commanded McLaws' brigades for extended periods—Semmes, Wofford, Kershaw, and Barksdale—had training or experience as a professional soldier. The norm in the army was a mix of about one-half professionals among the brigades of most divisions. No other division operated for any extended period with all-amateur leadership at the brigade level. Despite that considerable disadvantage McLaws put together a solid record as a division commander.

After fighting under the wildly unpredictable Major General John B. Magruder on the Peninsula early in 1862 McLaws took over much of Magruder's command after the Seven Days'. During the Maryland Campaign September 4–22, 1862, the division forged one of the key preliminary successes on Maryland Heights above Harpers Ferry. At Sharpsburg on September 17 elements of McLaws' command made up the largest part of a Confederate force that stumbled onto the greatest Southern tactical triumph on the field when it routed Major General John Sedgwick and Major General Edwin V. Sumner in the West Woods. McLaws faced two personal controversies in the aftermath of the campaign. He resolved a quarrel with his failed subordinate Brigadier General Howell S. Cobb, who was leaving the army. A disagreement with Brigadier General John B. Hood apparently smoothed out, but McLaws, handwritten note on the envelope holding a conciliatory missive reads: "Relative to the lies of J. B. Hood."

The assignment to defend the riverbank at Fredericksburg in December 1862 suited McLaws perfectly. E. P. Alexander said of McLaws, "Few of our generals equalled him in...the pains he took in many matters of little detail." Of his Fredericksburg role Alexander wrote: "McLaws was about the best general in the army for that sort of job, being very painstaking...& having a good eye for ground. He had fixed up his sharpshooters all along the river to the Queen's taste." Moxley Sorrel of Longstreet's staff commented in the same vein that while McLaws was "not brilliant...or quick...he could always be counted on and had secured the entire confidence of his officers and men."

The following spring McLaws commanded a detachment sent from Chancellorsville on May 3, 1863, to meet a crisis at Salem Church. His performance there irritated General R. E. Lee, who grumbled the next day that "a great deal of valuable time had already been uselessly lost" and that "no body knew exactly how or where the enemy's line of battle ran." No doubt the episode contributed to Lee's decision not to give McLaws a corps command when the army was reorganized that month in the wake of the death of Major General "Stonewall" Jackson.

Lieutenant General James Longstreet, who was McLaws' fond patron and immediate superior, insisted that the promotion system was rigged against McLaws because he was not from Virginia. A few weeks later patron and protege had a massive falling-out over Longstreet's demeanor at Gettysburg in July. In a letter written to his wife immediately after the battle McLaws declared that his sponsor was "a humbug, a man of small capacity, very obstinate, not at all chivalrous, exceedingly conceited, and totally selfish." The impact of McLaws' disgust with his corps commander on his own military career was of course dramatic and negative.

When Longstreet saw his campaign in East Tennessee come to a pathetic end at Knoxville in November 1863, he lashed out at McLaws and two other generals with court-martial charges. Longstreet filed six specific complaints against McLaws in connection with the grotesquely mismanaged attack on Fort Sanders. Five of the six charges were simply and unequivocally untrue, as attested by the unanimous testimony of more than fifty witnesses before the court. Longstreet understood little of what had happened and embarrassed himself in public as a result. The sixth charge against McLaws was equally mistaken, although not absolutely untrue. In the aftermath of the court-martial the War Department censured Longstreet for his conduct of the proceedings. One of his fellow sufferers at Longstreet's hands, Brigadier General Evander M. Law, wrote to McLaws at this difficult time that he had caught Longstreet in a new "infamous lie" and suggested that the lieutenant general "is most certainly on the wane both in and out of the army.... I believe we can oust him."

In fact, Longstreet was much more important to Lee and his army than were McLaws and the other victims of their corps commander's rage. In consequence, McLaws was transferred to the defense of Savannah, where he had begun his Confederate career four years before. There he endeavored to meet the hopeless responsibility of coping with a Federal flood tide surging toward the coast and then moving into South Carolina. A famous Confederate artillerist had described McLaws as "slow...but sure," and another gunner called him "one of the most dogged defensive fighters in the army." None of those characteristics could supply the missing means of defense, and Lafayette McLaws found nothing but defeat during the war's closing months.

McLaws returned home to an impoverished existence that approached genuine want. His antebellum friend U. S. Grant appointed McLaws to two sinecures under Federal patronage to bail him out. Even so, in 1886 McLaws wrote disconsolately: "I do not know what to commence on, unless it is Pea Nut vending, as I am without means, having lost all...." The former Confederate spent the later years of his life writing and speaking copiously on war topics, but little of that production reached print. The enormous volume of surviving manuscripts by McLaws represents perhaps the most extensive unused body of material on any Confederate major general, but his execrable handwriting renders that splendid mass of documentation difficult to retrieve.

General McLaws died in Savannah on July 24, 1897, and was buried there in Laurel Grove Cemetery.

Robert K. Krick

At the same sitting McLaws posed for this previously unpublished portrait. (Museum of the Confederacy, Richmond, Va.)

McLaws Papers, University of South Carolina, Chapel Hill.
McLaws Papers, Duke University, Durham, North Carolina.

✷ *Evander McNair* ✷

Evander McNair as colonel of the 4th Arkansas. The only known uniformed portrait to survive from the war. (*Confederate Veteran*)

Evander McNair was born in Richmond County, North Carolina, on April 15, 1820, near Laurel Hill. In 1821 his family moved to Mississippi, settling ultimately in Simpson County. In 1842 McNair became a merchant in Jackson and during the Mexican War served as 1st sergeant in Company E as part of Jefferson Davis' 1st Mississippi Rifles. In the mid-1850s he moved to Washington, Arkansas, and when the Civil War began, raised an infantry battalion of seven companies. This command eventually grew to regimental strength and took the designation 4th Arkansas Infantry with McNair as its colonel.

He was with Brigadier General Ben McCulloch in the battles at Wilson's Creek, August 10, 1861, and Pea Ridge, or Elkhorn Tavern, March 7–8, 1862. In the latter engagement his regiment was on the extreme right of Colonel Louis Hébert's brigade, and McNair reported that following the death of McCulloch and Brigadier General James McIntosh and after Hébert was captured, there was no other field officer present. He assumed command of the brigade, which at that time did not number more than one thousand, and ordered it to fall back on the reserves. In late March the brigade was composed of the 1st and 2d Arkansas Mounted (both dismounted), the 4th and 30th Arkansas Infantry, the 4th Arkansas Battalion, and J. T. Humphreys' Artillery.

He took the brigade across the Mississippi River, and was with Major General Edmund Kirby Smith in the Kentucky Campaign. After the Battle of Richmond on August 30, 1862, Brigadier General Thomas J. Churchill, who commanded the 3d Division, Army of Kentucky, reported: "I cannot speak too highly of the gallantry and coolness displayed by Colonels McNair and McCray throughout the entire day, and I have to thank them for the promptness and skill with which they executed all orders."

At the reorganization of the troops in the Department of East Tennessee under Kirby Smith about October 31, 1862, McNair commanded the 3d Brigade in the 2d Division of Major General J. P. McCown. He was promoted to brigadier general November 4, 1862. His brigade took part in the Battle of Stone's River, where McCown reported that McNair "exhibited cool and dauntless courage, as well as skill," in his handling of the command. On December 31 the commander of the 30th Arkansas recalled that the men had assaulted a battery but had halted to resupply their ammunition. When engaged in this, "General McNair was forced to retire from the field, to the deep regret of all." There is no report of McNair being wounded, but since almost all of the casualties in the brigade occurred on December 31 (42 killed, 330 wounded, and 52 missing), it is safe to assume he was probably among those not seriously wounded.

In January 1863 McNair was reported as part of Smith's Corps serving with Lieutenant General William J. Hardee at Shelbyville, Tennessee; on May 20–21 McNair's brigade joined General Joseph E. Johnston in Mississippi to aid in the defense of Vicksburg. In June Major General Samuel G. French was assigned to duty in Johnston's Department of the West, and he took command of a division composed of the brigades of McNair, Samuel B. Maxey, and "Shanks" Evans. Under Johnston at Jackson, McNair commanded a brigade composed of the 1st and 2d Mounted Riflemen (both dismounted), 4th Arkansas Infantry, 25th and 31st Arkansas (consolidated), and the 39th North Carolina. As the campaign took shape, McNair's Arkansas troops were consolidated into tighter commands. He was engaged on the retreat from Big Black, and on July 15 his line of skirmishers was sharply engaged but lost no ground.

After the surrender of Vicksburg McNair remained in Mississippi until September 1863 when he was ordered to Atlanta. McNair participated in the Battle of Chickamauga as part of Bushrod Johnson's corps and was wounded seriously around 9:30 A.M. on September 20. General Braxton Bragg later wrote that he "fell severely wounded while gallantly leading" his command in the "thickest of the fight." It was "gratifying to know that he was convalescing and will again

be found at the post of duty and danger." McNair returned to Mississippi, where Joseph E. Johnston noted in October that McNair's brigade, "reduced in the battle near Chattanooga," was only "a skeleton."

In January 1864 his brigade returned to Atlanta with Lieutenant General Leonidas Polk's Army of Mississippi. After the fall of Atlanta McNair was transferred to the Trans-Mississippi Department. He took over the Arkansas Infantry Brigade of Thomas P. Dockery, and Dockery was assigned to the Reserve Corps. On September 23, 1864, McNair was reported to have arrived at Brigadier General Thomas J. Churchill's division to assume command. He remained in Arkansas until the end of the war.

After the war he moved to New Orleans, then to Magnolia, Mississippi, and finally to Hattiesburg, where he died on November 13, 1902. He was buried at Magnolia at the home of his son-in-law.

Anne Bailey

Harrell, John M., *Arkansas*, Vol. X in Evans, *Confederate Military History*.

✭ *Dandridge McRae* ✭

No uniformed portrait of Dandridge McRae has been found. This dates from the late 1870s. (Miller, *Photographic History*)

Dandridge McRae was born on October 10, 1829, in Baldwin County, Alabama. At age twenty he graduated from South Carolina College and soon after moved to Arkansas where he began his practice as a lawyer. He acted as clerk of White County and the circuit courts for six years.

When the Civil War began, he served on Governor H. M. Rector's staff. On May 22, 1861, the governor appointed him special mustering officer to receive soldiers into the service of the state. On May 27 McRae was sent to Searcy to recruit; he had permission to receive men into the service and to subsist them at the expense of the state until they were mustered into the Confederate army.

In late June Brigadier General Ben McCulloch issued a proclamation calling the people of western Arkansas to arms, telling them that their state was threatened. The effect of the proclamation caused several hundred to gather at Fayetteville, and McCulloch ordered McRae to take command and make a demonstration on Springfield, Missouri. "The maneuver was well executed," reported McCulloch, "and had the effect of causing General [T. W.] Sweeny, then in camp at Springfield, to recall that portion of his force on its march to join Colonel [Franz] Sigel."

McRae participated August 10 in the Battle of Wilson's Creek as a lieutenant colonel in command of Arkansas Volunteers. During the battle it was said he led his men with the "greatest coolness and bravery," always in the front cheering the troops forward. At Pea Ridge (March 7–8, 1862) Major General Earl Van Dorn noted that the regiment under McRae should be "especially mentioned for their good conduct." He was promoted to brigadier general on November 5, 1862. He led a brigade in December at Prairie Grove, where Brigadier General Thomas C. Hindman observed that he "did noble duty."

He fought in the battle of Helena on July 4, 1863, in an attempt by Arkansas Confederates to offer some assistance to Vicksburg. McRae's brigade during the battle was composed of the 32d, 36th, and 39th Arkansas, as well as Marshall's Battery, a total of 1,227 men. Unfortunately, his actions angered Lieutenant General Theophilus H. Holmes, the district commander who led the Confederate attack. Holmes reported that he had ordered McRae to do one thing, but Major General Sterling Price had instructed him to do another. "After much delay," Holmes complained, McRae had followed Price's instructions, "but utterly failed to render the slightest aid" in his endeavor. Furthermore, McRae "was nowhere to be seen, while General [James] Fagan, with greatly reduced force, was being assaulted and driven back by the enemy, largely re-enforced."

Because of McRae's actions, Holmes insisted that he had been forced to withdraw. Price, however, came to the defense of McRae and wrote: "I must also commend the excellent discipline which General McRae maintains at all times in his brigade; the marked good sense and energy with which he conducted its march to Helena; the promptitude with which he has always obeyed my commands, and the earnest efforts which he made to reenforce General Fagan toward the close of the attack." In spite of Price's supportive remarks, McRae complained to Price on July 14: "I regret this, as General Holmes has, by his hasty remarks, done both my brigade and myself gross injustice, which requires at my hands a publication based upon my report, as, under the circumstances, that course is unavoidable." He asked for a court of inquiry into the matter, but before any action could be taken participated in the fight for Little Rock in September.

In October Holmes apparently was still miffed over the Helena incident, and on the 7th told Price that he had assigned McRae to him. "It was my impression that a copy of the order was made out," wrote Holmes, "relieving General McRae from duty with his command, and sent you." In March 1864 he was the commander in charge of Confederate forces in northeastern Arkansas and in early April was skirmishing in that area. It is reported that McRae fought with Price during the Red River Campaign, participating at Marks' Mills and Jenkins' Ferry.

A court of inquiry finally convened at Camden, Arkansas, on June 7, 1864, to examine the charges against McRae "of misbehavior before the enemy at the attack upon Helena," but the finding was that McRae's actions were "obnoxious to no charge of misbehavior before the enemy." McRae, however, resigned in 1864 and returned home to Searcy, where he resumed the practice of law.

In 1881 he became the deputy secretary of the state of Arkansas, served on the state chamber of commerce, and in various other public positions. He died at Searcy on April 23, 1899, and was buried there.

Anne Bailey

Harrel, John M., *Arkansas*, Vol. X in Evans, *Confederate Military History*.

✷ William MacRae ✷

Born at Wilmington, North Carolina, September 9, 1834, William MacRae was a civil engineer, prewar. In April 1861 he enlisted as a private in the Monroe Light Infantry Company and was elected captain May 1. That outfit became Company B, 5th North Carolina Volunteer Infantry Regiment on June 11, redesignated the 15th on November 14.

The 15th North Carolina reached Yorktown June 29, 1861, and remained there until transferred to Suffolk and Goldsboro in March 1862 following Confederate defeats in North Carolina. Greater danger, however, threatened Yorktown, so by April 15 the regiment was back on the Peninsula. It fought heavily April 16 at Lee's Mill, where its colonel was killed.

Throughout this period MacRae served so creditably that the 15th, when reorganizing for the war May 2, made him lieutenant colonel. His outfit saw no combat until Malvern Hill and was disastrously repulsed there; its new colonel was wounded out. MacRae, whose "calm courage" on July 1 won Major General John Magruder's praise, thenceforth led the regiment.

Later in 1862 MacRae fought at Crampton's Gap, Antietam, and Fredericksburg. For most of September 17 at Antietam he commanded Howell Cobb's brigade, containing the 16th and 24th Georgia infantry regiments, Cobb's Legion Georgia Infantry Battalion, and the 15th. MacRae's regiment transferred on November 26 to John R. Cooke's brigade, where it remained until Appomattox. The 15th thus helped repulse repeated Yankee assaults December 13 at Fredericksburg. It spent most of 1863, however, in the relative backwaters of South and North Carolina and Richmond,

fighting minor affrays at Gum Swamp and South Anna Bridge. MacRae had become its colonel February 27, 1863.

The brigade rejoined R. E. Lee's army in October—and promptly suffered disaster at Bristoe Station October 14. Cooke was severely wounded there. Following senior colonel Edward D. Hall's resignation December 31, MacRae temporarily commanded the brigade containing the 15th, 27th, 46th, and 48th North Carolina infantry regiments until Cooke returned in mid-April.

Still a colonel, MacRae battled May to June 1864, at the Wilderness, Spotsylvania, North Anna, Pole Green Church, Second Cold Harbor, and White Oak Swamp. His hard fighting and strict discipline attracted his superiors' attention. When command of another brigade in that division fell vacant with the wounding of Brigadier General William W. Kirkland near Gaines' Mill June 2, they transferred MacRae to lead it. He was appointed to the temporary rank of brigadier general June 23, ranking from June 22. Assigned to duty June 27, he assumed command on June 29 of Kirkland's brigade, containing the 11th, 26th, 44th, 47th, and 52d North Carolina infantry regiments.

As early as Bristoe Station MacRae had admired those soldiers, "for he loved brave men," recalled the 44th's major. Successful battle leaders know that "love" means "discipline." "Two brigades…, Cooke's and MacRae's…," reported the army's inspector general in September 1864, "are in specially good order and

William MacRae seems not to have left behind a uniformed portrait. This one is considerably postwar in vintage. (Miller, *Photographic History*)

136

commanded by two most excellent officers, who are strict disciplinarians, but who have great influence over their men in camp and on the field." MacRae, indeed, "was...a strict disciplinarian...," remembered the 11th's colonel, "and he rapidly brought the brigade to a high degree of efficiency." The brigade assistant adjutant general agreed: "Officers and men felt that laxity of discipline was at an end, and to the consequent grumbling in camp by a few, succeeded an absolute faith in the commander. His exact discipline prepared them for the trying ordeal through which they were to pass from now to the end." "General MacRae...," concurred an officer of the 26th, "changed the physical expression of the whole command in less than two weeks, and gave the men infinite faith in him and themselves, which was never lost, not even when they grounded arms at Appomattox."

His first fight as a brigadier, ironically, was a defeat: Globe Tavern, August 21. His next two onslaughts, Reams' Station August 25 and Poplar Spring Church September 30–October 2, proved splendidly successful. Although he was eventually driven out, his deep penetration at Hatcher's Run October 27 enhanced his fighting reputation. The decisive contribution of Brigadier General James Conner, Cooke, and especially MacRae on August 25 had earned Lee's personal commendation.

MacRae's overall service, August–October, won his promotion on November 5 to permanent brigadier general in the provisional army, ranking from November 4. He accepted November 15 and was confirmed January 17, 1865. Of the thirty-five temporary brigadier generals appointed under the act of May 31, 1864, only MacRae and David Weisiger were converted to that permanent rank in the provisional army.

MacRae continued serving at Hicksford, Hatcher's Run, Watkins' Farm, White Oak Road, Sutherland's Station, and Cumberland Church. Only 442 officers and men of his hard-fighting brigade remained to surrender with him at Appomattox.

Postwar MacRae was a railroad superintendent in North Carolina and Georgia. He died February 11, 1882, and was buried in Wilmington.

"No brigades in any army," recalled division commander Henry Heth, "surpassed in gallantry those of John R. Cooke and William MacRae....The record made by Cooke's and MacRae's brigades is one of unbroken glory...." The 47th's member-historian regarded MacRae as "the equal of any brigadier in the army." The 44th's commander perceived that "Nature had endowed [MacRae] with a type of personal courage which made him absolutely indifferent to danger;"his courage had with it a certain quality rarely possessed by any to the same extent. He made all around him brave. It mattered not how appalling the fire..., his presence always steadied the men, who seemed to imbibe his spirit." And an officer of the 26th summarized that "General MacRae soon won the confidence and admiration of the brigade, both officers and men. His voice was like that of a woman; he was small in person, and quick in action....He could place his command in position quicker and infuse more of his fighting qualities into his men, than any officer I ever saw. His presence with his troops seemed to dispel all fear, and to inspire every one with a desire for the fray."

MacRae, indeed, ranks as one of the great battle brigadiers of the Army of Northern Virginia. Preserving Petersburg for forty-two weeks demanded generalship at many levels; the strategic masterfulness and moral courage of Lee and the grand-tactical skill of corps and division commanders, certainly, but also the hard-fighting leadership of brigadiers. No brigadier surpassed MacRae in defeating repeated Union drives against Petersburg.

Richard J. Sommers

Clark, Walter, *Histories of the Several Regiments and Battalions from North Carolina in the Great War, 1861-'65* (Goldsboro, N.C., 1901).

Heth, Henry, *The Memoirs of Henry Heth*, edited by James L. Morrison (Westport, Conn., 1974).

Hill, Daniel Harvey, Jr., *North Carolina*, Vol. IV in Evans, *Confederate Military History*.

Jordan, Weymouth T., and Manarin, Louis H., *North Carolina Troops, 1861-1865: A Roster* (Raleigh, 1975).

Stedman, Charles M., *Memorial Address:...A Sketch of the Life and Character of General William MacRae, with an Account of the Battle of Reams' Station* (Wilmington, N.C., 1890).

"Prince John" Magruder seems not to have been photographed in a regulation Confederate uniform, but he posed gladly in this adaptation of his own design. (Museum of the Confederacy, Richmond, Va.)

⭐ *John Bankhead Magruder* ⭐

John B. Magruder was born at Port Royal, Virginia, on May 1, 1807, of Scots ancestry. He attended the United States Military Academy in the class of 1830 and achieved a solid scholastic record there. After placing tenth out of sixty-three cadets during his first year, young Magruder dropped several positions during his second and third years and finished fifteenth among forty-two graduates in 1830. Only William Nelson Pendleton and Magruder became familiar Confederate names out of that rather undistinguished class. Magruder fared less well in the rankings of cadets by conduct, standing 188th out of 215 cadets at West Point in 1830. He also fared poorly in impressing young women at this stage of his life, according to a Fredericksburg matron who wrote that Magruder "was the butt of all the girls, he was so stupid and conceited."

Second Lieutenant Magruder entered the United States Army with the 7th Infantry, but he only served with that arm for a little more than one year. When he transferred at the same rank to the 1st United States Artillery on August 11, 1831, John Magruder began an association with the regiment that brought him opportunities and attention in the Mexican War. He won promotion to 1st lieutenant on March 31, 1836, and to captain on June 18, 1846. The latter promotion came after Magruder had fought with distinction at the Mexican War battle of Palo Alto. He also earned brevet rank of major, to date from April 18, 1847, for gallant and meritorious conduct at Cerro Gordo. A few months later Magruder added to his admirable record with a battlefield performance at Chapultepec that resulted in another brevet, to lieutenant colonel. Magruder's command in Mexico included a subordinate who won as much attention and promotion as his chief—Lieutenant Thomas J. Jackson, who was still more than a dozen years short of earning his immortal *nom de guerre*, "Stonewall."

Before his stellar performance in the Mexican War, Magruder's postings had included some time in Texas and a stint fighting the Seminoles in Florida. After Mexico he served in Maryland and California and at Fort Leavenworth and commanded a post at Newport, Rhode Island. He resigned from the U.S. Army effective April 20, 1861, immediately after his native state seceded. The newly resigned brevet lieutenant colonel promptly received a commission as colonel of infantry. As was typical of hundreds of such initial commissions, Magruder's ranked from March 16, 1861, although it was dated May 21. In less than five months Magruder received two promotions and reached his highest Confederate rank. He became a brigadier general appointed on June 17, effective the same day. On October 7, 1861, he was appointed major general, also effective October 7.

General Magruder assumed command of the Confederate forces stationed on Virginia's Peninsula in May 1861 and began a year-long defense of that crucial ground. Troops under Magruder's command won a skirmish at Big Bethel on June 10 that despite its very modest proportions won wide attention as the first "battle" of the war in Virginia. During his antebellum assignment in Newport Magruder had become fond of high society affairs, and he carried such trappings into his Confederate headquarters. The general's "lordly air and brilliant ability to bring appearances up to the necessities of the occasion" earned him the nickname "Prince John" Magruder. A South Carolinian described Magruder's attire as fitting the legend—no uniform, but rather a "black felt hat and black overcoat with cape." The general also spoke in a peculiar style that added to his mystique. "He does not speak very plainly," wrote an otherwise complimentary soldier, and a Richmond woman noted that Magruder "lisps and swears at the same time," with comical results.

"Prince John" needed all of the style and flair that he could muster during the spring of 1862, when McClellan's Federal army descended on the Peninsula. Magruder won a high reputation for himself during this period for the clever subterfuges he energetically employed to screen his weakness from

A variant from the same sitting. (Louisiana State University, Baton Rouge, La.)

his foe. Some of his zealous measures seem wildly visionary with hindsight, such as when he requisitioned 242 bolts of cotton and black cambric in October 1861 (well past the early war gimmickry phase) to make "badges" to distinguish his men from the enemy. During the dreadful confusion incumbent on the congressionally imposed elections early in 1862 Magruder had mixed success in holding his units together. A Louisianan under him wrote home in March, "I have lost all confidence & it is no doubt the case with all the troops"; those being assigned elsewhere "seem glad to get from under Magruder." Brigadier General Lafayette McLaws, Magruder's ranking subordinate, was intensely disgusted with his superior by late spring. Another soldier, however, called Magruder "a splendid officer and brave commander," and a chaplain who had heard much grumbling about the general was surprised to find him "a very unpretentious and likeable gentleman."

Magruder's performance during the Seven Days' Campaign remains the most widely discussed and best remembered of his Confederate roles. Throughout the week-long defense of Richmond and especially at Malvern Hill July 1, the general behaved so excitedly and irrationally that accusations of drunkenness circulated freely. Magruder was "a very brilliant man, but unfortunately addicted to intemperance" (Colonel Eppa Hunton); "depressed, and I fear was drinking" (Colonel T. R. R. Cobb); "drunk during the action, was common talk among troops" (J. W. Lokey, 20th Georgia). Captain Greenlee Davidson of Virginia, who was "posted near" Magruder at Malvern Hill, described to Major General A. P. Hill how Magruder "seemed to be laboring under the most terrible excitement. The wild expression in his eyes and his excited manner impressed me at once with the belief that he was under the influence of some powerful stimulant...He was certainly the most excited General officer I have ever met upon a battlefield and in my opinion was totally incapacitated for the high command he held." Magruder's defenders denied the allegations and cited a combination of nervous tension, lack of rest, and medication.

Soon after the Seven Days' ended, Magruder was assigned to the Trans-Mississippi, but he returned to Richmond on orders to face the rumors in circulation. Magruder levied charges against Lieutenant Colonel R. H. Chilton of General R. E. Lee's staff in connection with the controversy. In October 1862 Magruder was assigned to Texas. His efforts in that area included typically energetic measures to defend the state's lightly guarded coast. Innovative cottonclad steamers augmented Magruder's force. On the first day of 1863 he captured Galveston in a famous raid that counted among its spoils a Federal vessel in the harbor.

Early in 1864 Magruder dispatched a sizable portion of his strength to help Lieutenant General Richard Taylor resist the Federal onset in Louisiana. He remained himself with his Texas command to the end of the war, then emigrated to Mexico and served in the army of Maximilian. When Maximilian's regime fell, Magruder returned to the United States. He scratched out a meager existence by lecturing for a time, then took up residence in Houston, Texas, where he died on February 18, 1871. Magruder was buried in Galveston.

Robert K. Krick

Hotchkiss, Jedediah, *Virginia*, Vol. III in Evans, *Confederate Military History*.

Long, Armistead L., "Memoir of General John Bankhead Magruder," *Southern Historical Society Papers*, Vol. XII.

Another, damaged pose, from the same sitting. (Library of Congress)

William Mahone's almost painful thinness is evident in this late-war portrait, made probably in the winter of 1864-65. (William A. Turner Collection)

⭐ *William Mahone* ⭐

The future general, railroader, and U.S. senator was born on December 1, 1826, in Southampton County, Virginia. His parents were Fielding Jordan and Martha Drew Mahone. In this Southside county of large plantations destined to be the locale of Nat Turner's Rebellion a few years later, the senior Mahone kept an ordinary. As a boy, "Billie," carried the mail from Jerusalem (Courtland) to Hills Ford (Emporia). He matriculated at Virginia Military Institute, from which he graduated in 1847. While teaching at Rappahannock Military Academy, Mahone continued to study engineering. He was hired as an engineer by the Orange & Alexandria Railroad, then under construction, and in 1851 went to work for the Norfolk & Petersburg Railroad. By the winter of 1860–61 he held three key positions with the latter railroad—president, chief engineer, and superintendent. He had married in 1855, and when Virginia left the Union, he, his wife, and their three children were living in Petersburg.

Although he was apolitical, Mahone, upon learning of Virginia's secession, secured appointment as quartermaster general of state forces. On April 20, 1861, he was elected and commissioned lieutenant colonel of the 4th Virginia Artillery Regiment and on May 2 colonel of the 6th Virginia Infantry Regiment. He was initially assigned to the Department of Norfolk. In the autumn and winter of the war's first year he reported to Major General Benjamin Huger and was commander of a four-thousand-man brigade. As such, he was promoted brigadier general on November 16, to rank from November 16. Upon the Confederate evacuation of the Norfolk area and the city's May 10, 1862, surrender to Union forces, Mahone on the 15th assumed responsibility for the defense of Drewry's Bluff. Earlier in the day the Confederate batteries there had repulsed a Union naval squadron that had ascended the James River.

Mahone and his brigade in late May were assigned to the division commanded by General Huger and participated in the Battle of Seven Pines, where on June 1 they saw savage combat against a II Corps division. During the Seven Days' Mahone, an eccentric hypochondriac whose headquarters baggage included his milk cow, clashed with the foe at King's School House on June 25; failed General Robert E. Lee on June 30 at Glendale when his men engaged in a wood-chopping contest against the Federals rather than pushing boldly ahead; and at Malvern Hill on July 1, with his Virginians, was among those who closed to within seventy-five yards of the Union lines northwest of the Crew House.

In the mid-July reorganization of the Army of Northern Virginia, Mahone's brigade was assigned to Richard H. Anderson's division of James Longstreet's corps. At Second Manassas while gallantly leading his four Virginia regiments in Longstreet's August 30 onslaught, Mahone was wounded. His injuries were so severe that he did not return to duty until mid-October. Because of the fortunes of war Mahone and his brigade—the 6th, 12th, 16th, 41st, and 61st Virginia—although present at three great battles that took place between December 1862 and July 1863 and in the Bristoe Station and Mine Run campaigns of the autumn of 1863, were spared many of the horrors of war. At Fredericksburg December 11–16, although under arms, they were posted in a sector of rifle-pits that was not attacked. At Chancellorsville Mahone skirmished with the Union vanguard on the last day of April 1863 and on May 1 spearheaded the Orange Turnpike counterattack that led Joseph Hooker to lose his nerve and yield the initiative to General Lee. At Salem Church on May 3 Mahone battled John Sedgwick. Mahone's leadership during the Chancellorsville battle earned a commendation from General Anderson, who called attention to his "bold, skillful, and successful management" of his brigade.

In the mid-May reorganization of the army Anderson's division was assigned to Lieutenant General A. P. Hill's newly constituted III Corps. At Gettysburg Mahone's men were in reserve, saw no action except as skirmishers, and consequently

The absence of insignia on the collar and the pin on the blouse suggests that this portrait was taken at a different sitting, though whether earlier or later cannot be determined. (Library of Congress)

suffered the least casualties of any of Lee's infantry brigades.

During the last eleven months of the war Mahone's star ascended, and he became arguably Lee's best general, both as a division commander and as a leader of detached forces of corps strength. Mahone's rise began on May 6, 1864, at the Wilderness, when he led brigades—his own, William T. Wofford's, Joseph R. Davis', and "Tige" Anderson's—in one of the war's most devastating counterattacks, which surprised and rolled up Winfield S. Hancock's left flank in the woods south of the Orange Plank Road and hurled back the dismayed and disorganized Federals. Only the accidental wounding of Longstreet by some of Mahone's Virginians prevented an overwhelming Confederate victory. As a result of the reorganization mandated by the wounding of Longstreet and the loss of other senior officers in the Wilderness that saw Richard Anderson placed in temporary command of Longstreet's corps, Mahone assumed command of Anderson's III Corps division.

At Spotsylvania on May 10 Mahone performed with credit in the fight south of the Po River, in which one of Winfield Hancock's divisions was mauled, and on the North Anna on May 23 he gained some success in the attack on the Union V Corps that had crossed the river at Jericho Mills. At Cold Harbor on June 3 one of his five brigades was instrumental in closing the breach that Hancock's human wave attack had made in the Rebel line south of Boatswain Creek.

Mahone and his division crossed the Appomattox River on June 18 and for the next nine months played a key role in the defense of his home town, the capture of which became a focal point of the war in Virginia. On June 23 Mahone and Major General Bushrod Johnson savaged the proud II Corps in the battle of the Jerusalem Plank Road, capturing hundreds of prisoners, four cannon, and several stands of colors. Five weeks later on July 30 the Federals exploded eight thousand pounds of powder under Elliott's Salient and attacked with three IX Corps divisions. Mahone, in the ensuing struggle for the "Crater," first contained the Yankees and then routed them with terrible slaughter. Commenting on Mahone's role in the fight, W. H. Stuart of the 61st Virginia wrote, "The whole movement was under his immediate and personal direction, and to him, above all, save the brave men who bore the muskets, belongs the honor and credit of recapturing the Confederate lines." His leadership was recognized by his promotion to major general on August 3, 1864, to rank from the Battle of the Crater.

In August Mahone and his troops battled the foe north of the James at Fussell's Mill and south of Petersburg in the Battle of the Weldon Railroad and at Reams' Station. In the latter fight the Confederates routed two II Corps divisions, capturing nine cannon, twelve stands of colors, and 2,150 soldiers.

Some two months later on October 28 at the battle of the Boydton Plank Road, Mahone and his division crossed Hatcher's Run and at first swept all before them, capturing six cannons and four hundred prisoners. The tide turned as General Hancock called in reinforcements and Mahone was beaten back, with the loss of several hundred prisoners. Mahone's next battle—the last before the April 1 and 2 disasters that compelled the Confederates to evacuate Petersburg and Richmond—was Hatcher's Run February 7, 1865. His was the only one of Hill's three divisions to retain its organization on the night of April 2, and with A. P. Hill dead, Mahone was assigned to James Longstreet's corps.

April 7, the day after Sayler's Creek, started badly for Mahone when Union soldiers seized High Bridge. Later in the day at Cumberland Church Mahone more than held his own when attacked by the II Corps, his frequent antagonists. Mahone and his division were still with General Lee at the April 9 Appomattox Court House surrender.

Mahone returned to railroading. Between 1867 and 1870 he took advantage of legislation enacted by the Virginia General Assembly to gain control of three railroads connecting Norfolk and Bristol and organized them into the Atlantic, Mississippi & Western, with steamboat connections at Norfolk and a franchise to extend his trunk line to the Ohio River. In 1869 he supported Republican Gilbert C. Walker in the latter's successful campaign for governor. Employing his railroad lobby, he gained control of the *Richmond Whig* editorial page and used this to secure the election of a group of legislators loyal to his interests. Such power politics aroused hostility, and Mahone was called "Railroad Ishmael" and "King of the Lobby."

Governors Walker and James Kemper in succession dumped him; twice he backed off when challenged to duels; in the 1873 panic he lost his railroad to a hostile receivership; and in 1877 his efforts to secure the nomination for governor at the Conservative convention failed. Undaunted, in 1879 he organized and became

Mahone from his late-war sitting. The device on the breast pin is a five-pointed star, whose significance is obscure. (William A. Turner Collection)

Another image from the same sitting. Mahone wears the star pin on his hat now. (U.S. Army Military History Institute, Carlisle, Pa.)

leader of the "Readjusters," who championed a partial repudiation of the state's huge debt and populist legislation. The Readjusters triumphed at the polls in 1879 and 1881, and in 1880 Mahone was elected to the U.S. Senate.

There he used his vote and committee assignments to win the plaudits of northern and western Republicans, attracting the wrath of the Southern Bourbons. In 1882 Mahone's "Coalitionists" sent a second senator and several representatives to the U.S. Congress. These successes made Mahone undisputed boss of the state's Republican party. His political power had crested, however, and he won no more elections. He had shown how to drive a wedge into the "Solid South" but not how to maintain the split. Mahone died in Washington, D.C., October 8, 1895, and was buried in Petersburg's Blandsford Cemetery. His gravesite is identified by a handsome memorial erected by the United Daughters of the Confederacy.

Edwin C. Bearss

Blake, Nelson M., *William Mahone of Virginia, Soldier and Political Insurgent* (Richmond, 1925).

DePeyster, J. W., "A Military Memoir of William Mahone, Major-General in the Confederate Army," *Historical Magazine* Vol. X (Morrisania, N.Y., 1871).

Hotchkiss, Jedediah, *Virginia*, Vol. IV in Evans, *Confederate Military History*.

A final pose from the same session. (Chicago Historical Society)

✷ James Patrick Major ✷

James Patrick Major was born on May 14, 1836, in Fayette, Missouri. He attended West Point, graduating in 1856 twenty-third out of forty-nine. His first assignment in the Regular Army was at Carlisle Barracks, Pennsylvania, but he joined the 2d U.S. Cavalry on the Texas frontier in the spring of 1857. He served on detached duty as the adjutant for Major Earl Van Dorn for over a year, and the two men developed what the major called an "intimate" friendship. While in Texas Major married a sister-in-law of Tom Green, who was then serving as clerk of the Texas supreme court. In February 1861 2d Lieutenant Major was in Texas delivering letters for the United States government, but resigned from the Regular Army on March 21. He immediately joined the Confederacy, and in April Samuel Cooper said Major was "specially detailed to bear dispatches to Texas."

The next month he was reported on Van Dorn's staff at San Antonio. Major remained in Texas about three months, during which time Brigadier General Van Dorn took the surrender of some of the Federal forces. In the summer he joined the Missourians with Brigadier General Sterling Price and took part in the Battle of Wilson's Creek August 10. During the battle Brigadier General Franz Sigel was ambushed by Major, who was directing the mounted troops. Major reported: "General Sigel and his men fought with desperation but were unable to withstand the terrific charge of our gallant men, before whose deadly aim of Western men they fell like chaff." Missourian John B. Clark, at that time a major, heaped praise on Major for his actions and called him the "gallant colonel" (he was a lieutenant colonel).

Major returned to Texas, and in March 1862 Governor Francis Lubbock complained that he was one of the men raising troops in the state for service in the Confederate army. Lubbock protested that this made his own job of raising troops difficult, and he wrote that Major, "late of the Second Cavalry, who distinguished himself in the great Wichita Indian fight under Van Dorn, and at the battle of Oak Hills under General McCulloch, has been commissioned by the Secretary of War to raise a regiment of lancers."

Although Major's plan to raise lancers failed, he returned in March to Arkansas, where he was ordered to superintend and control the organization of some regiments in Arkansas around Devall's Bluff and Jacksonport. He had not arrived in time to take part in the Battle of Pea Ridge March 7–8, but he accompanied Van Dorn across the Mississippi River, serving as lieutenant colonel of artillery and acting chief of artillery on the general's staff.

In September 1862 Van Dorn recommended Major for promotion to brigadier general, but no action was taken on this request. He served with Van Dorn at Corinth, but after Van Dorn's assassination at his headquarters at Spring Hill, Tennessee, in May 1863 Major returned to the Trans-Mississippi. On May 19 Major was ordered by Lieutenant General Edmund Kirby Smith, head of the department, to report to Major General Richard Taylor in Louisiana to take over a cavalry brigade. Smith told Taylor that Major would "make a most efficient commander of a cavalry brigade." He was given a brigade that in December included the 1st Texas Partisan Rangers under Walter P. Lane (by war's end to become a brigadier general); 2d Texas Cavalry

The only known genuine uniformed portrait of General Major was made during the last two years of the war. (Southern Historical Collection, University of North Carolina, Chapel Hill, N.C.)

Battalion, Arizona Brigade, under George W. Baylor; and the 3d Texas Cavalry Battalion, Arizona Brigade, under George T. Madison.

Major's command fought with Brigadier General Tom Green in the Louisiana campaigns in the summer and fall of 1863, and during these months Taylor had nothing but praise for both Green and Major. On June 18 Major captured and burned two Federal steamers at Plaquemine and took sixty-eight prisoners. In July Taylor had reported that Major "swept" the country along the Mississippi River and "successfully and brilliantly carried out his instructions." He fought in the Battle of Bayou La Fourche July 13 and at Bayou Bourbeau November 3. Major did such an excellent job with his Texas cavalry that Taylor wrote in July that his conduct had "been above all praise. He has shown energy, industry, and capacity which render him fit for any command, and I respectfully recommend and request that his command as colonel commanding brigade may be made permanent, as I am sure the interest of the service and the country will be promoted by his promotion." When nothing came of this, Taylor wrote in November: "I beg leave to repeat the recommendation previously forwarded for the promotion of Colonel Major. This officer has for some months been in command of a brigade and has shown marked energy and ability. On the 3d instant he led a brilliant and effective charge on the enemy's line." Kirby Smith endorsed this request, and Major was appointed a brigadier general on July 25, to rank from July 21, 1863.

When a threat to Texas developed in the late autumn of 1863, Green and Major were ordered to return to Galveston. In January 1864 Major was at Virginia Point on the coast and remained there until relieved by Brigadier General William Steele in late March. When Major General Nathaniel Banks began his Red River Campaign in the spring of 1864, both Green and Major were instructed to return to Taylor's command. Major arrived at Mansfield on April 6 and the next day was ordered to Pleasant Hill, where he was placed in charge of the cavalry advance and outposts. He fought with distinction in the battles at Mansfield and Pleasant Hill and was with Tom Green when Green was killed at Blair's Landing on April 12. On May 3 Major captured a transport that bore the 120th Ohio Regiment, taking over 270 prisoners. His cavalry brigade inflicted severe damage on the fleet as it passed down the Red River.

After the Red River Campaign ended, Major's brigade became part of Major General John A. Wharton's division and served in Louisiana and southern Arkansas. He was paroled at New Iberia, Louisiana, on June 11, 1865.

Following the war he lived abroad in France, then returned to the United States to take up farming in Louisiana and Texas. Major died on May 7, 1877, in Austin, Texas. Since his second marriage was to a sister of General Paul O. Hébert of Louisiana, he was buried in his in-laws' tomb at Donaldsonville, Louisiana.

Anne Bailey

Roberts, O.M., *Texas*, Vol XI in Evans, *Confederate Military History*.

✵ *George Earl Maney* ✵

George Earl Maney was born at Franklin, Tennessee, on August 24, 1826. He attended the Nashville Seminary and graduated from the University of Nashville in 1845. On May 28, 1846, Maney volunteered to serve in the military during the Mexican War. He became a 2d lieutenant in what eventually was designated Company L, 1st Tennessee Infantry. Although he had enlisted for one year, he was honorably discharged on September 7, 1846, at Camargo, Tennessee, because of physical disability. On March 6, 1847, he was commissioned a 1st lieutenant in the regular U.S. Army, and the following month he was assigned to the 3d Dragoons. After mustering out on July 31, 1848, Maney studied law and was admitted to the Tennessee bar in 1850. He practiced law in Nashville, where he married Bettie Crutcher on June 23, 1853.

Maney continued his law practice in Nashville until the commencement of the Civil War, at which time he entered Confederate service as captain of the Hermitage Guards. Before this company officially became Company D, 11th Tennessee Infantry, Maney was elected colonel on May 8, 1861, of the 1st (Feild's) Tennessee Infantry. Organized at Nashville on May 9, the 1st Tennessee went into camp at Allisonia, Franklin County. Soon relocated to Camp Cheatham, Robertson County, the men drilled there until July 10, when the regiment was ordered to Staunton, Virginia. At Valley Mountain it joined the 7th and 14th Tennessee regiments to form Brigadier General Samuel R. Anderson's brigade in Brigadier General William W. Loring's division, Army of the Northwest. The regiment participated in Brigadier General Robert E. Lee's inglorious Cheat Mountain campaign in western

Virginia (September 10–15). Transferred to Brigadier General Thomas J. "Stonewall" Jackson's command at Winchester on December 8, the regiment fought at Bath, Hancock, and Romney in January of 1862. Maney's attention to detail and his ability to discipline his men were noticed by his superiors early in the war. When Jackson ordered Loring to detach one regiment for a hazardous flanking movement at Bath, Loring selected Maney's.

The regiment was at Winchester when the fall of Forts Henry and Donelson prompted Maney to request the transfer of his regiment to the west. When the request was approved on February 17, the regiment departed for Knoxville, where it was divided, five companies going to Cumberland Gap and five, under Maney, proceeding to Corinth. Initially assigned to command the 2d Brigade in Major General Benjamin F. Cheatham's division of Major General Leonidas Polk's corps, Maney received orders to guard the extreme Confederate right with his battalion during the advance on Shiloh. When Maney reached the battlefield at about 2:30 P.M. on April 6, Cheatham ordered Maney to take lead the units of his choice in an attack. Supplementing his battalion with the 9th and 19th Tennessee regiments, Maney carried a stubbornly held Federal position which precipitated his enemy's withdrawal to the river. Cheatham described it as "one of the most brilliant, as it was certainly one of the most decisive, moments of the day." On April 7 Maney was ordered to reinforce the hard-pressed extreme right with his battalion.

The only known uniformed portrait of General Maney dates from after Shiloh. (Museum of the Confederacy, Richmond, Va.)

Again, with Maney leading, the battalion's counterat-tack repulsed the Federal advance.

When the army was reorganized after the battle, Maney's performance earned him promotion to brigadier general on April 18, to rank from April 16. As part of Major General Cheatham's division Maney's predominantly Tennessee brigade suffered severe casualties at Perryville October 8, and was again heavily engaged at Murfreesboro December 31, 1862–January 2, 1863. Following that battle the brigade encamped near Shelbyville, where it remained until June 27 when it departed for Chattanooga. After distinguishing itself at Chickamauga September 18–20, the brigade took part in the seizure of Missionary Ridge on September 22. On October 22 the brigade accompanied Major General William H. T. Walker's division on an expedition into East Tennessee. Officially transferred to Walker's division on November 12, the brigade returned to Chattanooga in time to participate in the struggle for Missionary Ridge on November 25. Maney received a wound in the right arm while sup-porting Major General Patrick Cleburne's successful defense of Tunnel Hill during this engagement.

The brigade went into winter quarters at Dalton, Georgia, on November 27. On February 20, 1864, it returned to Cheatham's division. After being attached to Major General Alexander P. Stewart's division at Resaca on May 16, 1864, the brigade returned to Cheatham's division at Adairsville the following day. Detached on May 26 at New Hope Church, the brigade was to attack the Federals near Dallas in conjunction with Major General William B. Bate's division. As before, on the following day it returned to Cheatham's division. At Kennesaw Mountain on June 27 Maney's brigade distinguished itself by holding the section of earthworks associated with the struggle nicknamed the "Dead Angle." On July 22 Maney commanded Cheatham's division during the Battle of Atlanta. He also led the division at Jonesboro on August 31, but that evening he was granted a leave of absence, having been certified disabled by a surgeon. Accompanying Lieutenant General William J. Hardee to Savannah, Maney never again held field command. He was paroled at Greensboro, North Carolina, on May 1, 1865.

In 1868 Maney became president of the Tennessee & Pacific Railroad; in 1876 he was the Republican nomi-nee for governor, but he withdrew before the election. Remaining in the Republican party, Maney served in the state legislature and ardently campaigned for his

party's presidential candidates. President Chester A. Arthur appointed him minister resident to Colombia on May 19, 1881, and Maney held this post during the critical period when European nations were attempt-ing to establish a guarantee of neutrality of any intero-ceanic canal. Reassigned to Bolivia on April 17, 1882, he served as minister resident and consul general at La Paz. On June 20, 1889, President Benjamin Harrison appointed Maney minister resident to both Paraguay and Uruguay. Promoted to envoy extraordinary and minister plenipotentiary on September 23, 1890, he remained in that position until June 30, 1894, when he retired to Washington, D.C. His death came unexpect-edly in Washington on February 9, 1901. He was buried in Mount Olivet Cemetery in Nashville.

Lawrence L. Hewitt

Porter, James D., *Tennessee*, Vol. VIII in Evans, *Confederate Military History*.

[Tennessee] Civil War Centennial Commission. *Tennesseans in the Civil War: A Military History of Confederate and Union Units with Available Rosters of Personnel* (Nashville, 1964).

⭐ *Arthur Middleton Manigault* ⭐

Arthur Middleton Manigault was born into a prominent South Carolina family on October 26, 1824, in Charleston. The son of a wealthy rice planter, he received a good education but withdrew from the College of Charleston in 1841 to enter the export business. Manigault also became interested in military affairs and served as sergeant major of the local militia. Because of his experience Manigault was made a lieutenant in the famous Palmetto Regiment when the Mexican War began. Serving under Winfield Scott, he fought in five battles from Vera Cruz to Mexico City and suffered three wounds, none serious. After the war Manigault returned to Charleston and became a commission merchant before moving to near Georgetown to plant rice. There he was elected captain of the North Santee Mounted Rifles, a local militia company.

After South Carolina seceded in 1860, Manigault was placed on the staff of Brigadier General P. G. T. Beauregard at Charleston. He was present at the bombardment of Fort Sumter and in May 1861 was a lieutenant colonel serving as Beauregard's inspector general. Six weeks after the fall of Fort Sumter Manigault was appointed colonel of the 10th South Carolina Regiment and was placed in command of the First Military District of South Carolina under Robert E. Lee. Headquartered at Georgetown, he erected fortifications and batteries along the coast. However, Major General John Pemberton, who replaced Lee in South Carolina, ordered Manigault to dismantle the works and abandon his positions. Manigault then briefly served in Charleston under Brigadier General R. S. Ripley, but after the Battle of Shiloh (April 6–7, 1862) was ordered west with his regiment to join Major General John J. M. Withers' brigade near Corinth, Mississippi.

Manigault was in constant service for months afterward but saw no heavy combat. He did engage in some skirmishing during the evacuation of Corinth, where he temporarily commanded the brigade. Likewise, during the Kentucky invasion Manigault saw some skirmishing but was not heavily engaged. Murfreesboro, however, changed this pattern. During the Confederate attack on December 31, 1862, Manigault was in temporary command of Patton Anderson's brigade, which served at the "hinge" in General Braxton Bragg's line as his left flank swept to the right. The brigade suffered heavily, often being enfiladed by Federal fire, but Manigault kept going. Two assaults failed, but the third one pushed the Yankees back and his brigade captured a battery of artillery. Withers, in whose division Manigault served, wrote, "His command had been subjected to a most trying ordeal, and had suffered heavily. The calm determination and persistent energy and gallantry which rendered Colonel Manigault proof against discouragements had a marked influence on and was admirably responded to by his men." By the end of the day Manigault had lost 530 men. Fortunately his brigade was not heavily engaged for the remainder of the battle.

On April 30, 1863, Manigault received his promotion to brigadier general, effective April 26. Bragg recommended him for this star in November 1862, but no action was taken, prompting Manigault to claim that his promotion was delayed by unnamed political enemies in the War Department. His first major battle as a

General Manigault has not left behind a uniformed portrait that has come to light. This one is considerably after the war. (Miller, *Photographic History*)

brigadier was at Chickamauga. On September 19, 1863, Manigault's brigade was at Lee and Gordon's Mill, where it saw some light skirmishing. On September 20 it was placed on the extreme left of the army and moved forward to attack Major General George Thomas' men along thickly wooded ridges. The Yankee line overlapped Manigault's brigade and poured an enfilading fire upon him, forcing him to withdraw. He renewed the attack, however, and fought fiercely for several hours before being sent with a force to try and flank Thomas out of his position. When the Confederates attacked, they hit Major General Gordon Granger's corps. The battle surged back and forth at close quarters, and once Manigault's 10th South Carolina lost its colors. The Rebels then fell back, regrouped, and charged again, this time recapturing the flag. Manigault later remembered Chickamauga to have been the hardest-fought battle of his career. His brigade lost 656 men out of 2,025 engaged, and he estimated that at one time three hundred were shot down within three minutes.

Manigault's brigade helped surround the Federals in Chattanooga and was entrenched on Missionary Ridge when the Yankees counterattacked on November 25. Manigault ordered his provost guard to shoot any unwounded soldiers leaving the field, but his brigade was finally overwhelmed and fell back. Manigault barely escaped himself by galloping through what he described as a fiery gauntlet of several thousand bullets.

Manigault saw almost continuous service in the Atlanta Campaign as part of Major General Patton Anderson's division. He was slightly wounded in the hand at Resaca (May 14–15), where he lost 110 men. Although only lightly engaged at New Hope Church, he was in the thick of the fight at Peachtree Creek July 20. There his brigade, aided by another, managed to overrun sixteen Federal cannons but was only able to drag away six of the guns at a cost of four hundred men. On July 28, 1864, he was shocked when Lieutenant General Stephen D. Lee ordered his lone brigade to attack a large entrenched Union force on Lickskillet Road. Manigault reluctantly obeyed and failed twice to dislodge the enemy. He then angrily watched as five Confederate brigades were massed together and unsuccessfully assaulted the same position. Having witnessed numerous similar incidents of poor leadership, Manigault was quite vocal in criticizing Confederate generals when he wrote his memoirs shortly after the war. The Battle of Jonesboro (August 31—September 1)

further weakened his brigade, although Manigault acknowledged that his men did not fight with their usual élan. Four months of trench warfare had greatly sapped their spirits.

Manigault's exhausted brigade accompanied General John Bell Hood on his Tennessee invasion in late 1864. At Franklin November 30 he led his men against the strong Union line and was quickly cut down by a bullet that clipped his ear and cut a groove across the side of his skull. Although the wound did not appear to be serious at first, Manigault was out of the war after having led his brigade in thirteen battles and thirty skirmishes.

Manigault returned to South Carolina and became a rice planter near Georgetown after the war. In 1880 he was elected the adjutant and inspector general of the state and held that position until his death. Manigault died on August 17, 1886, at South Island from the long-term effects of his head wound. He was buried in the Magnolia Cemetery, Charleston, South Carolina.

Terry L. Jones

Tower, R. Lockwood, ed., *A Carolinian Goes to War: The Civil War Narrative of Arthur Middleton Manigault, Brigadier General, C.S.A.* (Columbia, 1983).

John S. Marmaduke is a brigadier in this post-November 1862 portrait, as indicated by collar and buttons. (William A. Turner Collection)

✶ John Sappington Marmaduke ✶

On March 14, 1833, a son was born to Meredith Miles and Lavinia Sappington Marmaduke, who were then living on a farm near Arrow Rock, Missouri. They named their baby John Sappington in honor of his maternal grandfather, a prominent Saline County physician. John received his primary and secondary education in the Saline County schools and at Lexington's Masonic College. He attended Yale for two years and then transferred to Harvard. While in his first year at the latter school he received an appointment to the U.S. Military Academy, where he reported on July 1, 1853. He graduated as number thirty in the class of 1857 and was commissioned a brevet 2d lieutenant in the 1st U.S. Infantry. The next month he became a 2d lieutenant and joined the 7th U.S. Infantry, then posted at Fort Laramie. He and his unit participated in the 1858–59 Mormon Expedition to Utah.

The crisis sparked by Abraham Lincoln's election and the secession of the seven states of the lower South found Marmaduke stationed at Fort Webster in New Mexico Territory. Deeply troubled by the threatened breakup of the Union, he secured a furlough to visit Missouri to review the situation with his father, who in 1844 had briefly served as governor of the state. The father favored the Union but told his son to make his own decision. Lincoln's April 15, 1861, call for seven hundred and fifty thousand volunteers and Governor Claiborne F. Jackson's incendiary and ringing response was a clarion call to action, and Marmaduke resigned from the Old Army on April 17 and was commissioned a colonel in the

prosecessionist state guard by the governor. At Boonville on June 17 Union forces routed the state guard and sent it scurrying into southwest Missouri. Disenchanted with the state guard and its leadership, he resigned his colonelcy, traveled to Richmond, and was commissioned a 1st lieutenant in the Confederate army. He returned to the Trans-Mississippi, joined Brigadier General William J. Hardee's staff, and was promoted lieutenant colonel and assumed command of the 1st Arkansas Infantry Battalion. In October Marmaduke crossed the Mississippi and joined the Army of Central Kentucky posted near Bowling Green. On January 1, 1862, he became colonel of the reorganized unit, which was redesignated the 3d Confederate Infantry.

Marmaduke and his regiment fought at Shiloh with Colonel R. G. Shaver's brigade. His regiment "bore the guiding colors of the brigade" as it swept across Seay's cotton field, hammered the Federals, and helped rout Everett Peabody's brigade from its camps. He was wounded in the fighting on April 7 and hospitalized for several days. By April 17 he was back on duty and was assigned to lead a newly constituted brigade in Hardee's corps. He and his brigade participated in the Siege of Corinth and the retreat to Tupelo.

Marmaduke has altered his uniform buttons into rows of threes, indicating a major general, though Confederate regulations never mandated such an arrangement. This would date the image to being taken after hostilities ceased, since he was in prison when promoted to that grade in March 1865. (William A. Albaugh Collection)

In mid-September Marmaduke, having been detached from Braxton Bragg's army, crossed the Mississippi and reported to Major General T. H. Holmes' Little Rock headquarters. On September 28 he was assigned to duty as an acting brigadier general in Major General Thomas C. Hindman's I Corps, Army of the West. In command of Hindman's cavalry division—Cols. Joseph O. Shelby's, Charles A. Carroll's, and Emmett MacDonald's brigades—he clashed with the Federals at Cane Hill and was conspicuous at the Battle of Prairie Grove from the opening gun through the retreat across the Boston Mountains.

He was commended by Hindman, who noted in his report that Marmaduke had not been confirmed as a brigadier and declared that if the War Department had been present at Prairie Grove or at Shiloh, "the act of confirmation could not be too long delayed." This letter had the desired result, and Marmaduke was promoted to brigadier general, to rank from November 15.

Marmaduke next led his horse soldiers on two raids that thrust deep into Missouri. The first began on the last day of 1862 with the division's departure from Lewisburg, Arkansas, and ended January 25 at Batesville, Arkansas, and saw engagements at Springfield and Hartville, Missouri. The second raid began on April 17 when Marmaduke left Jackson, Arkansas; crested on the 26th when the Confederates attacked Cape Girardeau and were repulsed; and ended when they recrossed the St. Francis River at Chalk Bluff on May 2. At Taylor's Creek on May 11 Marmaduke engaged and defeated a twelve-hundred–man cavalry column.

Marmaduke and his two-brigade division had an active role in the July 4 attack on Helena, which saw the Rebel infantry repulsed with frightful casualties. He commanded the army's cavalry that opposed the advance of Frederick Steele's army from Helena to the approaches to Little Rock (August 10–September 6). On the last day, despite Major General Sterling Price's efforts, Marmaduke met Brigadier General L. Marsh Walker in a duel—"pistols at ten paces to fire and advance." Marmaduke had questioned Walker's courage at the Helena battle. Walker was mortally wounded, and Marmaduke was placed under arrest by General Price, but upon the "almost unanimous request" of Marmaduke's officers Price ordered him to resume his command.

There were too many Yankees, and Little Rock was surrendered. Soon thereafter Marmaduke was formally released from arrest by district commander Holmes.

On October 25 Marmaduke attacked Pine Bluff with his four-brigade division and was repulsed.

On March 23, 1864, General Steele's army marched out of Little Rock en route to Louisiana and an anticipated rendezvous with N. P. Banks' army on Red River. Marmaduke and his division, picketing the line of the Ouachita, harassed and slowed Steele's columns in a fight at Elkins' Ferry (April 3–4) and in clashes on Prairie d'Ane. Frustrated and running short of supplies, Steele turned aside and occupied Camden. At Poison Spring April 18 Marmaduke, in cooperation with Brigadier General Samuel B. Maxey's mixed Texas-Choctaw-Chickasaw division, routed a Union brigade and captured a wagon train. He led the pursuit of Steele's columns on their retreat from Camden and spearheaded the Confederate attacks during the initial phase of the battle at Jenkins' Ferry on April 30.

Marmaduke with one of his brigades entered Lake County, Arkansas, and in late May and early June attacked Union shipping plying the Mississippi. This led to the June 6 fight at Lake Chicot with a Union landing force. He returned to Missouri on September 19, leading one of the three columns into which General Price had divided his army. His division participated in the ill-starred attack on Fort Davidson (September 27) and the fights at the Little Blue (October 21), Byram's Ford (October 23), and the Marais des Cygnes and Mine Creek (October 25). In the last engagement Marmaduke, William Cabell, and five hundred of their men were overwhelmed and captured. On March 18, 1865, while imprisoned at Fort Warren, Massachusetts, Marmaduke was made a major general, the last Confederate officer to be promoted to that rank. He was released in August and sailed for Europe to recuperate.

Upon returning to Missouri, Marmaduke made his home in St. Louis and enjoyed some success, first as a commission merchant and then as an insurance agent. From 1871 to 1874 he was editor of the St. Louis *Journal of Agriculture*, and from 1880 to 1885 he was a member of the Missouri Railway Commission. In 1880 he was an unsuccessful candidate for the Democratic nomination for governor. Four years later he again sought that office. He was nominated by the Democrats and elected. Standing more than six feet tall and still looking like a soldier, he took office in January 1885. A major problem confronting his administration was regulation of the railroads. The bill for this purpose, which he championed, was defeated. Undaunted, he called the assembly into special session, by use of strong-arm tactics carried the day, and had the satisfaction of signing into law a regulatory measure. Marmaduke also dealt firmly and fairly with a bitter railroad strike that was settled with little loss of property and no loss of life.

Governor Marmaduke died at Jefferson City on December 28, 1887, a year before the expiration of his term. The life-long bachelor was buried there.

Edwin C. Bearss

Cullum, George W., *Biographical Register of the Officers and Graduates of the U.S. Military Academy*, Vol. II (Washington, 1940).

Moore, *Missouri*, Vol. XII in Evans, *Confederate Military History*.

Wright, Marcus J., *General Officers of the Confederate Army...* (New York, 1911).

Another pose from the same sitting, almost certainly made in July 1865 or later. (Louisiana State University, Baton Rouge)

☆ *Humphrey Marshall* ☆

No genuine uniformed pose of Humphrey Marshall has been found. This portrait may be wartime, but more than that cannot be said. (National Archives)

Lawyer, politician, and general, Humphrey Marshall was born in Frankfort, Kentucky, on January 13, 1812. After local education he entered West Point in 1828 and graduated four years later, forty-second in a class of forty-five. Commissioned in the cavalry, he participated in the Black Hawk War. Marshall resigned his commission in less than a year, studied law, and was admitted to the bar, and soon established a successful practice in Louisville.

Active in the state militia, he raised the 1st Kentucky Cavalry Regiment in 1846 and was commissioned as its colonel. He and it performed well for Zachary Taylor at the Battle of Buena Vista, where he charged a much larger force.

Marshall's military reputation helped him win elections to the U.S. House of Representatives as a Whig in 1848 and 1850. He left Congress in 1852 to become the nation's commissioner to China. After his return to Kentucky Marshall won elections to the House as a Know-Nothing in 1854 and 1856. He campaigned actively for John C. Breckinridge in 1860, then supported the call for a border states peace convention and Kentucky's policy of neutrality. Learning that he would probably be arrested, Marshall fled the state.

After a visit to President Jefferson Davis, Marshall was commissioned a brigadier general on October 30, 1861, to rank from the same day, and given the small Army of Southwest Virginia and Eastern Kentucky. Thereafter he contended that he had been given an independent command and had been promised enough troops and other support to enable him to recover Kentucky for the Confederacy.

An inch under six feet and weighing over three hundred pounds, Marshall was ill suited to mountain campaigning. Warned that he was an attractive target for bushwhackers, Marshall said that he would surround himself with fat staff officers. Once asked why he was camped in an almost inaccessible location, he replied that he was not afraid of the Yankees, he was trying to dodge Confederate major generals.

Unable to raise a large enough force to win Kentucky and plagued by a chronic shortage of food and other supplies, Marshall had an undistinguished Civil War career. Affronted when Major General George B. Crittenden was given a command, Marshall offered his resignation on November 30, 1861. Persuaded to continue, he encountered Colonel James A. Garfield in the battle at Middle Creek on January 10, 1862, a small engagement which each commander claimed to have won. Marshall's best showing was at Princeton, Virginia, in May 1862 when he checked the advance of Union Brigadier General Jacob D. Cox and saved the Lynchburg-Knoxville Railroad and some important lead and salt works.

Major General E. Kirby Smith was sent to Knoxville in March 1862, and Marshall submitted his resignation in June. But a major Confederate invasion of Kentucky was being planned and Marshall was persuaded that his participation might be of help. He applied for reinstatement as of June 23, and while it may have never been acted on by Congress, Marshall was treated as if he had never resigned. When Braxton Bragg and E. Kirby Smith moved into Kentucky, Marshall was to cooperate by advancing from the eastern mountains. His pace was likely to be slow since he would be under Kirby Smith's command when they joined forces. Marshall moved to Mount Sterling where he would be in position to intercept George Morgan when he abandoned the Union position at Cumberland Gap.

George Morgan managed to escape to the Ohio River, and Marshall's forty-five hundred men had still not reached Lexington on the eve of the Battle of Perryville. Following that indecisive struggle on October 8, 1862, a Confederate council of war decided to leave the state. Marshall remained in Kentucky for a time, then withdrew to his haven in southwestern Virginia. In April 1863 he ventured back into his native state in a cavalry raid that accomplished little. Relieved of his command that month and ordered to report to General Joseph E. Johnston at Chattanooga, Marshall delighted many Confederate officials by resigning on June 17, 1863.

Humphrey Marshall wrote more and longer reports and letters than any other brigadier general in the Confederate armies. Disregarding the chain of command, he directed many of them to President Davis, General Lee, and the secretary of war. Lee responded with his usual tact and patience on May 1, 1862: "I think I have not succeeded in making myself clear in my letter." Davis was often less restrained. "When success is attainable, you have not been required to lose the opportunity," he informed the complaining general on August 27, 1862. He was even more direct on September 19: "No one can have an independent command. Cooperation is necessary to success, and the Senior officer present for duty must command the whole." No compact had been made between Marshall and the Confederate government. Such rebukes had little effect upon the obese and verbose Kentuckian; he simply sent another epistle.

After returning to civilian status Marshall practiced law in Richmond. In February 1862 Kentucky soldiers and refugees elected him as the Eighth District's representative in the Confederate Congress. He served on the Military Affairs Committee, and his eloquence and persistence made him an influential member. While he favored granting the president extensive powers to draft men, including slaves, and to control transportation facilities, he opposed the administration's attempt to raise taxes and to suspend the writ of *habeas corpus*.

Marshall fled to Texas in 1865 but in November was allowed to go to New Orleans. There he continued his profession until President Andrew Johnson removed his civil disabilities in December 1867. Marshall resumed his legal career in Louisville, where he died on March 28, 1872. He was buried in the Frankfort state cemetery.

Lowell H. Harrison

Duke, Basil W., *Reminiscences of General Basil W. Duke, C.S.A.* (Garden City, N.Y., 1911).

Guerrant, Edward O., "Marshall and Garfield in Eastern Kentucky," in *Battles and Leaders of the Civil War* (New York, 1887), I, pp. 393–97, and "Operations in East Tennessee and Southwest Virginia," IV, 475–479.

Levin, H., *The Lawyers and Lawmakers of Kentucky* (Chicago, 1897).

✳ *James Green Martin* ✳

James Green Martin, the son of William and Sophia Scott Daugé Martin, was born at Elizabeth City, North Carolina, on February 14, 1819. He was educated in local common schools and at St. Mary's boys school in Raleigh and received an appointment to the United States Military Academy. He reported at West Point on July 1, 1836, and was graduated as a member of the class of 1840. His standing was fourteenth in a class that included William T. Sherman (sixth), George H. Thomas (twelfth), and Richard S. Ewell (thirteenth).

Commissioned a 2d lieutenant in the 1st Artillery, Martin on his initial assignment went to Houlton, Maine. This was in the year before the Webster-Ashburton Treaty of 1842 rang down the curtain on the Potato War with Great Britain and settled the Maine–New Brunswick boundary dispute. In the years before 1846 he pulled duty at Fort Sullivan (1843–44) and Hancock Barracks (1844–45), also in Maine, and at Fort Adams, Rhode Island, as well as an 1845–46 detail to the U.S. Coast Survey.

Martin campaigned with Zachary Taylor's army in northern Mexico and fought at Monterrey September 20–23, 1846. Along with most of the regulars, he was transferred to Winfield Scott's army that winter and on February 17, 1847, promoted 1st lieutenant. He participated in the siege of Vera Cruz (March 9–27), the Battle of Cerro Gordo (April 18), the march to the Valley of Mexico, and the August 20 battles of Contreras and Churubusco on the approaches to Mexico City. Two weeks before, on August 5, he had been promoted captain. In the latter fight he was seriously wounded, suffering the amputation of his right arm. He emerged from the Mexican War with a brevet rank as major for gallantry in the August 20 battles.

Martin during the years between 1848 and 1861 was stationed at a number of posts as quartermaster—Fort Monroe (1848–55), Schuylkill Arsenal (1857–58), Nebraska City (1858–59)—in the small peacetime army. In April 1861 he was on staff duty at Fort Riley, Kansas.

Martin resigned his commission on June 17, 1861, and offered his services to North Carolina Governor John W. Ellis. He was commissioned a captain of cavalry and appointed adjutant general of the ten regiments of North Carolina troops then being raised. As such he had a key administrative role in the organization, equipping, and mustering in of North Carolina troops for Confederate service. Responding to his recommendation, Governor Ellis employed ships to run the blockade and bring in war materiel and consumer goods from Europe.

On September 28, 1861, Martin was named commander of state troops with the rank of major general of North Carolina militia. Successes scored by Union troops under Major General Ambrose E. Burnside in carrying the war into the North Carolina Sounds alarmed the state, and Martin, appreciating the gravity of the situation, raised twelve thousand more men than the North Carolina quota established by the secretary of war. Many of these troops were rushed to Virginia to first confront the Army

There is some confusion about General James Martin. The photo customarily identified as being him shows a man in colonel's insignia, a rank that Martin never held. This image reveals his rank as major general of North Carolina militia from his buttons. Identified as Martin, this picture was previously erroneously identified as being General Rufus Barringer. (U.S. Army Military History Institute, Carlisle, Pa.)

of the Potomac along the Yorktown-Warwick line and then oppose Major General George B. McClellan's snail-like advance up the Peninsula.

In May Martin, having successfully met this challenge and tiring of a desk job, requested a field assignment. On May 17 he was promoted brigadier general, to rank from May 15, in the provisional Confederate States army but resigned on July 25. He was reappointed on August 11 to rank from the date of his first appointment and was confirmed by the Senate on September 10, 1862. In August he was named commander of the District of North Carolina with headquarters at Kinston. He and his men did not see action quickly. Some fourteen months later, on October 25, 1863, he was directed to organize a brigade from troops posted in the district and be prepared to meet the enemy. With his brigade—the 17th, 42d, 50th, and 66th North Carolina infantry regiments—he went into camp near Wilmington. Within weeks it was reportedly as "well-drilled and equipped a command as the Confederate army possessed."

Martin saw his first Civil War combat at Newport Barracks on February 2, 1864, when his brigade participated in the campaign, directed by Major General George E. Pickett, aimed at defeating Union forces holding the New Berne enclave. The riverline advance of Major General Benjamin F. Butler's Army of the James and its May 5 landings at and occupation of Bermuda Hundred and City Point led to a call for reinforcements, and Martin and his brigade were rushed north, the last of his troops reaching Petersburg on May 13. Martin was assigned to hard-drinking Major General W. H. C. Whiting's command and was present on the 16th when Whiting botched the Port Walthall attack. On May 20 Martin and his North Carolinians—now assigned to Lieutenant General D. H. Hill's command—earned the plaudits of their comrades when they charged and routed the enemy from their forward rifle-pits covering the Bermuda Hundred line. After scoring this victory Martin was hoisted on his men's shoulders and carried through the encampment to the shouts of "Three cheers for old one wing." The stern disciplinarian was surprised by this display of his soldiers' affection.

On May 21 Martin's brigade was transferred from D. H. Hill's command and assigned to Major General Robert Hoke's division and on the 31st crossed the James River and made a forced march to Cold Harbor. On June 1 and again on the third Martin and his Carolinians posted north of Boatswain's Swamp repulsed the Army of the Potomac's human wave assaults.

From June 3 to nightfall on the 12th the brigade battled Yankee sharpshooters, and General Robert E. Lee—in the belief that Lieutenant General U. S. Grant would attack again—told Martin that he held the key to the Cold Harbor line and inquired, "As your troops have not been in many battles, can they be relied on in a crisis?" Martin responded that his North Carolinians were equal to Lee's veterans. But, he added, showing foresight, "Grant will soon disappear from our front, cross to the Southside and move against Petersburg." To counter Grant's crossing of the James, Hoke's division was rushed to Petersburg on June 15, arriving just in time to prevent the city's capture by Union troops who had overwhelmed the Confederate defenders and breached the Dimmock line. Martin battled and battered onrushing soldiers of the Army of the Potomac on the eastern approaches to Petersburg June 16–18. Grant then abandoned his sledgehammer frontal attacks, and the nine and one-half month siege of Petersburg had begun.

On June 28, his health compromised by the strain and exposure of duty in the trenches, Martin was relieved of duty with the Army of Northern Virginia and established his command post at Burke's Station with responsibility for guarding the bridges and trestles on the Southside and Danville railroads. Then in mid-July he was assigned to command of the District of Western North Carolina, headquartered at Asheville. Soon after his departure from Petersburg, General Lee commended Brigadier General W. W. Kirkland, Martin's successor, on the brigade's faithful obedience to orders. Whereupon Kirkland reminded Lee that the praise was largely due his predecessor. Lee answered, "General Martin is one to whom North Carolina owes a debt she can never repay."

General Martin and his command were included in the April 26, 1865, surrender effected by General Joseph E. Johnston at Durham Station, and he was paroled at Waynesboro, North Carolina, May 10.

In the postwar years Martin read law and became a successful attorney with offices in Asheville. During these years he was a leading Episcopal layman, being elected as a delegate to the general conventions of his church. He died in that city on October 4, 1878, and was buried there.

Edwin C. Bearss

Cullum, George W., *Biographical Register of Officers and Graduates of the U.S. Military Academy*, Vol. II (Washington, 1940).

Hill, D. H., *North Carolina*, Vol. V in Evans, *Confederate Military History*.

☆ *William Thompson Martin* ☆

General William Martin's portrait in uniform has not been found. This was taken in the 1880s (Warners, *Generals in Gray*)

William T. Martin was born on March 25, 1823, in Glasgow, Kentucky. An 1840 graduate of Centre College, Martin moved to Natchez, Mississippi, where two years later he studied law and opened a practice in the city. He served several terms as a district attorney in the years before the Civil War. An avowed Unionist Whig, Martin nevertheless embraced the Confederate cause and recruited a cavalry company that he led to Richmond in the spring of 1861.

Martin's men were organized with fellow Mississippians into the Jeff Davis Legion. On November 11, 1861, Martin, now with the rank of major, led part of the legion against Federals near Falls Church, Virginia, capturing prisoners, wagons, and horses. By the spring of 1862 Martin was promoted to lieutenant colonel and commanded two squadrons of the legion in Brigadier General J. E. B. Stuart's ride around George McClellan's Union army on the Peninsula in June. Promoted to colonel, he participated in the Seven Days' and Sharpsburg campaigns.

On December 2, 1862, Martin received his brigadier-generalcy, effective the same day, and was transferred to the Western theater. During March and April 1863 he commanded a two-brigade division of cavalry in the Tullahoma, or Middle Tennessee, Campaign. Throughout the summer of 1863 the Mississippian led his division in the operations of General Braxton Bragg's Army of Tennessee. At the Battle of Chickamauga September 19–20 Martin's division fought in Major General Joseph Wheeler's cavalry corps. That fall he participated in Lieutenant General James Longstreet's campaign against Union forces at Knoxville. He was promoted to major general on November 12, 1863, effective November 10.

During the spring and summer of 1864 Wheeler's cavalry corps opposed the advance of William T. Sherman's Union command on Atlanta. When Sherman closed on Atlanta in August and September, the Confederate cavalry raided into Tennessee. Finally, when the Federals marched from Atlanta to Savannah at the end of the year, Wheeler's troopers were the only Confederate forces to offer serious resistance. Throughout the months Martin ably led his division. Early in 1865 Martin was assigned to command of the District of Northwest Mississippi.

Martin returned to his adopted state and home town after the war. A staunch Democrat, he served as a delegate to Democratic national conventions for thirty-two years and served in the state senate for a dozen years. He also was a trustee of the state university and of Jefferson College. In 1884 his company completed the construction of the Natchez, Jackson & Columbus Railroad. This solid if unspectacular cavalry officer died in Natchez on March 16, 1910, and was buried in City Cemetery.

Jeffry D. Wert

Connelly, Thomas Lawrence, *Autumn of Glory: The Army of Tennessee, 1862–1865* (Baton Rouge, 1971).

Hooker, Charles E., *Mississippi*, Vol. VII in Evans, *Confederate Military History*.

A beautiful early-war portrait of Maury as colonel on Van Dorn's staff. (William A. Turner Collection)

⋆ *Dabney Herndon Maury* ⋆

Maury was born on May 21, 1822, in Fredericksburg, Virginia. After the death of their father Dabney and a brother were raised by their uncle, Matthew Fontaine Maury. Dabney graduated from the University of Virginia in 1842 and then studied law there and under a judge at Fredericksburg. He did not care for the law and entered West Point, graduating in 1846. Brevetted a 2d lieutenant, Maury joined the Regiment of Mounted Rifles (later the 3d U.S. Cavalry). He served in the Mexican War, during which he won a brevet of 1st lieutenant for gallant and meritorious conduct at Cerro Gordo. An enemy musket ball shattered his left arm, permanently crippling it, and he returned to the United States to recuperate.

During the years prior to the Civil War Maury served from 1847 to 1852 as a professor and instructor at West Point; spent four years on the frontier in Texas; was superintendent of the cavalry school at Carlisle Barracks, Pennsylvania, until 1860; and, as a captain, was assistant adjutant general of the Department of New Mexico. He turned in his resignation in May 1861 when he learned of the secession of Virginia, and the War Department dismissed him on June 25.

Maury traveled to Richmond and in July received commissions as a captain of cavalry in the Regular Confederate Army, colonel of cavalry in the Virginia state forces, and lieutenant colonel in the provisional army. On July 19 the War Department assigned him as adjutant general to General Joseph E. Johnston at Manassas, but on August 23 he was reassigned as adjutant general to Major General Theophilus H. Holmes, commander of the Department of Fredericksburg.

Maury remained on Holmes' staff until February 1862 when he was promoted to colonel and ordered to become chief of staff to Major General Earl Van Dorn, who had just been placed in charge of the Trans-Mississippi Department. He performed outstanding service at the Battle of Pea Ridge (Elkhorn Tavern) March 7–8. Van Dorn wrote: "Colonel Maury was of invaluable service to me both in preparing for and during the battle. Here, as on other battle-fields when I have served with him, he proved to be a zealous patriot

and true soldier; cool and calm under all circumstances, he was always ready, either with his sword or his pen." For his conduct Maury received a promotion to brigadier general on March 18, 1862, to rank from March 12.

He accompanied the Army of the West to Corinth, Mississippi, and in late April was placed in command of a brigade in Major General Samuel Jones' division. During the evacuation of Corinth he had charge of the army's rear guard. He was given command of a division of three brigades in the Army of the West in June. Maury worked hard at drilling and instructing his troops. Some of the volunteers hated him for his strict discipline, but after serving under him in battle they gained great respect for him and nicknamed him "Little Dab."

He led his men in the battles of Iuka September 19 and Corinth October 3–4, and received praise from Major General Sterling Price for his role in the latter engagement. Maury was promoted major general on November 4, to rank from the same day, and took his division to Vicksburg in December. After commanding at Snyder's Bluff for several months he went to support Major General William W. Loring's forces defending Fort Pemberton in early April 1863.

On April 15 Jefferson Davis ordered Maury to Knoxville to assume command of the Department of East Tennessee. Less than two weeks later the War Department ordered him to go to Mobile, Alabama, and replace Major General Simon B. Buckner as commander of the District of the Gulf. Maury assumed the latter position on May 19 and held it until the end of the war. Davis had specifically selected Maury to take over at Mobile and had great confidence in his abilities. During the remainder of the conflict Davis would not allow any senior major generals to be assigned to the district, where they might outrank Maury. One of Maury's men remembered him as "'every inch a soldier', but then there were not many inches of him. The soldiers called him 'puss in boots,' because half of his diminutive person seemed lost in a pair of the immense cavalry boots of the day. He was a wise and gallant officer."

As commander of the District of the Gulf Maury proved a competent, trustworthy general. He pushed

Probably a mid-1862 portrait taken after Maury was made brigadier but before his promotion to major general. (U.S. Army Military History Institute, Carlisle, Pa.)

One of a series of late-war portraits from a sitting, with the buttons on his blouse arranged as for a major general. (Library of Congress)

the construction of Mobile's defenses and was selfless when called upon to send men or supplies to other points of the Confederacy. Maury recognized the city's place in the Confederacy's overall war strategy and acted accordingly. He deserves credit for accepting his role and performing his job most capably. In June 1863 Maury's command was upgraded to a department, but it was redesignated as a district within the Department of Alabama, Mississippi, and East Louisiana in January 1864. Federal naval vessels bombarded Fort Powell in Mississippi Sound in February and March 1864, but its defenders successfully withstood the pounding.

On July 26 Maury assumed temporary command of the Department of Alabama, Mississippi, and East Louisiana and held that position until Lieutenant General Richard Taylor assumed command on September 6. During Maury's absence Admiral David G. Farragut's Union fleet steamed into Mobile Bay, destroying the small Confederate naval force there and capturing, in conjunction with land forces, Fort Morgan, Fort Gaines, and Fort Powell. Maury again exercised temporary departmental command from November 22 to December 11 while Taylor was away in Georgia. Federal forces moved against the eastern defenses of Maury's district in March 1865, capturing Spanish Fort on April 8 and Fort Blakely the next day. Maury ordered an evacuation of Mobile, and he left the city with his army's rear guard on April 12. When his forces reached Meridian, Mississippi, they were formed into an infantry division in Taylor's army.

Maury and his men were surrendered at Cuba Station, Alabama, on May 8. He returned to Fredericksburg and opened the Classical and Mathematical Academy for boys, where he taught for a time. Then Maury moved to New Orleans to become an express agent, and later he operated a naval stores manufacturing establishment in nearby St. Tammany Parish. He organized the Southern Historical Society in 1868 and served as the chairman on its executive committee until 1886. Maury was U.S. minister to Colombia from 1885 to 1889. When he returned to the United States, he lived with his son in Peoria, Illinois. Maury died there on January 11, 1900, and was buried in Fredericksburg.

Arthur W. Bergeron, Jr.

"Dabney Herndon Maury," Southern Historical Society Papers, XXVII (1899), pp. 335–49.

Maury, Dabney H., *Recollections of a Virginian* (New York, 1894).

A handsome profile from the late-war sitting. (Southern Historical Collection, University of North Carolina, Chapel Hill, N.C.)

Another portrait from the same sitting. (Warner, *Generals in Grey*)

Samuel B. Maxey as colonel of the 9th Texas Infantry in 1861-62. (Courtesy of Lawrence T. Jones)

⋆ *Samuel Bell Maxey* ⋆

Samuel Bell Maxey was born on March 30, 1825, at Tompkinsville in Monroe County, Kentucky. In 1834 his parents, Rice and Lucy Pope Bell Maxey, moved to Clinton County, where the young Maxey attended school. At seventeen he received an appointment to West Point, graduating in 1846, next to last in his class of fifty-nine—a group that included such notables as George B. McClellan, "Stonewall" Jackson, and George Pickett (although Pickett actually graduated below Maxey). Maxey was assigned to the 7th Infantry Regiment and fought in the Mexican War, in which his only brother, William Henry Maxey, died. He was promoted to 1st lieutenant for gallantry in the battles of Contreras and Churubusco in August 1847. After Mexico City fell he was in charge of one of the districts into which the city was divided.

Following the war he returned to Jefferson Barracks in St. Louis, Missouri, and began to read law in his spare time. On September 17, 1849, he resigned from the U.S. army, studied law seriously, and opened a practice with his father at Albany, Kentucky. The two men moved in 1857 to Texas, where they established a law office at Paris in Lamar County. Maxey served as the district attorney in 1858 and 1859. In 1861 he was elected to the Texas Senate, but declined to serve when military duty called; his father replaced him.

Maxey organized the Lamar Rifles, which later became part of the 9th Texas Infantry, and joined General Albert Sidney Johnston in Kentucky. He was appointed a brigadier general on March 7, 1862, to rank from March 4. General Joseph E. Johnston sent him to Chattanooga to collect and reorganize troops, and while there he attacked the rear-guard garrisons of Major General Don Carlos Buell's army at Stevenson, Bridgeport, and Battle Creek, Alabama. He was transferred to Port Hudson, Louisiana, to take part in the defense of the Confederate positions on the Mississippi River. On May 23 he took his brigade to Jackson, Mississippi, to join Joseph E. Johnston. In June when Major General Samuel G. French was assigned to duty in Johnston's Department of the West, he assumed command

of a division composed of the brigades of Evander McNair, Samuel B. Maxey, and "Shanks" Evans. Maxey fought under French during the retreat from the Big Black.

On August 18, 1863, Maxey was assigned to the Trans-Mississippi Department and ordered to report to Lieutenant General Theophilus H. Holmes at Little Rock. General Edmund Kirby Smith, who was Maxey's friend, was having trouble in his command structure. Brigadier General William Steele, who headed the Indian Territory, was unpopular among the troops, partly because of his Northern birth. When Steele requested a transfer Smith appointed Maxey to replace him. On December 11, 1863, Maxey was assigned to command that district with headquarters at Doaksville and had the difficult job of trying to bring order out of confusion. He organized the Indians and earned their respect; he was particularly careful that no race or color line should be drawn in determining the ranking of officers.

In April 1864 he was instructed to bring his troops to Arkansas to replace the Confederates who had headed for Louisiana to stop Union Major General Nathaniel Banks' move up the Red River. Maxey took part in the Camden Campaign and participated in the controversial battle on April 18, 1864, at Poison Spring, where over three hundred Federal soldiers, over half of them black, were killed or wounded as they tried to escape. In fact, the bloodshed might have been much worse had Maxey not arrived, assumed command of the Confederates, and called off the pursuit. Maxey, however, became the scapegoat for those who believed the Southerners should have finished the victory by rounding up all the escaping soldiers.

Nevertheless, Maxey was familiar with the controversial Confederate reactions along the Mississippi River toward black soldiers. Although he had left Port Hudson before the battle there, he knew that the fighting had made headlines as the first major engagement involving blacks. Moreover, Maxey had achieved his objective at Poison Spring; he had destroyed a Union wagon train of almost two hundred wagons and thus forced the Union commander Major General Frederick Steele to retreat. Major General Sterling Price reported that he wanted to "acknowledge the prompt and effective support rendered me by Brigadier-General Maxey and his troops. Leaving the District of the Indian Territory, which he commanded, he joined me at a time when the necessity for reenforcements seemed greatest and until relieved from duty here after the evacuation of Camden by the Federal forces continued to perform most efficient service."

On May 9, 1864, Maxey resumed command of the Indian Territory. Kirby Smith promoted him to major general, to rank from April 18. Although there is some question whether this was confirmed by Richmond, Maxey signed all official documents as a major general for the remainder of the war. Smith, however, continued to have problems within his department. On January 9, 1864, Brigadier General Douglas Cooper had been made commander of the Indian troops, serving in a unique position as go-between for the Confederate government. In July 1864 the Confederate War Department finally issued instructions giving Cooper command of the entire district; he would replace Maxey. Smith wrote Richmond requesting that the government cancel Maxey's removal order. Smith felt that Maxey "has with skill, judgment, and success administered his duties" and "serious injury would result to the service were this order enforced." Smith backed Maxey and believed that Cooper was not a good choice. Unfortunately Richmond did not agree; Cooper even visited Richmond to further his promotion. When Smith learned that the order must be carried out, he delayed it for several weeks. On February 21, 1865, however, Maxey was relieved and Cooper took his place.

Maxey was put in command of a division of dismounted cavalry on April 25, 1865. He resigned on May 26, 1865, and returned to Paris, Texas, where he resumed the practice of law. He held various political positions and was offered a post as judge of the Eighth District of Texas. He did not accept, however, because he had designs on a United States Senate seat. He served in the United States Senate for two terms until he was defeated for reelection in 1887. Maxey died on August 16, 1895, at Eureka Springs, Arkansas, and was buried in Evergreen Cemetery, Paris, Texas.

Anne Bailey

Horton, Louise, Samuel Bell Maxey: A Biography. (Austin, Tex, 1974).

Nunn, W. C., *Ten More Texans in Gray* (Hillsboro, Tex, 1980).

Another rare portrait of Maxey following his promotion to brigadier. (Courtesy of Lawrence T. Jones)

✫ *Hugh Weedon Mercer* ✫

The only known uniformed portrait of Hugh Mercer shows him as a brigadier, and may have been taken any time after October 1861. (William A. Turner Collection)

The grandson and namesake of revolutionary war Brigadier General Hugh Mercer, who was mortally wounded at Princeton, Hugh Weedon Mercer was born on November 27, 1808, at "The Sentry Box," Fredericksburg, Virginia. Finishing third among the thirty-three graduates in the West Point class of 1828, he was appointed a brevet 2d lieutenant in the artillery on July 1, promoted to 2d lieutenant that same day, and assigned to the 2d Artillery. Initially assigned to the artillery school for practice at Fort Monroe, Virginia, he served as aide-de-camp to Brigadier General Winfield Scott (1832–34). As a member of Scott's staff Mercer was stationed in Charleston, South Carolina, during the Nullification Crisis of 1832–33. In 1834 he served briefly at the Augusta Arsenal. Promoted to 1st lieutenant on October 10, 1834, Mercer was assigned to quartermaster duty at Fort Oglethorpe in Savannah. He resigned his commission on April 30, 1835, married into a local family, and settled in Savannah. In 1841 he began working as a cashier at the Planters' Bank, a position he retained until 1861. Between 1835 and 1845 he served as a 1st lieutenant in the Chatham Artillery; he remained active in the militia until 1861.

Mercer entered Confederate service as colonel of the 1st Volunteer Georgia Regiment. He spent most of the war in Savannah because of his extensive knowledge of the city's defenses. Initially he served under Brigadier General Alexander R. Lawton, commander of the Department of Georgia with headquarters at Savannah. Anxious to assert greater control over the coastal defenses of his state in October 1861, Governor Joseph E. Brown offered Mercer a commission as major general of state forces. Rather than accept Brown's proposition Mercer opted for promotion to brigadier general in the Confederate army on October 29, 1861. On November 5 Lawton's department was merged into a new department under the command of General Robert E. Lee, who was responsible for defending the coasts of South

Carolina, Georgia, and east Florida. By November 10 Mercer was defending the Georgia coast near Brunswick with approximately two thousand troops. Ordered to assume command of the Second Military District of South Carolina on May 26, 1862, Mercer was ordered back to Georgia on June 6 to relieve Lawton, who had been transferred to Virginia.

In August 1862 Mercer supported the impressment of the first slaves and free blacks into Confederate service, contending that these men were desperately needed to construct fortifications. When he began this labor program, he requested slave owners to rent one-fifth of their able-bodied slaves to the government, which would provide both their transportation and their rations. Initially his appeals were well received by the public, but the slave owners throughout Georgia soon responded to his request with "a howl of indignant condemnation." When Mercer attempted to impress laborers, public opposition became so strong that the Confederate government revoked Mercer's authority to seize slaves. Continuing to believe in the program, Mercer now had to rely upon Governor Brown and local sheriffs to provide him with slaves to work on the fortifications.

On December 28, 1862, General P. G. T. Beauregard expanded Mercer's district to include the entire state of Georgia except for the defenses of the Apalachicola River. Relieved of this command on April 26, 1864, Mercer was ordered to reinforce General Joseph E. Johnston in northwestern Georgia.

Mercer, along with the 1st Volunteer, 54th, 57th, and 63d Georgia regiments, which comprised almost all of the infantry in his former district, reached Dalton during the first week of May. Because it had not been depleted by combat and the rigors of field duty, Mercer's brigade was the largest in the Army of Tennessee. The battle-hardened veterans of Johnston's army viewed Mercer's men as being green and dubbed them "New Issue" and the "Silver Fork brigade." Despite their comparatively easy duty at Savannah, Mercer had trained and disciplined his men well. After they had proved themselves in their first engagement at Dalton, they too were veterans and no longer objects of derision.

Assigned to Major General William H. T. Walker's division of Lieutenant General William J. Hardee's corps, between May 7 and May 20 Mercer's brigade lost four killed and forty-one wounded. Walker praised the brigade for its performance in skirmishes around Marietta and at the Battle of Kennesaw Mountain June 27.

Between July 20 and September 1 the brigade lost forty-six killed, two hundred wounded, and fifty-nine missing, more than half on July 22 during the Battle of Atlanta. Walker was killed that morning and Mercer commanded the division, apparently to Hardee's satisfaction.

Because of Mercer's health, however, General John B. Hood did not consider him a suitable division commander. On July 24 Hood disbanded Walker's division and transferred Mercer's brigade to Major General Patrick R. Cleburne's division. The following morning Mercer resumed command of the brigade and reported to Cleburne. That evening he was relieved. When queried about this arrangement, General Braxton Bragg replied that Mercer, "whose age and physical inability unfit him for active service, I propose to order to Savannah." Mercer's uncertain health was undoubtedly responsible for the following statement in Cleburne's report of August 7: "If General Hardee expects Mercer's brigade to do any good a brigade commander is immediately necessary. Its present commander is not efficient." Mercer apparently commanded the brigade for the last time on August 31 near Jonesboro when, against orders, he made a successful but impetuous charge across the Flint River in pursuit of the fleeing Federals in an effort to drive them from yet another line of fortifications. Limited by his physical inability to remain in the field, he was relieved from duty that evening. He accompanied Hardee to Savannah, where he remained until its evacuation in December. Mercer was paroled at Macon on May 13, 1865.

By 1866 Mercer was engaged in the banking business in Savannah. Relocating to Baltimore in 1869, he worked as a commission merchant for three years. His health continued to decline, and in 1872 he moved to Baden-Baden, Germany, for a change of climate. He died there on June 9, 1877, and is buried there in an unknown grave.

Lawrence L. Hewitt

Derry, Joseph T., *Georgia*, Vol. VI in Evans, *Confederate Military History.*

Heitman, Francis B., *Historical Register and Dictionary of the United States Army, From Its Organization, September 29, 1789, to March 2, 1903* (Washington, 1903).

⋆ *William Miller* ⋆

William Miller probably sat for this portrait while colonel of the 1st Florida Infantry. (Museum of the Confederacy, Richmond, Va.)

William Miller was born in Ithaca, New York, on August 3, 1820; his parents moved to Louisiana with him while he was still an infant. After attending Louisiana College he studied law. He fought as an enlisted man under Major General Zachary Taylor during the Mexican War. Upon his return to the United States Miller moved to Pensacola, Florida, and established a law practice. In the late 1850s he also began operating a saw mill in Santa Rosa County.

He entered Confederate service in 1861 as the major in command of the 1st Florida Battalion. In late May or early June of 1862 Miller's battalion was merged with the remnant of the 1st Florida Regiment, which had been reduced to a battalion of six companies earlier that spring. Miller became colonel of the consolidated unit, which became known as the 1st Florida Regiment. As part of Brigadier General John C. Brown's brigade of Major General J. Patton Anderson's division, he led his regiment during General Braxton Bragg's invasion of Kentucky. After Brown was wounded in the early fighting at Perryville October 8, Miller assumed command of the brigade and his performance promised a glorious, promotion-filled career in the army.

Returning to Tennessee, the 1st Florida was united with the 3d to form the 1st and 3d Florida Consolidated Regiment. Miller commanded the new organization, which formed part of Brigadier General William Preston's brigade of Major General John C. Breckinridge's division. At Murfreesboro Miller's regiment was not heavily engaged on December 31 but around 4:00 P.M. on January 2, 1863, Miller led his regiment in a "magnificent but disastrous charge." Several Union brigades occupied a stretch of high ground immediately north of Stone's River, and Miller participated in Breckinridge's attempt to seize their position. Leading his men up the heights, Miller pressed on, his Floridians driving the Federals down the opposite slope. Pursuing the fleeing enemy, Miller started down the slope after them, but his command was now exposed to the fire of sixty Federal cannon on the opposite bank of the river. Union gunners quickly zeroed in, and Miller was wounded during the ensuing carnage, which stopped the Confederate advance. Miller's refusal to leave his men until the fighting had ended and his personally seeing to their safe withdrawal caused him to figure prominently in the official report filed by his brigade commander. The 1st and 3d Florida Consolidated began the charge with 531 officers and men; of these, five were killed, seventy-three were wounded, and forty-one were reported missing.

Returning to Florida for what proved to be a lengthy convalescence, Miller was appointed head of the C.S.A. Conscript Bureau for the Southern District of Florida and Alabama. On March 4, 1864, Union Brigadier General Alexander Asboth, Miller's western Florida nemesis who was headquartered at Fort Barrancas, reported that Miller was about to lead three hundred troopers in a raid on East Bay "for the purpose of gathering up all deserters and refugees secreted in the woods and abandoned farms...." Asboth reported on April 16: "Smaller parties [less than 2,000 each], under command of Colonel Miller, are controlling the country between Escambia and Blackwater Rivers (Escambia County), scouting down to Gashorn's Point, where a schooner of ours, while collecting logs, was fired upon and driven back on the 10th instant." Actually, all of Miller's forces combined totaled only about twelve hundred troops of all arms.

His abilities to raise forces and to limit Federal forays into the interior demonstrated to the Confederate government that he had sufficiently recovered to return to field duty. On August 2, 1864, the War Department relieved "Colonel" Miller as commandant of conscripts in Florida and ordered him to report for duty with the 1st and 3d Florida Consolidated, which was then serving as part of the Army of Tennessee near Atlanta. That same day, however, Miller was also commissioned a brigadier general.

On August 31 the newly commissioned brigadier surprised Major General Samuel Jones when he arrived at his headquarters at Charleston, South Carolina, and requested orders. Officially Jones was in the dark, but he surmised from a letter he had seen written by President Jefferson Davis to Florida Governor John Milton that Miller was to command the District of Florida. Finally, orders issued on September 8 placed Miller in command of the reserve forces of the state of Florida. Apparently this assignment did not sufficiently challenge Miller, and he offered his services to Brigadier General John K. Jackson, commanding the District of Florida with headquarters at Lake City. Jackson, who desperately needed qualified subordinates at the time, accepted Miller's offer and assigned him to command Sub-District No. 1. Jackson notified his superiors of this action on September 28. The War Department responded the following day by transferring Jackson and assigning Miller to command the District of Florida in addition to commanding the Florida reserves. On October 31 Miller had ninety-four officers and 1,220 men present for duty with fourteen cannon.

Reports from Asboth indicate that Miller continued to counter successfully every Federal incursion. And although burdened down with administrative paperwork, occasionally found an opportunity to return to the field. On March 2, 1865, Major General Jones assumed command of the District of Florida, and Miller commanded most of Jones' field troops. Miller participated in the repulse of a Federal amphibious expedition directed against St. Marks and Tallahassee in mid-March, and Jones' report of March 20 indicated that Miller did an outstanding job of containing Federal forays despite his inadequate force. Miller's success was primarily due to the constant overestimating of his forces by the Federals. As late as April 17 Asboth reported Miller's force to be twice its actual size.

When the war ended, Miller moved to Washington County; he continued in the lumber industry and diversified his operations by adding extensive agricultural holdings. Miller served in the state legislature in 1885 and was elected to the state senate in 1886 and again in 1903. He died on August 8, 1909, at Point Washington, Florida. First buried in the yard of his home, he was reinterred in St. John's Cemetery in Pensacola.

Lawrence L. Hewitt

Dickison, J. J., *Florida*, Vol. XI in Evans, *Confederate Military History*.

✮ *Young Marshall Moody* ✮

Young Moody stands at right. His collar insignia is blurred but appears to show at least one star, implying that this portrait was made either as lieutenant colonel or colonel of the 43d Alabama, though the button arrangement on his blouse is only that of a captain. (Cook Collection, Valentine Museum, Richmond, Va.)

Born in Chesterfield County, Virginia, on June 23, 1822, Young Marshall Moody moved to Alabama at the age of twenty. He settled in Marengo County, where he successively taught school, worked as a merchant, and served as clerk of the circuit court in the county. Appointed to that position in 1856 and elected to it in 1858, he resigned the post in 1861 to join the army.

Moody entered Confederate service as a captain in the 11th Alabama Infantry, which organized at Lynchburg, Virginia, in 1861. On October 22 the 11th Alabama was apparently assigned by the War Department to the brigade of Brigadier General Cadmus M. Wilcox of Major General James Longstreet's division, which formed part of General Pierre G. T. Beauregard's Potomac District, Department of Northern Virginia. Four days later, however, General Joseph E. Johnston ordered the brigade attached to the II Corps of the Army of the Potomac, and on November 14 the brigade formed part of that corps, which was commanded by Major General Gustavus W. Smith. On November 16 the War Department amended its orders of October 22 and now provided that Wilcox command a brigade of five Alabama regiments in Major General Earl Van Dorn's division in the Potomac District. The conflicting orders of Johnston, Beauregard, and the War Department apparently never resulted in a physical relocation of the regiment, which by mid-January 1862 was one in Wilcox' brigade of Smith's division in Beauregard's Potomac District. This organizational structure continued until March 23, when Wilcox' brigade was assigned to Major General Theophilus H. Holmes' command and ordered to report to Richmond. Six days later the brigade departed Richmond for Yorktown, where it would remain until Moody's departure, if in fact Moody had not already left the regiment to assist Archibald Gracie,

Jr., major of the 11th Alabama, in organizing a new regiment.

It is possible that recruiting efforts were initiated in late March and the 43d Alabama was organized in Mobile in May with Gracie as colonel and Moody as lieutenant colonel. Immediately ordered to Chattanooga, it formed part of Brigadier General Danville Leadbetter's brigade of Brigadier General Henry Heth's division. On August 10 Moody commanded the 43d when Gracie led it and another regiment on an expedition to Huntsville, Tennessee, where they routed approximately four hundred Unionists. During the invasion of Kentucky, Gracie led the brigade and Moody the regiment, although they saw little action in the Bluegrass State.

Moody became colonel of the regiment on November 4, following Gracie's promotion to brigadier general. As part of Gracie's brigade the 43d Alabama spent the winter of 1862–63 garrisoning Cumberland Gap. With the exception of an absence in late April Moody remained at Cumberland Gap with the 43d until August 3, when the regiment was ordered to Knoxville. Continuing on to northwestern Georgia, Moody led the regiment with distinction at Chickamauga on September 20. Moody was one of five officers in Gracie's brigade that Brigadier General William Preston, their division commander, praised for their "valuable services." Gracie reported that Moody, "always at the head of his regiment on the march, maintained the same position on the field, rallying and encouraging his men." The ninety-nine casualties in Moody's regiment included the lieutenant colonel and six company commanders.

The brigade was assigned to Major General Simon Bolivar Buckner's division following Chickamauga but was actually commanded by Brigadier General Bushrod Johnson. After participating in the siege of Chattanooga, the division was ordered to East Tennessee on November 22, but only two brigades, including Gracie's, departed before the balance was ordered back to Missionary Ridge the following day. After participating in the siege of Knoxville, which ended on December 4, Johnson's division fought on December 14 at Bean's Station, where Moody assumed temporary command of the brigade following the wounding of Gracie and the brigade's suffering casualties of twenty percent. The brigade then entered winter quarters at Morristown.

Ordered to Virginia in May 1864, Moody commanded the brigade during its relocation. Assigned to the division under Major General Robert Ransom, Jr., it occupied fortifications along the James River near Petersburg. Gracie led the brigade during the fighting at Drewry's Bluff (May 12–16), where Moody was severely wounded in the ankle. Upon his recovery Moody rejoined his regiment, which had remained in the trenches protecting Petersburg. By mid-August the brigade was again in Johnson's division, and by October 31 the division had been assigned to Lieutenant General Richard H. Anderson's IV Corps of the Army of Northern Virginia.

When Gracie was killed on December 2, 1864, Moody assumed command of the brigade, which consisted of the 41st, 43d, 59th, and 60th Alabama regiments and the 23d Alabama Battalion. He was promoted to brigadier general March 13, 1865, to rank from March 4. Moody's Alabamans remained in the trenches about Petersburg until the town was evacuated during the night of April 2. Although they were constantly fighting, a typical daily report for the brigade during the siege would read: "Nothing of importance has occurred along the line during the last twenty-four hours…killed, 1; wounded, 3." During a Confederate assault on March 25, however, the Federals captured the battle flag of the 43d Alabama. Suffering from an illness, Moody was confined to a wagon during the retreat westward. Although he was captured with the wagon train on April 8, the day before General Robert E. Lee surrendered at Appomattox Court House, Moody was paroled with his brigade: sixty-three officers and 515 men.

From Appomattox Moody went to Mobile. His success in business there influenced him to open a branch in New Orleans. Traveling to the Crescent City in the late summer of 1866, Moody contracted yellow fever. He died in New Orleans on September 18 and was interred there. Moody was described as having a "soldierly bearing, six feet in height, slender and erect," and a "very gentle disposition, and loved by the men of his command as a friend and protector, whom they obeyed because they held him in high esteem."

Lawrence L. Hewitt

Wheeler, Joseph, *Alabama*, Vol. VIII in Evans, *Confederate Military History*.

⭐ *John Creed Moore* ⭐

Moore was born in Hawkins County, Tennessee, on February 28, 1824. He attended neighborhood schools until he was sixteen and then spent four years at Emory and Henry College in Virginia. Moore graduated seventeenth in a class of forty-three at West Point in 1849. Entering the artillery service, he fought in the Seminole War of 1849–50. After several years of garrison duty on the frontier Moore resigned as a 1st lieutenant in 1855. He became a civil engineer and ran a railroad line in eastern Tennessee. In 1860 Moore took a position as a professor at Shelby College in Kentucky. He entered the Confederate army as captain of Company B, 1st Louisiana Heavy Artillery, on March 24, 1861.

He resigned on April 15, having received appointment as captain in the Regular Confederate army, and went to Galveston, Texas, to organize the defenses of that place. Brigadier General Earl Van Dorn, commanding the Department of Texas, recommended that the War Department authorize Moore to raise an infantry regiment. He organized a unit and became colonel of the 2d Texas Infantry on September 2. After drilling his men in camps at Galveston, Houston, and Beaumont, Moore received orders to go to Corinth, Mississippi, where his regiment arrived on April 1, 1862. Moore and his men were assigned to Brigadier General John K. Jackson's brigade, Brigadier General Jones M. Withers' division, II Corps, Army of Mississippi.

The Texans saw heavy fighting on the Confederate right flank during the first day at Shiloh on April 6, and were present at the surrender of Brigadier General Benjamin M. Prentiss' Union troops. Withers praised Moore, whom he said "displayed great gallantry" in the attack. The next day Moore exercised command of a temporary brigade of three regiments. Withers and General Braxton Bragg recommended him for promotion, and he was made a brigadier general on and to rank from May 26. (Moore had assumed command of a brigade in late April during the operations at Corinth.)

In June Moore was given command of a brigade in Brigadier General Dabney H. Maury's division of the Army of the West. Major General Sterling Price ordered Moore to Tupelo on September 16. There he was to organize and forward to the army a group of exchanged prisoners that had been designated to reinforce it. Moore led his brigade in the Battle of Corinth October 3–4, 1862. His men saw heavy fighting on the first day, capturing three enemy camps and a redoubt. The next day Moore's brigade attacked into the town, captured a Federal battery, and were finally driven out by a Union counterattack. While helping cover the army's retreat at Hatchie Bridge the next day, some of Moore's men were overrun by an enemy assault. Maury's division participated in the marches and skirmishes of Major General Earl Van Dorn's army in northern Mississippi during the next two months and was ordered to Vicksburg in late December.

The men went into camp near Snyder's Mill. For some unknown reason, on February 5, 1863, Lieutenant General John C. Pemberton asked that Moore be replaced in command of his brigade by Brigadier General Winfield S. Featherston, but the latter received a brigade in another division. On March 12 Moore's brigade was ordered to Yazoo City to support Major General William W. Loring's troops in stopping the Union Yazoo Pass Expedition. Moore and his men remained in the area until late April when they returned to the vicinity of Vicksburg.

A previously unpublished version of the only known uniformed photo of General Moore, dating from after May 1862. (Alabama Department of Archives and History, Montgomery, Ala.)

By this time Major General John H. Forney had replaced Maury as divisional commander. During the battles in the rear of Vicksburg in mid-May Pemberton assigned Moore to guard the river front at Warrenton and the approaches to Vicksburg from the lower ferries of the Big Black River. Moore's brigade took a position on the right of Forney's division in the Vicksburg trenches when the army fell back. His men occupied entrenchments on both sides of the Baldwin Road. On May 22 they repulsed several determined assaults by Union troops, and Moore's old regiment captured two enemy flags.

Moore was paroled at the surrender of Vicksburg on July 4, 1863. When exchanged in September, Moore's brigade had been reduced to three regiments, and his men went into camp at Demopolis, Alabama. Maury, now commander at Mobile, requested on August 31 that Moore be ordered to the District of the Gulf to take over Brigadier General Samuel B. Maxey's old brigade, but one of Maxey's colonels was promoted and given command of the brigade. Maury repeated his request for Moore's services on September 9, saying, "His ability, skill, and experience will be most important to me at this time." The War Department did not immediately act upon this request. About November 1 Moore and his brigade were ordered to reinforce General Braxton Bragg's army at Chattanooga. Moore was assigned to Major General Benjamin F. Cheatham's division, then temporarily commanded by Brigadier General John K. Jackson.

Placed on the northern slope of Lookout Mountain, the brigade took up positions near the Craven House, which Moore made his headquarters. He led his men to the aid of Brigadier General Edward C. Walthall's brigade during the Battle of Lookout Mountain on November 24. The Federals pushed Walthall's men back, but Moore was able to stop the enemy's advance with assistance from Brigadier General Edmund W. Pettus' brigade. He and his men fell back to Missionary Ridge about 2 A.M. on November 25. Union troops routed Jackson's brigade, which was stationed on Moore's right, after they broke through the Confederate center during the Battle of Missionary Ridge. Moore rallied some of Jackson's men and held back the Federals until dark, when he was ordered to retreat.

After these battles Moore joined Walthall and Pettus in criticizing Jackson's conduct at Lookout Mountain. They contended that Jackson had failed to give them proper instructions or inform them of the dispositions of troops on the mountain. In the years following the war Moore softened his criticism of Jackson.

On November 23 the War Department had ordered Moore to report to Mobile, but he did not report to his new station until early December. Maury placed him in command of the "eastern division" of the district on December 10. Moore resigned his commission on February 3, 1864, perhaps because of his assignment to an inactive theater. He appears to have returned to Galveston after his resignation.

Moore returned to teaching after the war and lived in Mexia and Dallas. He died on December 31, 1910, at Osage, Texas, and was buried there.

Arthur W. Bergeron, Jr.

Moore, John C., "Battle of Lookout Mountain," *Confederate Veteran,* VI (1898), pp. 426–29.

Roberts, O. M., *Texas,* Vol. XI in Evans, *Confederate Military History.*

Wooten, Dudley G., ed., *A Comprehensive History of Texas, 1685 to 1897,* 2 vols. (Austin, 1986).

✶ *Patrick Theodore Moore* ✶

A previously unpublished portrait of Patrick Moore as colonel of the 1st Virginia Infantry. (William A. Turner Collection)

Moore, near the war's close, as a brigadier, taken in Richmond in the winter of 1864-65. (Museum of the Confederacy, Richmond, Va.)

Patrick Moore was born on September 22, 1821, in Galway, Ireland. The son of a British diplomat, Moore came with his family to Canada in 1835 and then to Boston. In 1850 the twenty-nine-year-old Irishman settled in Richmond, Virginia, and became a merchant. He later joined a local militia company, rising to the rank of captain. When Virginia seceded in April 1861, Moore was commissioned colonel of the 1st Virginia.

Moore and the 1st Virginia were assigned to the brigade of James Longstreet at Manassas. On July 21 at the First Battle of Manassas while leading the regiment in a charge, Moore suffered a severe head wound that incapacitated him from field command. Both Colonel James Longstreet and Brigadier General P. G. T. Beauregard cited him in their reports for his conduct.

After his recovery Moore joined the staff of General Joseph E. Johnston as a volunteer aide-de-camp, serving under the general until the latter's wound at the Battle of Fair Oaks on May 31, 1862. During the Seven Days' Campaign he served in a similar capacity on the staff of Longstreet.

For the next two years Moore was assigned to court-martial duty in Virginia. In the summer and fall of 1864 he assisted Brigadier General James Kemper in the organization of the state's reserve forces. On September 23, 1864, Moore was promoted to brigadier general, effective October 20, and given a brigade of local defense troops in Lieutenant General Richard S. Ewell's corps. In April 1865 Moore's troops joined the Confederate retreat from Richmond and Petersburg. Although no record exists, he was probably captured in the debacle at Sayler's Creek on April 6. He was paroled on the 30th at Manchester, Virginia.

The war ruined Moore's mercantile business, so he opened an insurance agency in Richmond after the conflict. He died in the former Confederate capital on February 19, 1883, and was buried in Shockoe Cemetery.

Jeffry D. Wert

Hotchkiss, Jedediah, *Virginia*, Vol. III in Evans, *Confederate Military History.*

Another pose, probably from the same sitting. (Cook Collection, Valentine Museum, Richmond, Va.)

A variant pose of Moore made at the same sitting. (National Archives)

☆ *John Hunt Morgan* ☆

For some reason, almost all uniformed portraits of General John Hunt Morgan show evidence of artists' retouching. This was taken at the time of his wedding in 1863 or shortly thereafter. (Museum of the Confederacy, Richmond, Va.)

The favorite hero of the Civil War to many Kentuckians, John Hunt Morgan was born in Huntsville, Alabama, on June 1, 1825, but his family moved to Lexington, Kentucky, in 1831. Educated at home and at a local school, he entered Transylvania University in 1842. Suspended for dueling in 1844, he never resumed his studies. Refused a Marine commission in 1845, Morgan enlisted in Humphrey Marshall's 1st Regiment of Mounted Volunteers in 1846 when the Mexican War started. Soon promoted to 1st lieutenant, his major action was in February 1847 at Buena Vista, where Marshall's regiment performed well.

He became a successful businessman and a well-known man about town. Active in the state militia before it was terminated in 1854, he indulged his military tastes three years later by organizing an elite group called the Kentucky Rifles. Pro-Southern during the secession crisis, Morgan was relatively inactive, perhaps because his invalid wife died on July 21, 1861. After Kentucky's neutrality ended, Morgan and his rifles slipped away during the night of September 20, 1861, and joined the Confederate army near Bowling Green. Morgan became so engrossed in harassing the Federals with small raids, attacks on outposts, and imaginative deceptions that he was not sworn into Confederate service until October 27.

His raids and reconnaissance excursions continued after the Confederates withdrew from the state in mid-February 1862. The daring captain of a cavalry company, Morgan received favorable attention throughout the South, and on April 4, 1862, he was promoted to colonel. Six feet tall and 185 pounds, with dark hair and beard and blue-gray eyes, he was a dashing, romantic figure.

Morgan participated in a minor way at Shiloh (April 6–7, 1862), the only major battle of his Civil War career. His continued exploits in Tennessee and Kentucky attracted both attention and recruits, and he built his 2d Kentucky Cavalry Regiment to some nine hundred men and began acting as if he was a brigadier general.

Morgan was nearly captured at Lebanon, Tennessee, on May 6, 1862, but, still free, he destroyed important railroad tunnels at Gallatin on August 12, and with the aid of part of the 1st Kentucky Infantry Brigade, he eliminated a Union detachment of over two thousand men at Hartsville on December 7. Most of his growing fame, however, came from his raids into Kentucky. The first came in July 1862 when he looped through the central Bluegrass. During the late summer he returned with the Braxton Bragg–Kirby Smith invasion of the state, but he missed the Battle of Perryville on October 8, 1862. Instead of accompanying the Confederate army on its retreat, Morgan doubled back through the central part of the state and left via Hopkinsville. He was promoted to brigadier general on December 11, effective the same day, the day before his marriage to twenty-one-year-old Martha (Mattie) Ready of Murfreesboro. His Christmas Raid at the end of 1862, with 3,900 men—the most he ever commanded—resulted in the destruction of two large railroad trestles north of Elizabethtown and enhanced his reputation for that kind of warfare.

Morgan's leadership declined after 1862. Increased Union effectiveness was partly responsible, but even his brother-in-law and loyal second-in-command, future brigadier Basil Duke, suggested that Morgan's infatuation with his new bride diverted his attention from military affairs. (Another brother-in-law was Lieutenant General A. P. Hill.)

His reputation tarnished by some defeats in Tennessee, Morgan embarked upon his "great raid" in July 1863. Disobeying orders, he crossed the Ohio River at Brandenburg and created intense excitement in Indiana and Ohio. When he surrendered near West Point, Ohio, he had only a few hundred weary survivors with him. General Braxton Bragg, who had earlier praised Morgan, decided that "...Morgan never returned from a raid without his command broken and dissipated, with more lost than gained from the undertaking." Morgan did not work well under close supervision. Duke put it as gently as possible when he wrote: "He did not display so much ability when operating immediately with the army as when upon

An early-war portrait that some evidence suggests to be Morgan, probably as captain of the Lexington Rifles in 1861. (Museum of the Confederacy, Richmond, Va.)

Another early-war portrait believed to show Morgan, this time with a beard, and probably dating from later in 1861. (Courtesy of Dale S. Snair)

Though no uniform insignia is evident, Morgan is probably colonel of the 2d Kentucky Cavalry in this view. (Courtesy of Hunt-Morgan House, Lexington, Ky.)

An 1863 or 1864 portrait, probably his best known. (Museum of the Confederacy, Richmond, Va.)

Very likely taken at Morgan's last sitting before his death. (Museum of the Confederacy, Richmond, Va.)

A very slight variant from the last sitting. (Museum of the Confederacy, Richmond, Va.)

detached duty." Concerned about the decline in Morgan's usefulness, General William J. Hardee suggested to General Joseph E. Johnston, "Would it not be well for you to send for Morgan and have some talk with him?"

Imprisoned in the Ohio Penitentiary in Columbus, Morgan and six of his officers made a spectacular escape on November 27, 1863. In an effort to rehabilitate his reputation Morgan raided Kentucky again in 1864, departing quickly before he could be ordered not to go. Plundering and other outrages occurred, particularly at Mount Sterling, but Morgan refused his officers' request for immediate punishment of the offenders. He missed the steadying influence of Duke, still a prisoner, who had managed much of the discipline. George Prentice, editor of the Louisville *Journal*, once declared that "Someone might hit Duke on the head and knock Morgan's brains out." Morgan, who could not discipline himself, was unable to discipline his command.

Yet they had a last moment of glory at Cynthiana, Kentucky, on June 11, 1864, when they forced the surrender of General Edward H. Hobson and six hundred men. But Morgan ignored his own principles of hit-and-run warfare and remained encamped there. The next morning his command was surprised and smashed by General Stephen Burbridge. After this debacle Morgan was made commander of the Department of Western Virginia and East Tennessee. Charges continued to mount, and on August 22 he was relieved of departmental command. On August 30 Morgan was suspended from command, and a court of inquiry was ordered to convene in Abingdon on September 10.

But a Union force was threatening, and Morgan, ignoring his suspension, continued to direct his troops. Surprised at Greeneville, Tennessee, on September 3, 1864, he was killed by a rifle shot while trying to escape. Buried in Richmond, Virginia, his remains were reinterred in the Lexington, Kentucky, cemetery on April 17, 1868.

Lowell H. Harrison

Duke, Basil W., *History of Morgan's Cavalry* (Cincinnati, 1867).

Holland, Cecil Fletcher, *Morgan and His Raiders* (New York, 1943).

Ramage, James A., *The Life of General John Hunt Morgan* (Lexington, Ky., 1986).

Thomas, Edison H., *John Hunt Morgan and His Raiders* (Lexington, Ky., 1975).

✳ *John Tyler Morgan* ✳

Morgan was born on June 20, 1824, in Athens, Tennessee. He received his only formal education in a pioneer school there. His family moved to Calhoun County, Alabama, in 1833, and from that time the only teaching he got came from his mother. Morgan continued to read books that became available to him while he assisted his family in farming. Later he studied law in Tuskegee and in 1845 was admitted to the Alabama bar. Morgan practiced law in Tuskegee until 1855 when he moved to Dallas County. He then practiced in both Selma and Cahaba. In 1860 he was an elector on the ticket of John C. Breckinridge. His county elected him to the state secession convention early the next year, and he voted for the ordinance that took Alabama out of the Union.

Major General Jeremiah Clemens of the state militia appointed Morgan to his staff after the convention adjourned, and Morgan saw some duty at Fort Morgan. He resigned his position after that fort was transferred to the Confederate government in March 1861. The next month he enlisted in the Cahaba Rifles as a private. His company became Company G, 5th Alabama Infantry Regiment, and Morgan was elected major of that unit when it was organized on May 1.

The 5th Alabama, commanded by Colonel Robert E. Rodes, received orders to go to Virginia and was engaged in a skirmish at Fairfax Courthouse on July 17. General Pierre G. T. Beauregard praised Morgan for his role in the engagement, writing that he "acted with intelligent gallantry." Morgan's regiment was not engaged in the First Battle of Manassas four days later. By that time the regiment's term of service had expired in May 1862; Morgan had been promoted to lieutenant colonel. At the reorganization of the unit, he resigned and returned to Alabama to recruit a regiment of mounted troops.

His new command was mustered into service at Oxford, Alabama, on August 11, 1862, as the 51st Alabama Partisan Rangers. Morgan received orders in September to help protect the counties in northern Alabama through which the Mobile & Ohio Railroad ran. As Union troops were withdrawn from the area to oppose General Braxton Bragg's invasion of Kentucky, Morgan led his men into Middle Tennessee. He had orders to guard the Nashville & Chattanooga Railroad and to harass enemy soldiers stationed around Nashville.

In October the 51st Alabama joined Brigadier General Nathan Bedford Forrest's command. The men saw their first action in an attack on Federal pickets near Nashville on November 5. Morgan's command joined Brigadier General Joseph Wheeler's cavalry after Bragg's army returned to Tennessee from Kentucky. The Alabamans skirmished with Federal cavalry at LaVergne on December 26 and captured more than fifty enemy wagons in the vicinity four days later. Morgan and his men fought under Wheeler during the Battle of Murfreesboro December 31, 1862–January 2, 1863. They continued serving under that commander during the early months of the latter year.

Morgan was appointed a brigadier general on June 6, 1863, to succeed Rodes, who had been promoted to

No uniformed portrait of John T. Morgan has yet surfaced. This dates from the 1870s or later. (Virginia Historical Society)

major general. While on his way to Virginia, Morgan learned that the 51st Alabama had fought an engagement at Elk River Ford and that his former lieutenant colonel had been killed. He therefore declined the promotion and returned to his regiment. Morgan then assumed command of a brigade of Alabama regiments in Brigadier General William T. Martin's division. The brigade fought several skirmishes during the opening stages of the Chickamauga Campaign. Morgan led his men in the Battle of Chickamauga September 19–20, 1863, and was praised by Wheeler for his gallantry. Morgan's brigade participated in Wheeler's raid on Major General William S. Rosecrans' communications September 30–October 17.

Jefferson Davis appointed Morgan a brigadier general on November 17, 1863, to rank from November 16. The brigade accompanied Wheeler's cavalry to Knoxville and engaged in several skirmishes near there during Lieutenant General James Longstreet's campaign against the city. When Wheeler returned to the Army of Tennessee in late November, Martin assumed command of Longstreet's cavalry and Morgan took over Martin's old division of two brigades. Morgan's division covered the rear of Major General Lafayette McLaws' division during the retreat from Knoxville. Union troops attacked Morgan's men at Russellville on December 10 but were repulsed. The division fought again at Mossy Creek on December 29, and Martin complimented Morgan for his gallantry in that engagement.

Federal cavalry forces attacked Morgan's division near Fair Gardens on January 27, 1864, and routed it. The enemy captured Morgan's flag and his servant, and it is said that he barely escaped capture himself. Longstreet ordered Martin's cavalry to Dalton, Georgia, in mid-March. Morgan resumed command of his brigade when the troops reached the Army of Tennessee. Martin's horses were in such poor condition that his division was declared unfit for field service and was stationed near Rome to refit. On May 17 Morgan and his brigade reinforced infantry forces at Rome, which was threatened by Union troops. Shortly afterward Morgan was accused of drunkenness and placed under arrest. Brigadier General William W. Allen was given command of his brigade.

On August 5 Morgan was released from arrest and ordered to report to Brigadier General William H. Jackson. He was to collect the stragglers of the cavalry corps and "organize them for efficient service."

Shortly afterward he assumed command of two cavalry units that were to act as a reserve force. His men operated at first on the army's right flank. By August 31 his men were stationed at East Point, helping to protect it. During the next several days Morgan's little brigade helped to cover the army's flank as it retreated from Atlanta. The brigade acted for a time in a temporary division under Brigadier General Alfred Iverson and accompanied the army on its operations against the railroad from Chattanooga to Atlanta in October 1864.

Morgan served briefly under Wheeler while the latter opposed Major General William T. Sherman's March to the Sea. Later he was detached to help recruit new soldiers in Alabama. Morgan's last duty apparently was in attempting to raise and organize black troops in Alabama and Mississippi for the Confederate army. He was said to have been in the latter state when the war ended.

After the surrender Morgan returned to his law practice in Salem. He was a Democratic party elector in the presidential election of 1876 and was elected to the United States Senate in that year. Morgan was continually reelected and served in that body until his death. He supported states rights and white supremacy and favored construction of a canal through Central America. In his fifth term Morgan joined the Populist party. He died in Washington, D.C., on June 11, 1907, and was buried at Live Oak Cemetery in Selma.

Arthur W. Bergeron, Jr.

McMahon, C. W., "John Tyler Morgan of Alabama," *Confederate Veteran*, XXXIII (1925), pp. 408–409.

Owen, Thomas M., *History of Alabama and Dictionary of Alabama Biography*, 4 vols. (Spartanburg, S.C., 1978).

Wheeler, Joseph, *Alabama*, Vol. VII in Evans, *Confederate Military History*.

⋆ Jean Jacques Alfred Alexander Mouton ⋆

Mouton was born on February 18, 1829, in Opelousas, Louisiana, the son of a future governor of that state. He received his early education from Jesuit priests at St. Charles College in Grand Coteau. Mouton received an appointment to West Point and graduated thirty-eighth out of forty-four in the class of 1850. Although he was commissioned a lieutenant in the 7th United States Infantry, he resigned from the army on September 16, 1850, to return to his native state and become a planter. Mouton managed his father's plantation for two years and then became an assistant engineer for the New Orleans, Algiers, Attakapas, & Opelousas Railroad Company. He left this position in the latter part of 1853, purchased some land from his father, and operated his own sugar plantation.

In 1855 the governor of Louisiana appointed him as a brigadier general in the state militia. Mouton helped organize and drill vigilance committees to combat bands of outlaws who plagued the prairies of southwestern Louisiana, and succeeded in breaking up the bandits' organization. Shortly after the formation of the Confederate States of America, President Jefferson Davis commissioned Mouton as a captain in the provisional army.

On June 19 he assumed command of the Confederate Infantry School of Practice at Baton Rouge. This battalion of four companies of Confederate recruits moved to New Orleans on July 4, and Mouton resigned as their commander on July 16. He returned to Lafayette Parish and raised an infantry company. Taking his men to Camp Moore near Tangipahoa, he was elected

lieutenant colonel of a six-company battalion about September 28. The battalion was soon increased and on October 5 was mustered in as the 18th Louisiana Infantry Regiment. Mouton was elected colonel of the new unit.

He took his regiment to New Orleans for drill and instruction. About December 18 the regiment was placed in a brigade commanded by Brigadier General Daniel Ruggles. Ruggles' brigade left New Orleans on February 16, 1862, to reinforce General Pierre G. T. Beauregard's forces at Corinth, Mississippi. Ten days later Mouton led his regiment, an artillery battery, and a detachment of cavalry to Pittsburg Landing on the Tennessee River to observe and defend that vicinity. Mouton's troops fought a brief skirmish there on March 1, driving off the Federal gunboats *Tyler* and *Lexington*.

The 18th Louisiana soon established a camp at Monterey, Tennessee, and continued to picket the area for about three weeks before returning to Corinth. For a brief time during this period Mouton commanded a brigade of two regiments, a battalion, and a battery. Mouton's regiment made up part of Colonel Preston Pond's brigade of Ruggles' division, II Corps, in the Battle of Shiloh. On April 6 Mouton's men charged a superior enemy force and were driven back with a loss of about two hundred men killed and wounded. Mouton's clothes and saddle had a dozen bullet marks after the assault, and his horse was shot from under him. In the fighting on April 7 Mouton received a slight but painful wound in the face. He

---

Alfred Mouton, probably as colonel of the 18th Louisiana in the first year of the war. (Museum of the Confederacy, Richmond, Va.)

began recovering while in camp at Corinth, but when he became ill with erysipelas, he went to New Orleans for treatment.

For his gallantry at Shiloh Mouton was promoted to brigadier general on April 18, 1862, to rank from April 16. He had to escape from New Orleans when the Union fleet steamed up to the city, and he traveled to his home to continue his recovery. Mouton returned to duty in mid-October, at which time Major General Richard Taylor, commander of the District of West Louisiana, placed him in charge of the troops in the Bayou La Fourche region of the district. Union forces moved against Mouton's men later in the month. He failed to dispose his men properly to meet the threat, and then an attack of rheumatism prevented him from leading them in the battle at Labadieville fought on October 27. The Federal victory in that engagement forced Mouton to order his forces to retreat to the lower Bayou Teche region. There he ordered the erection of fortifications on Bisland Plantation near Centerville to prevent the Federals from advancing up the bayou.

Mouton retained command of Taylor's forces in south Louisiana until February 1863 when Brigadier General Henry H. Sibley replaced him. Mouton then took charge of a small brigade of Louisiana infantrymen. During the Battle of Bisland April 12–13, Mouton exercised immediate command of all of Taylor's troops on the east side of Bayou Teche, and his men repelled several Union attacks. On April 23 Taylor relieved Sibley from duty because of his poor conduct during the campaign, and Mouton again became commander of the forces in south Louisiana. Taylor ordered him to harass remaining Union troops in that region after the main Federal army marched against Port Hudson, but Mouton failed to take any aggressive steps to carry out those orders. He saw no real battlefield experience during the campaigns in south Louisiana during the remainder of 1863.

About December, Taylor formed a division of Mouton's old brigade and a Texas infantry brigade commanded by Brigadier General Camille J., Prince de Polignac, and he placed Mouton in charge of the division. Mouton's men marched to the area of Monroe in that month to cover the crossing of weapons from east of the Mississippi River. When the Red River Campaign began in March 1864, Mouton's division formed an integral part of Taylor's army. His men participated in the Battle of Mansfield on April 8 and

suffered heavy losses in helping to defeat Major General Nathaniel P. Banks' Federal forces. During the battle Mouton was killed by a number of Union soldiers who had started to surrender to him but then retrieved their muskets when they saw he was alone. One of Mouton's soldiers called him "one of the finest looking officers I ever saw" and said that Mouton was an outstanding drillmaster and a strict disciplinarian. Taylor wrote of Mouton: "While an excellent officer in the field, of great gallantry and fair qualifications, he is, I fear, unequal to the task of handling and disposing of any large body of troops." An officer serving under Mouton shared this judgment: "He never was made for an independent commander."

Buried initially in the cemetery at Mansfield, Mouton's body was moved to the family plot in Lafayette in 1867.

Arthur W. Bergeron, Jr.

Arceneaux, William, *Acadian General: Alfred Mouton and the Civil War* (Lafayette, 1981).

Bergeron, Arthur W., Jr., ed., *Reminiscences of Uncle Silas: A History of the Eighteenth Louisiana Infantry Regiment* (Baton Rouge, 1981).

✯ *Allison Nelson* ✯

No uniformed view of General Nelson is known. This portrait was probably taken when he sat in the Texas legislature in 1859-61. (Museum of the Confederacy, Richmond, Va.)

Born in Fulton County, Georgia, on March 11, 1822, Allison Nelson was a lawyer who entered politics in 1848 when he served one year in the Georgia legislature. Although he was Atlanta's mayor in 1855, Nelson was more interested in military affairs than in politics. During the Mexican War he raised a volunteer company and was elected its captain. He also served in the Cuban war for independence and was made a brigadier general by the Cuban leader Narcisco Lopez. In the mid-1850s he traveled westward and became involved in proslavery activities in "Bleeding Kansas." Finally, in 1856 Nelson moved to Bosque County, Texas, and became one of Texas' adopted sons. There he earned a reputation for being an effective Indian fighter and was elected to the Texas legislature in 1859.

Favoring secession, Nelson served in the 1861 secession convention. After secession he helped raise the 10th Texas Regiment and was elected its colonel. Nelson did an admirable job in equipping and training the raw recruits and was sent to join Major General Thomas Hindman's force in Arkansas. Hindman was impressed with Nelson and praised his well-equipped regiment. In June 1862 his men entrenched at Devall's Bluff with three guns to harass Union gunboats on the White River. Nelson was soon reinforced with an additional regiment, a battalion of infantry, and three artillery batteries. His force skirmished with a number of Federal gunboats and transports and turned them back before they reached Devall's Bluff.

Acting on Major General Theophilus Holmes' recommendation, Confederate authorities promoted Nelson to brigadier general on September 26, 1862, effective September 12. One day after contracting a fever, on September 28, he was given command of Holmes' 2d Division. He died in camp near Austin, Arkansas, on October 7, 1862, and was buried in Little Rock. General Holmes wrote, "I have the painful duty to perform of reporting the death of Brigadier-General Nelson, who commanded a division. He is an irreparable loss to me."

Terry L. Jones

Roberts, O. M., *Texas*, Vol. XI in Evans, *Confederate Military History*.

Webb, Walter Prescott, ed., *The Handbook of Texas* (Austin, 1952).

A previously unpublished portrait of General Nicholls taken after October 1862. (Museum of the Confederacy, Richmond, Va.)

Francis Redding Tillou Nicholls ★

Francis R. T. Nicholls was born on August 20, 1834, in Donaldsonville, Louisiana. The son of a prominent state legislator and judge, he was educated at local schools and the Jefferson Academy in New Orleans. In 1851 Nicholls entered West Point and graduated twelfth in his class four years later. He was commissioned a 2d lieutenant in the artillery and was sent to Fort Myers, Florida, during the Seminole crisis. He and eleven men garrisoned an isolated outpost known as Fort Deynaud for several months but never even saw an Indian. Nicholls then was transferred to Fort Yuma, California, where he fell ill. In 1856 he resigned from the army because of his illness and entered law school at the University of Louisiana (now Tulane University). He had just begun practicing law at Napoleonville when the Civil War began.

Organizing the Assumption Guards, Nicholls merged it with his brother's company to form a new unit called the United Guards. This company quickly disbanded, however, over a dispute about terms of enlistment. Nicholls then organized the Phoenix Guards and was elected captain. In June 1861 his company was placed in the 8th Louisiana Volunteers, and an election was held for regimental officers. Some of Nicholls' men accused him of using the company as a stepping stone to a higher rank. To allay this fear, Nicholls promised he would remain their captain for the duration of the war. Thus when others nominated Nicholls for colonel, he refused to campaign and instead supported Captain Henry Kelly. Just before the vote his men released him from his pledge, and Nicholls was elected lieutenant colonel. It was generally believed he would have been elected colonel without opposition had it not been for the promise made to his men.

Nicholls first saw combat July 21 at First Manassas, where his regiment received some artillery fire while in reserve at Mitchell's Ford. During Major General "Stonewall" Jackson's Valley Campaign Nicholls accompanied the 8th Louisiana, part of Richard Taylor's brigade, to Front Royal, Virginia, where he commanded the skirmish line during the short engagement there. On May 25, 1862, his regiment was placed on Taylor's far left during the attack on Winchester. In this assault Nicholls' left elbow was shattered by a ball that took him out of action. In an attempt to save his arm, the surgeons waited a week before deciding that amputation was necessary. As the doctors operated, the Confederate army retreated up the Valley and left Nicholls to be captured. For some time afterward rumors spread that he had been captured in civilian clothing and was arrested as a spy. These stories were unfounded, however, and Nicholls was exchanged in September.

After being exchanged Nicholls was temporarily sent to Texas. He was there in June 1862 when he was promoted to colonel and given command of the 15th Louisiana Volunteers. Nicholls was unable to return to this regiment in Virginia, however, and stayed in Texas. On October 14, 1862, he was appointed brigadier general, to rank from October 14, and was given command of the 2d Louisiana Brigade, Army of Northern Virginia. Nicholls was pleased but adamant in his assertion that he had not applied for either promotion.

Nicholls returned to Virginia and his brigade in January 1863. His first engagement as brigade commander was at Chancellorsville. Serving in Jackson's Corps,

A bust portrait possibly from the same sitting. (Museum of the Confederacy, Richmond, Va.)

197

Nicholls' youth is evident. He is not yet thirty, but the war's ravages on him are obvious. (Cook Collection, Valentine Museum, Richmond, Va.)

A pose from what was likely Nicholls' last wartime sitting. (Courtesy of the New-York Historical Society, New York City)

Nicholls' brigade was in the second line of the attack on May 2 when Jackson crushed the Federal flank. While trying to collect his men after dark, Nicholls came under artillery fire. A solid shot ripped through his horse and tore off Nicholls' left foot. He was later found by an ambulance crew, but they left him for dead after discovering his severed leg and empty sleeve. Fearing he would bleed to death, Nicholls felt his leg and "found to my utter surprise that the wound did not bleed at all." He was finally carried to a hospital by his men in a makeshift blanket litter. After suffering two serious wounds in his first two major battles, Nicholls was believed by his men to be jinxed.

Nicholls recuperated in Lynchburg and was eventually given command of that post, since he was unfit to retake the field. There in June 1864 he faced the Yankee raiders of Major General David Hunter alone before being aided by Lieutenant General Jubal Early's corps. Shortly afterwards Nicholls was transferred to the Trans-Mississippi Department, where he commanded the Volunteer and Conscript Bureau for a brief period before the Confederate surrender.

After the war Nicholls entered Louisiana politics. In 1876 his Democratic friends nominated "all that is left of General Nicholls" for governor. Nicholls also quipped that he might as well be governor because he was too one-sided to be a judge. The election was a hotly contested one, and both parties claimed victory. Both refused to concede, and a dual government was set up in Louisiana before the federal authorities finally recognized Nicholls as governor. To his dying day Nicholls declared he had made no political deals to win this recognition.

After his governor's term expired, Nicholls spent a few years in semiretirement, dabbling in law and business ventures in New Orleans. In 1886 he was appointed to the board of visitors for the United States Military Academy, serving for a time as its president. In 1888 he was elected to a second term as governor and helped rid Louisiana of the notoriously corrupt Louisiana Lottery Company. From 1892 to 1911 Nicholls was on the Louisiana supreme court, sometimes serving as chief justice. He died on his plantation near Thibodeaux on January 4, 1912, and was buried in Thibodeaux's St. John's Episcopal Cemetery.

Terry L. Jones

Jones, Terry L., *Lee's Tigers: The Louisiana Infantry in the Army of Northern Virginia* (Baton Rouge, 1987).

Lathrop, Barnes F., ed., "An Autobiography of Francis T. Nicholls, 1834–1881," *Louisiana Historical Quarterly*, XVII (1934).

Francis Nicholls as Lieutenant colonel of the 8th Louisiana in late 1862 after release from prison and amputation of his left arm. (Courtesy of Evans J. Casso)

✴ *Lucius Bellinger Northrop* ✴

Surprisingly, no portrait of General Northrop in uniform has been found. This was probably taken very soon after the war. (Warner, *Generals in Gray*)

One of the most controversial generals in the Confederate service, Northrop was a native of Charleston, South Carolina, born September 8, 1811. In 1827 he secured an appointment to the United States Military Academy at West Point, where as a first-year cadet he may have become acquainted with a graduating senior, Jefferson Davis. Northrop himself graduated in 1831 and soon went to the West, where he became a lieutenant in the Dragoon regiment commanded by Colonel Henry Dodge, that formed at Missouri's Jefferson Barracks in 1833. Fellow lieutenants were Davis, Theophilus Holmes, Edwin Sumner, and others, with whom close friendships soon grew. Davis and Northrop especially became intimate friends and formed a mutual dislike for their crusty Major Richard Mason. That fall Northrop marched with the regiment to Fort Gibson, Arkansas, where he became known as a fun-loving and not especially meticulous young officer who rather thought his friend Davis to be "too rigid in the minutiae of the service."

Indeed, Northrop was lax enough to get himself into trouble. In the fall of 1834, aged just twenty-three, he already evidenced a tendency to frail health and left his regiment without permission in order to recuperate. Davis himself was ordered to arrest his friend though no court-martial ensued. In December, however, he was confined to quarters for negligence of duty when he attended a horse race instead of overseeing a working party, then ignored the order and left his tent anyhow, resulting in formal charges. The court-martial was held in January 1835, though Northrop suffered no lasting injury from the proceedings, and then immediately afterward he testified in defense of his friend Davis at *his* court-martial, thus cementing a special tie and already close relationship.

The balance of Northrop's service in the Old Army was undistinguished until 1839, when he took a wound in the Seminole War that put him out of active service almost completely. He spent the next several years at home in Charleston recuperating, while still on sick leave from the army, and during that time studied medicine in the North and even commenced to practice briefly, at least on himself. For the rest of his life he would be sickly and probably a hypochondriac, prone to such odd remedies as wearing newspapers inside his shirt to keep out the cold and ward off rheumatism. The army dropped him from its rolls in 1848 for practicing a profession, but when his friend Davis became secretary of war in 1853, Northrop was soon reinstated and promoted to captain, though he stayed on sick leave until 1861 and continued his medical practice without interference.

When secession came Northrop was among the first to go to Montgomery, Alabama, to offer his services and apparently to capitalize on his friendship with the new Confederate president. He and Davis were often seen walking together deep in discussion, and one of Davis' first appointments made Northrop a colonel in charge of the Commissary Department.

In this post for almost four years, Northrop would stir up controversy and animosity and earn for himself the almost universal obloquy of soldiers and civilians alike. In some degree, he never had a chance. The fact of his being a favorite of the President's guaranteed some criticism, for as a vocal opposition party grew within the Confederacy, all friends of Davis, especially those he sustained in the face of manifest demonstrations of incompetence, came under fire. Furthermore, the task of feeding the growing armies of the Confederacy was a nightmare job, involving not just finding the foodstuffs but also managing to get it to the armies. Worst of all, however, was Northrop's utter lack of ability for the task. He could not organize, nor could he manage either men or resources efficiently. By 1863, if not before, he had lost the respect of almost everyone in the War Department, a condition made worse by Davis' obstinate support of him and Northrop's equally obvious—to his foes— fawning and sycophancy with the President.

Eventually, however, even Davis grew impatient with his old friend and relations became strained by 1864, with Davis more than once indulging in out-

bursts that sent Northrop away from him sulking. As if to make up, Davis appointed Northrop a brigadier on November 26, 1864, but thereafter did not risk sending the appointment on to the Senate for confirmation, as surely it would have been rejected. A wave of indignation swept official circles when Northrop's commission became known and the new general became even more officious and self-important than before.

In the end Northrop had to go. When Davis sought to appoint Major General John C. Breckinridge secretary of war, Breckinridge made Northrop's removal a condition of acceptance and the president gave in. On February 15, 1865, he was formally replaced though actually relieved of duty on January 30. Within three weeks his successor, Isaac M. St. John, was winning plaudits from Lee for having his army better fed than it had been for months during the last of Northrop's tenure.

Northrop traveled with the fleeing government at war's end but was taken prisoner in North Carolina on June 20 and imprisoned for four months on suspicion of starving Federal prisoners of war. He returned to Charlottesville, Virginia, where he farmed as his health allowed until 1890 when he became paralyzed and went into the Pikesville, Maryland Confederate Home. There he died on February 9, 1894, and was buried in Baltimore's New Cathedral Cemetery. While his devotion to the Confederate cause can hardly be doubted, it is also evident that he would have served it best by staying home and practicing medicine. In uniform, Northrop only added to his nation's ills.

William C.Davis

Evans, Clement A., *The Civil History of the Confederate States*, Vol. I in Evans, *Confederate Military History*.

Hay, Thomas R., "Lucius B. Northrop; Commissary General of the Confederacy," *Civil War History*, IX (March 1963).

✫ *Edward Asbury O'Neal* ✫

No uniformed portrait of General O'Neal has come to light. This probably dates from his years as governor of Alabama in the 1880s. (Virginia Historical Society)

An excellent illustration of the vagaries of making generals in the Confederacy was presented by Edward A. O'Neal, born September 20, 1818, in Madison County, Alabama. His Irish-born father died when the infant Edward was but three months old, and his mother raised him and his older brother to manhood. O'Neal attended LaGrange College, graduating first in his class in 1836, then studied law for several years before being admitted to the Alabama bar in 1840. O'Neal opened his own practice in Florence and devoted the next two decades to the law and local politics. He served as solicitor of the local judicial circuit and ran unsuccessfully for Congress from his district. More to the point, he early identified himself with the more ardent secessionist sympathizers in the state.

When war came in 1861, O'Neal enlisted in what was to become the 9th Alabama and was elected its major upon formal organization on June 26, 1861. Four months later on October 21 he was promoted to lieutenant colonel and then in March 1862 assumed the colonelcy of the 26th Alabama effective April 2. The regiment saw its first active field service on the Virginia Peninsula in the fighting at Williamsburg May 5 and Seven Pines May 31–June 1. At the latter O'Neal was wounded while commanding his regiment in the brigade of Robert Rodes during operations on the Williamsburg Road. His horse was killed under him, and O'Neal himself was felled by a shell fragment.

O'Neal was back on duty by late summer and marched with the Army of Northern Virginia into Maryland. He temporarily commanded Rodes' Alabama brigade but returned to his own regiment only to be wounded in the thigh during the Battle of Boonsboro on September 14. Again O'Neal recuperated and again returned to the army. With Rodes absent once more O'Neal was given command of the Alabama brigade consisting of the 3d, 5th, 6th, 12th, and 26th regiments and subsequently led the brigade May 1–4, 1863, at Chancellorsville. In the fighting on the morning of May 3 O'Neal was wounded yet again while leading the brigade against Federal positions just north of the Orange Plank Road. His injury was serious enough to put him out of action but not so severe that he had not rejoined his command for the Gettysburg Campaign in June and July. Impressed with O'Neal's performance, General Robert E. Lee recommended that he be promoted to brigadier and permanent command of the brigade, Rodes having risen to divisional command. President Davis made the appointment effective June 6 and sent it to Lee, but the Battle of Gettysburg interfered.

During the fighting on the afternoon of July 1, Lee ordered Rodes to send his division in an attack against the faltering Union center on the Mummasburg Road. The assault was not well managed by Rodes, and O'Neal himself did not accompany his brigade in the movement. Worse, he did not send his command toward the point mandated by Rodes and allowed a fourth of his men to sit out the attack entirely. O'Neal's brigade was resoundingly repulsed, putting another brigade to rout in the process and endangering Rodes' remaining brigades for a time. Apparently this performance shook Lee's opinion of O'Neal, for he never gave the colonel his promotion to brigadier and instead withdrew his recommendation, leading Davis to cancel the promotion. Moreover, permanent command of Rodes' old brigade now went to another officer.

Colonel O'Neal remained with the army in Virginia through the Mine Run Campaign in the fall, then returned to Alabama during the winter to recruit replacements, having reverted to command of only his old regiment. When Union Major General William T. Sherman and General Joseph E. Johnston began their movements from Dalton, Georgia, in the spring of 1864, O'Neal was ordered to join James Cantey's brigade, and he once more rose to brigade command by default when Cantey assumed a division in the subsequent operations in the Atlanta Campaign. O'Neal led the 17th, 26th, 29th, and 37th Alabama regiments throughout the campaign May to September; then for unknown reasons he was relieved not only of command of the brigade but was also removed from his regiment, which was subsequently led by a mere captain. His removal came just after Johnston's replacement by General John B. Hood, though this may have been coincidental. His many wounds may have unfitted him for field service or he may have failed to give superiors satisfaction, as at Gettysburg. Whatever the cause, O'Neal was assigned the inglorious task of chasing deserters in northern Alabama for the duration of the war.

O'Neal returned to Florence and his law practice after the surrender and after a decade assumed prominence in state Democratic affairs. He rose through a succession of state offices and in 1882 was elected governor, winning a second term two years later. After leaving office O'Neal returned to the law until he died November 7, 1890. He was buried in Florence. In the wake of his death any judgment of O'Neal's activities must be equivocal. Certainly he lost Lee's confidence and perhaps that of Johnston or Hood as well. His commission as a brigadier was never confirmed by the Senate nor was the document itself ever given to him, making him, in a way, a general who never was.

William C. Davis

Bigelow, John, *The Campaign of Chancellorsville* (New Haven, Conn., 1910).

Wheeler, Joseph, *Alabama*, Vol. VII in Evans, *Confederate Military History*.

✦ *Richard Lucian Page* ✦

No uniformed portrait of General Page has been found. His resemblance to his first cousin Robert E. Lee is evident in this 1880s portrait. (Albert G. Shaw Collection, Virginia Historical Society, Richmond, Va.)

Page was born in Clarke County, Virginia, on December 20, 1807. He was appointed as a midshipman in the United States Navy on March 12, 1824. Page served on a number of vessels on a number of stations during the succeeding years. He was promoted lieutenant on March 26, 1834, and to commander on September 14, 1855. He served in the Pacific squadron during the Mexican War and spent two years as assistant inspector of ordnance at the Norfolk navy yard.

When Virginia seceded in April 1861, Page was again ordnance officer at that navy yard, and he resigned his commission to accept an appointment as an aide to Governor John Letcher. In that capacity Page began organizing a navy for the state. He also supervised the erection of and commanded batteries on the lower James River and other streams in that area. Page received a commission as commander in the Confederate navy on June 10 and became ordnance officer of the navy yard at Norfolk.

During the Battle of Port Royal, South Carolina, on November 7 he was second in command to Captain Josiah Tattnall. He returned to the Norfolk area and commanded batteries at Cedar Point, Barrel Point, Pagan Creek, and Gloucester Point during succeeding months. Page helped man a cannon in the Sewell's Point battery during the operations of the *Virginia* in Hampton Roads in March 1862, and the gun crew fired on several Union vessels. About this time he was promoted to the rank of captain.

Page supervised the removal of machinery and other stores from Norfolk to Charlotte, North Carolina, upon the evacuation of the former place. He established shops and laboratories at Charlotte for the manufacture of projectiles, gun carriages, and other naval supplies. Eventually the Charlotte Naval Works constructed marine engines, shafts, and other heavy equipment. In March 1863 Page became commanding officer of the Savannah squadron but was replaced in May when he returned to Charlotte. Confederate naval historian J. Thomas Sharf wrote that during Page's service there the works "became of inestimable value to the Confederacy."

Jefferson Davis arranged for Page's appointment as a brigadier general in the army on March 7, 1864, effective March 1, and had orders issued to him to report for duty at Mobile, Alabama. Major General Dabney H. Maury had requested promotion of an army officer to replace Brigadier General Edward Higgins as commander of the outer defenses of Mobile Bay. Davis decided instead to promote Page and assign him to that post. There is no evidence why Davis chose Page, but his correspondence indicates that he did not approve of the man Maury had recommended.

Page reached Fort Morgan on March 12 and quickly made a favorable impression on the officers and men of the garrison. One of the officers wrote: "We are very well pleased with our new general, although he hasn't found out the difference between a fort and a ship yet. He is a tall erect old fellow with the air of a man who has seen service and been accustomed to exercise command. A great disciplinarian, but very quiet and gentlemanly with it all." From his headquarters in Fort Morgan Page commanded the 3d Brigade, District of the Gulf, which consisted of the garrisons of Fort Morgan, Fort Gaines, and Fort Powell. Rumors of an impending Union naval attack on Mobile Bay began to grow during the summer, making Page apprehensive and pessimistic. He had no confidence in any of the Confederate warships in the bay except the ironclad ram *Tennessee*. Some of Page's subordinates had as little faith in those gunboats and less in their commanders. A lieutenant expressed the opinion that the officers of the Mobile squadron had caused the confusion he saw in General Page's mind, thus hindering his ability to command the fort. On the eve of the Battle of Mobile Bay Maury seemed disposed to replace Page, writing, "General Page is too despondent. He seems to see only the weak points of these forts. We need a buoyant man there."

Admiral David G. Farragut's Federal squadron ran into the bay past the forts on August 5 despite the best efforts of the Confederate cannoneers to stop them.

The commander of Fort Powell evacuated his post that night. On the evening of August 8 the officer in charge of Fort Gaines went aboard Farragut's flagship to negotiate a surrender of his garrison. While he was away, Page visited Gaines in an attempt to stop the proceedings but had no success. Page dubbed the surrender a "deed of dishonor and disgrace to its commander and garrison." The surrender of Fort Gaines occurred early the next morning, and that afternoon the Federals demanded an unconditional surrender of Fort Morgan after the fleet had bombarded it for several hours. Page refused, stating that he would hold out until he had no remaining means of defense.

The Federals established land batteries east of the fort, and those guns joined the ones of the fleet in pounding the fort for the next two weeks. Throughout all of the Federal bombardments Page moved about the fort sending officers and men to secure places while exposing himself a number of times to enemy fire. Finally Page decided on the morning of August 23 to surrender. A Federal general who witnessed the ceremonies recorded this description of the Confederate commander: "Page, in a plain suit of citizen's clothing, looked very stiff.... From the starched manner in which the late lord of Fort Morgan bore himself, I could well understand why our sailors had dubbed him 'Ramrod Page.'" Following the siege of Fort Morgan, Dabney Maury could find no fault in Page's actions there: "From all that is known of the conduct of this officer and the garrison under his orders, it is believed that they nobly strove to redeem the disgrace upon their arms inflicted by the hasty and unsoldierlike surrender of Fort Powell and Gaines."

Page was eventually sent to Fort Delaware and was released there on July 24, 1865. He returned to Norfolk and was superintendent of schools there from 1875 to 1883. Page died on August 9, 1901, at Blue Ridge Summit, Pennsylvania. He was buried in Cedar Hill Cemetery at Norfolk.

Arthur W. Bergeron, Jr.

Bergeron, Arthur W., Jr., *Confederate Mobile, 1861–1865* (Jackson, 1991).

Hotchkiss, Jedediah, *Virginia*, Vol. IV in Evans, *Confederate Military History*.

✸ Joseph Benjamin Palmer ✸

Palmer was born in Rutherford County, Tennessee, on November 1, 1825. Orphaned in infancy, he was raised by his grandparents. He matriculated at Union University in Murfreesboro, Tennessee, and in 1848 was admitted to the bar. The same year he was elected as a Whig to the state legislature representing Rutherford County and was reelected in 1851. Additionally, from 1855 to 1859 Palmer served as mayor of Murfreesboro. He opposed secession and supported the Constitutional Union ticket and its candidates, John Bell and Edward Everett, in the 1860 presidential campaign, arguing that the South should fight for its rights by remaining in the Union. But like most Southerners, he held that his first allegiance was to his state.

On the secession of Tennessee Palmer listened to her voice and raised a Rutherford County company of which he was elected captain. His company, along with nine others, was organized at Camp Trousdale on June 11, 1861, as the 18th Tennessee Volunteer Infantry. Palmer was elected colonel of the regiment at its initial muster. While posted at Camp Trousdale, the regiment was armed with substandard weapons—flintlock muskets. In September Palmer and his regiment were sent to Bowling Green, Kentucky, where they were brigaded with the 3d and 23d Tennessee under John Calvin Brown.

On February 8, 1862, Palmer and his unit were rushed to Fort Donelson to assist in the defense of that bastion, then threatened by a Union amphibious force that had captured Fort Henry on the 6th. Palmer led his men into battle on the 15th, and the next day they were included in the "unconditional surrender" of the thirteen thou-

in Boston harbor, Palmer was held there until his exchange in August. He rejoined the regiment's company officers and enlisted men, who had also been exchanged, at Vicksburg, Mississippi, on September 26. At the unit's reorganization, Palmer, given a vote of confidence, was reelected colonel. Palmer and his Tennesseans, traveling by rail, proceeded from Mississippi to Middle Tennessee where they reported to John C. Breckinridge on October 18 at Murfreesboro. Palmer was placed in charge of a brigade that included the 18th, 26th, 28th, and 32d Tennessee infantry regiments and a Georgia battery. He led the brigade at Stone's River from the beginning of the fight on December 31 until noon on January 2, 1863, when Brigadier General Gideon J. Pillow arrived from Chattanooga and took command. At 4 P.M. Palmer led his regiment in Breckinridge's savage but futile onslaught. Palmer was wounded in three places but refused to go to the rear until dark. His injuries proved to be so severe that they incapacitated him for duty until summer.

He rejoined the 18th Tennessee in time to participate in the Tullahoma Campaign (June 23–July 4) and the retreat across the Tennessee River. His regiment was assigned to John C. Brown's brigade, and on July 31 Brown's unit was one of the three brigades constituting Major General A. P. Stewart's "Little Giant" division. Palmer and his Tennesseans spent the last half of August and the first week of September in and around first Loudon and then Charleston, Tennessee. He and his regiment saw bitter fighting at Chickamauga on

General Palmer's only known uniformed portrait, probably taken in 1865. (Albert G. Shaw Collection, Virginia Historical Society)

208

September 19 and 20. On the former day in a savage attack near the Brotherton Cabin the brigade battered Horatio Van Cleve's Union division, surged across the Lafayette Road, and gained the Glenn-Kelly Road before being checked by James S. Negley's division and compelled to retreat. In this fighting Colonel Palmer was severely wounded as he led his men forward. General Brown, commenting on the advance and repulse, noted, "I felt deeply the loss of Colonel Palmer's services on the field, for with him on the right, the gallant [Edward C.] Cook in the center, and the brave [John M.] Lilliard on the left, I felt the utmost confidence in the unwavering steadiness of the line."

It took Palmer months to recuperate from this wound, and it was early July 1864 before he returned to duty. On doing so, he assumed command of Brown's brigade, then posted on the Chattahoochee, following the army's July 2 evacuation of the Kennesaw line. Carter L. Stevenson commanded the division and Lieutenant General John B. Hood the corps. Palmer's brigade was comprised of five Tennessee infantry regiments—the 3d, 18th, 26th, 32d, and 45th—and the 23d Tennessee Infantry Battalion. Hood soon succeeded Joseph E. Johnston as commander of the Army of Tennessee and S. D. Lee took over the corps. Palmer and his brigade participated in the defense of Atlanta July 29–August 25 and were under fire for twenty-six continuous days. On August 18 while on detached duty, he saw the greater part of his old regiment—the 18th Tennessee—outflanked and captured.

Four weeks after the evacuation of Atlanta, Palmer crossed the Chattahoochee at the head of his brigade in a campaign that saw General Hood maneuver and march through the mountains of northwest Georgia and take position at Tuscumbia and Florence, Alabama. He was promoted brigadier general on December 7, 1864, to rank from November 15, and on the 18th, three days before Hood put his columns in motion to begin his ill-fated Middle Tennessee campaign, Palmer's responsibilities increased when his and Colonel Alexander W. Reynolds' brigades—the 58th and 60th North Carolina and the 54th and 63d Virginia—were consolidated and he took command of the reorganized brigade. Palmer's brigade was fortunate in that it reached Franklin too late on the afternoon of November 30 to participate in that holocaust. Palmer and his brigade, when the army entrenched on the approach to Nashville, were detached on December 6 and sent to cooperate with Major General Nathan Bedford

Forrest's cavalry corps in wrecking the Nashville & Chattanooga Railroad and threatening Murfreesboro.

The next day Palmer and his brigade met the enemy in the battle of the Cedars, northwest of Fortress Rosecrans, and panicked, earning Forrest's ire. Palmer was still with Forrest on the evening of the 16th when news was received of Hood's Nashville disaster, and accompanied the cavalry corps on the march to Columbia, where on the evening of the 18th they rendezvoused with the army. On the retreat from Columbia to the crossing of the Tennessee River (December 20–28) Palmer led a two-brigade division that reported to Major General Edward C. Walthall and with Forrest's cavalry fended off pursuing Federal columns.

Palmer, after a halt to rest and reorganize his troops at Corinth in early January 1865, accompanied the Army of Tennessee on its roundabout redeployment to North Carolina. The army's decimated thirty-seven Tennessee infantry regiments and two battalions reporting to General Joseph E. Johnston were then consolidated into four regiments and assigned to a brigade led by Palmer. Palmer's brigade was attached to Major General Ben Cheatham's division. As a part of Lieutenant General William J. Hardee's corps they battled the enemy one last time March 19–21 at Bentonville, where they scored an initial success, capturing a number of prisoners. Palmer was included in the forces surrendered by General Johnston at Durham Station on April 26, and he was paroled at Greensboro, North Carolina, on May 1. Palmer had the responsibility of conducting the army's Tennessee troops back to their home state from North Carolina, marching them to Greeneville, Tennessee, from where they rode the railroad cars to Chattanooga.

In the postwar years Palmer resumed his Murfreesboro law practice, and though asked on several occasions to campaign for governor as a Democrat, he declined. He died at his Murfreesboro home on November 4, 1890, and was buried in the city's Evergreen Cemetery.

Edwin C. Bearss

Horn, Stanley F., ed., *Tennesseans in the Civil War: A Military History of Confederate and Union Units with Available Rosters of Personnel*, Pt. I (Nashville, 1964).

Neff, Robert O., *Tennessee's Battered Brigadier: The Life of Joseph B. Palmer* (1988).

★ *Mosby Monroe Parsons* ★

Mosby M. Parsons was born on May 21, 1822, at Charlottesville, Virginia, and headed west as a youth, settling in Cole County, Missouri. He read law, was admitted to the bar, and developed an extensive practice. Soon after the May 1846 declaration of war against Mexico he was elected and commissioned a captain in the 1st Missouri Mounted Infantry and served with distinction under Colonel Alexander Doniphan. He was cited for gallantry at the Battle of Sacramento February 28, 1847. Upon being mustered out of service Parsons returned to Missouri and his law practice. From 1853 to 1857 he was attorney general of Missouri and in the latter year was elected as a Democrat to the state senate.

During the crisis that followed the election of Abraham Lincoln as sixteenth president and the secession of the lower South, Parsons was an active and vociferous ally of Governor Claiborne F. Jackson in futile efforts to take Missouri out of the Union.

Pro-Union forces led by Brigadier General Nathaniel Lyon and Frank Blair having gained the upper hand, Parsons organized and commanded the 6th Division, Missouri State Guard, raised in the State's Sixth Congressional District in central Missouri. He held the rank of brigadier general. As such, he led the 6th Division in the battles of Carthage (July 5), Wilson's Creek (August 10), and the Siege of Lexington (September 12–20, 1861). During the retrograde from Lexington to Springfield and beyond, Parsons and his Missourians clashed with Kansas jayhawkers near Clintonville and on the Pomme de Terre October 12–13.

Parsons missed the Pea Ridge campaign but rejoined his division in late March 1862 on the march

place he assumed command of all the units of the Missouri State Guard in the Army of the West. Parsons and the guard made the trip by boat and then rail to Corinth, Mississippi, where they participated in the defense of that key railroad junction in May. In mid-July following the Confederate evacuation of Corinth and the retreat to the Tupelo area, Parsons and the guard were relieved of duty with Major General Earl Van Dorn's Army of the West and returned to the Trans-Mississippi, crossing the Mississippi River at Napoleon and reporting to Major General Thomas C. Hindman at Little Rock some three weeks later. Late September found Parsons posted at Yellville commanding a reinforced brigade of Missourians and Arkansans.

On November 5 Parsons entered Confederate service as a brigadier general, the same rank that he had held in the Missouri State Guard. By December 1 he and his brigade—the 7th, 8th, 9th, and 10th Missouri infantry regiments; Pindall's sharpshooters; and Tilden's four-gun Missouri Battery—were camped near Van Buren, where they were assigned to Brigadier General Daniel M. Frost's two-brigade division. Parsons and his Missourians met the enemy at Prairie Grove (December 7), and in his report of the battle Confederate commander Hindman noted that Parsons had done his "duty nobly." In view of critical shortages of forage and commissary supplies in the Fort Smith area Hindman reorganized his army's five military brigades (including Parsons') into a division and marched them to Little

The only known uniformed wartime portrait of Parsons, taken after November 1862. (Museum of the Confederacy, Richmond, Va.)

Rock. On April 1, 1863, Sterling Price, recently reassigned to the Trans-Mississippi, assumed command of the division.

Parsons at Helena on July 4 spearheaded the desperate but futile assault on Graveyard Hill, which cost his brigade 764 casualties. The Confederate infantry including Parsons and his brigade marched many miles but fought no battles during the ensuing five-week campaign that saw Union columns led by Frederick Steele advance out of the Helena enclave and capture Little Rock. On August 10 Parsons was posted at Des Arc, and on September 14 his troops, having evacuated Little Rock, were camped at Arkadelphia.

Parsons and his brigade spent the winter of 1863–64 at Camp Sumter near Spring Hill, Arkansas. N. P. Banks, supported by the Missouri Squadron, on March 16 occupied Alexandria, Louisiana, as the first stage in a campaign aimed at advancing up the Red River Valley, capturing Shreveport and carrying the war into Texas. On the 18th Parsons' Missourians along with three of the other four infantry brigades constituting Price's division broke camp and started for Louisiana. On March 24 they reached Shreveport, where there was a reorganization triggered by Lieutenant General Theophilus Holmes' relief from duty in the Trans-Mississippi and the reassignment of General Price as commander of the District of Arkansas. The reorganization placed Parsons in command of the two-brigade Missouri division and Brigadier General Thomas Churchill in charge of a two-brigade Arkansas division. Parsons took the field on April 4 and reached Mansfield on the evening of the 8th to find that Major General Richard Taylor's army had beaten Banks' vanguard earlier in the day. The next day Parsons fought the Yankees at Pleasant Hill, where his division lost 32 killed, 235 wounded, and 51 missing.

On April 14 with Banks' army in retreat and the Mississippi squadron checkmated, Parsons and his Missourians started on the return march to Arkansas where General Steele's army had advanced from Little Rock on March 23 and on April 15 had occupied Camden. Parsons reached the Camden area on the 22d, and when the Federals attacked the city on the 26th, he participated in the pursuit to the Saline, where the Confederates on the 29th overtook the foe. Parsons led his Missourians into the battle of Jenkins' Ferry the next day. General Price, commenting on the latter struggle fought in a rain-swollen swamp, called atten-

tion to Parsons' and Churchill's infantry divisions as having "fully sustained their old reputations."

In recognition of his leadership Lieutenant General Edmund Kirby Smith on May 11 assigned Parsons to duty as major general, to rank from April 30, the day of Jenkins' Ferry, but he was never confirmed in this rank by President Davis.

Parsons and his division spent the last seven months of 1864 in southern Arkansas. In September Parsons took position at Monticello. By mid-October he and his Missourians were back at Camden, with one brigade posted at Washington, which was then serving as the Confederate capital of Arkansas. The last five months of the war in the Trans-Mississippi saw Parsons wearing a number of hats. On February 15, in addition to his duties as the officer responsible for the defenses of Camden, he became acting commander of the District of Arkansas during the absence of Major General John B. Magruder. In mid-April Parsons and his division returned to Shreveport.

On May 12, 1865, Kirby Smith surrendered the forces in the Trans-Mississippi Department. Parsons, a "bitter ender," refused to sign a parole and struck out for Mexico. There he joined Maximilian's imperial forces. He was shot and killed by Juaristas, probably on August 15, 1865, near China on the San Juan River in the state of Nuevo León. The bodies of Parsons and his five comrades—including his brother-in-law and former adjutant, Captain A. M. Standish, and A. H. Conrow, a former member of the Confederate Congress—were buried in unmarked graves in that vicinity.

Edwin C. Bearss

Bay, William Van Ness, *Reminiscences of the Bench and Bar of Missouri* (St. Louis, 1878).

Conrad, Howard L., ed., *Encyclopedia of the History of Missouri* (New York, 1901).

⭑ *Elisha Franklin Paxton* ⭑

Elisha Franklin Paxton, generally known as Frank or "Bull," was born March 4, 1828, in Rockbridge County, Virginia, of English and Scots-Irish descent. Among his ancestors were veterans of the American Revolution and the War of 1812. He also numbered the famous Texan Samuel Houston among his distant cousins. The martial tradition of the Paxton clan did not influence Frank initially. He instead followed a scholarly course, displaying a studious personality. A roster of the schools that he attended makes manifest the level of his ability: Washington College (1845), Yale (1847), and the University of Virginia(1849). Paxton capped his academic accomplishments by graduating from the latter institution at the top of his class with a degree in law.

The young Virginian lived for a long time in Ohio and honed his legal abilities by prosecuting land claims. In 1854, however, he returned to Lexington in his native county and commenced a law practice that met with success despite the serious handicap of possessing "none of the natural gifts of the orator...." In addition to that blossoming career, Paxton undertook the duties of president for a local bank and apparently became something of a local leader.

Perhaps the most important aspect of Paxton's prewar life in Lexington was his close association with many of the future leaders of the Confederacy. "Stonewall" Jackson was a fellow Presbyterian and hence a friend, although relations were prickly between them in the years immediately preceding the war. William Nelson Pendleton and his son Sandie were Lexingtonians, and a whole crop of nascent Confederates matriculated yearly at the Virginia Military Institute. Those

acquaintances proved important in later years.

The stout, powerful figure of Frank Paxton that inspired his nickname of "Bull" belied the tenderness of his vision. A weakening of the eyes forced the premature end of Paxton's promising legal career in 1860. He found solace in the life of a gentleman farmer, and his zealous temperament made him a leader in the Lexington secession movement.

From the earliest days of the war Paxton proudly belonged to the Stonewall Brigade. He left Lexington as a lieutenant in the 5th Virginia Infantry; in his first battle he distinguished himself so greatly as to elicit praise from many, and an assignment to Brigadier General Stonewall Jackson's staff soon followed. Those heroic accomplishments had occurred at First Manassas on July 21, 1861. As the fighting reached its agonizing climax Paxton seized the flag of a Georgia unit, raced across the contested field leading a horde of Georgians and Virginians, and deposited the flag among some Union artillery pieces. On August 7 he received his reward by joining Jackson as aide-de-camp.

On October 14, 1861, Frank Paxton was commissioned major of the 27th Virginia Infantry. In that role he participated in the western Virginia wanderings of Jackson in the winter of 1861 as well as most of the legendary Valley Campaign in the spring of 1862. An incident in January 1862 left Paxton's feelings "much aggrieved," and he sought to resign. After reflection

---

Elisha Paxton appears probably as a lieutenant in the 27th Virginia in 1861 or 1862, though the uniform shows some signs of having been retouched by an artist. (Warner, *Generals in Gray*)

he withdrew his resignation but harbored ill feelings, although they had no specific target. In June the men of the 27th revealed their true feelings toward the strict major when they failed to reelect him. One subordinate wrote uncharitably that Paxton felt compelled to lead his men into battle "in perfect alignment and invariably when we were under a heavy fire he would give the order to dress the line...."

Bull Paxton resuscitated his career with the Army of Northern Virginia through the good offices of his old benefactor Stonewall Jackson, who tendered the unemployed veteran a post as volunteer aide on his staff. He served in that capacity through the fall of 1862, eventually with staff rank as major.

The landmark event of Paxton's military career involved much bitter feeling and is a glaring example of the political intrigues from which even the Army of Northern Virginia suffered. Because of his piety, discipline, and Lexington roots, Paxton always had been a wartime favorite of Jackson. On the strength of Jackson's recommendation Paxton was appointed brigadier general on and effective November 1, 1862, to command the Stonewall Brigade. The maneuver outraged the brigade's officers, particularly its more senior members. A pointed letter from Major General A. P. Hill to Major General "Jeb" Stuart succinctly summarized the opinion of the army: "*Paxton*, Brig. Gen!"

Paxton weathered the controversy, leading the brigade without serious incident at Fredericksburg in December. At the start of the new year the Bull ran afoul of Brigadier General William B. Taliaferro, who placed Paxton under arrest for disrespect with no appreciable results. The commander of the Stonewall Brigade soon returned to his men and prepared for what would be his final campaign.

General Paxton, like so many others, predicted his own death. His men had played a small role in the Battle of Chancellorsville by the evening of May 2, 1863, but a deadly fight was in the offing and Paxton knew it. He quietly spoke of his imminent death; he avoided emotion and merely spoke with a convincing sincerity that proved all too prescient. After a brief session with his Bible and his wife's picture Paxton led the advance of his brigade early on May 3. A Minié bullet through the breast killed him almost immediately.

Word of the death of Frank Paxton reached the ears of Lieutenant General Stonewall Jackson—himself grievously wounded—a few hours later. He was visibly moved by the report and honored Paxton posthumously

with a few laudatory remarks. The final sad twist to Paxton's life occurred on May 7. General Jackson's wife, having rushed to the deathbed of her husband, experienced the horror of seeing the coffin of her friend and neighbor Paxton excavated from its temporary resting place in the yard of the house at Guiney's Station in which her husband lay. Never far removed from his chief, Elisha Franklin Paxton finally found repose in Lexington, buried only a few feet from Jackson.

Robert E. L. Krick

Douglas, Henry Kyd, *I Rode With Stonewall* (Chapel Hill, 1940).

Paxton, Elisha Franklin, *Memoir and Memorials* (New York, 1905).

A previously unpublished portrait of General Payne, dating from the winter of 1864-65. (Museum of the Confederacy, Richmond, Va.)

A variant pose apparently taken at the same sitting. (William A. Turner Collection)

✶ *William Henry Fitzhugh Payne* ✶

William H. F. Payne was born on January 27, 1830, in Fauquier County, Virginia. A member of an old Virginia family, Payne was graduated from the Virginia Military Institute in 1849. The following year he studied law at the University of Virginia and then began a practice in Warrenton, the county seat of Fauquier. He prospered in the legal profession, and in 1856 the local citizens elected him commonwealth attorney.

When Virginia seceded in April 1861, Payne enlisted as a private, reporting for duty at Harpers Ferry. Within days, however, he was commissioned a captain of the Black Horse Cavalry, a company composed of men from Fauquier. The unit remained unattached until September 19, when it and five other companies were organized into the 4th Virginia Cavalry. Payne was appointed major of the regiment.

By the spring of 1862 the 4th Virginia was serving in the brigade of J. E. B. Stuart. At the Battle of Williamsburg May 5 Payne commanded the regiment and fell wounded and was captured. He remained in a Federal prison for nearly three months until exchanged. Returning to duty in September, Payne was promoted to lieutenant colonel and assigned to temporary command of the 2d North Carolina Cavalry, stationed at Warrenton. In February 1863 he rejoined the 4th Virginia, acting as its commander until June 8, when Colonel Sol Williams returned to duty. The next day, however, Williams was killed in action at Brandy Station and Payne assumed command of the regiment in W. H. F. "Rooney" Lee's brigade.

Payne distinguished himself during the Gettysburg Campaign. At Hanover, Pennsylvania, on June 30 Stuart's horsemen clashed with Union troopers. It was an engagement of charge and countercharge. The 2d North Carolina struck and routed the 18th Pennsylvania Cavalry, only to be repulsed by the 5th New York Cavalry. In the combat Payne's horse was killed under him, and he plunged into an uncovered vat of dye in a tannery yard. When he crawled out, he was colored a dark brown. He had sustained eleven saber cuts in the fighting and once again was captured.

Imprisoned at Johnson's Island in Ohio, Payne was released that fall, and while recuperating in a hospital in Lynchburg, Virginia, he commanded the troops in the town. During the summer of 1864 he was assigned to command of a brigade, comprised of the 5th, 6th, and 15th Virginia Cavalry, participating in the 1864 Shenandoah Valley Campaign. At the Battle of Cedar Creek October 19 Payne's three-hundred–man brigade led the Confederate surprise attack, with orders to dash into the Federal lines and endeavor to capture Union Major General Philip Sheridan at his headquarters. Although Sheridan was not there, the mission failed because of Federal resistance, but Payne's men fought well.

On November 4, 1864, Payne was promoted to brigadier general, effective November 11. During the conflict's final months, he commanded a mounted brigade in the Richmond-Petersburg lines. At Five Forks on April 1, 1865, he suffered a third wound and returned to his home in Warrenton. Federal troops found him there on the 14th and sent him back to Johnson's Island. The war finally ended for Payne on May 29 with his release.

The capable cavalry officer resumed his legal practice in Warrenton, serving as commonwealth attorney until 1869. Ten years later he was elected to one term in the state's house of delegates. He then relocated to Washington, D.C., where he was general counsel for the Southern Railway. Payne died in the capital on March 29, 1904, and was buried in Warrenton.

Jeffry D. Wert

Hotchkiss, Jedediah, *Virginia*, Vol. III in Evans, *Confederate Military History*.

Wert, Jeffry D., *From Winchester to Cedar Creek: The Shenandoah Campaign of 1864* (Carlisle, Pa., 1987).